EVOLVING LIFE *and* TRANSITION *to the* WORLD BEYOND

S0-EGK-821

To my dear friend Suzy—
As always Love is the Key—
Ron Radhopt

EVOLVING LIFE *and* TRANSITION *to the* WORLD BEYOND

The Fantastic Journey of the Body, Mind and Spirit

RONALD RADHOFF

BALBOA
PRESS
A DIVISION OF HAY HOUSE

Copyright © 2011 Ronald Radhoff

All rights reserved. No part of this book may be used or reproduced by any means, graphic, electronic, or mechanical, including photocopying, recording, taping or by any information storage retrieval system without the written permission of the publisher except in the case of brief quotations embodied in critical articles and reviews.

Balboa Press books may be ordered through booksellers or by contacting:

Balboa Press
A Division of Hay House
1663 Liberty Drive
Bloomington, IN 47403
www.balboapress.com
1-(877) 407-4847

Because of the dynamic nature of the Internet, any web addresses or links contained in this book may have changed since publication and may no longer be valid. The views expressed in this work are solely those of the author and do not necessarily reflect the views of the publisher, and the publisher hereby disclaims any responsibility for them.

The author of this book does not dispense medical advice or prescribe the use of any technique as a form of treatment for physical, emotional, or medical problems without the advice of a physician, either directly or indirectly. The intent of the author is only to offer information of a general nature to help you in your quest for emotional and spiritual well-being. In the event you use any of the information in this book for yourself, which is your constitutional right, the author and the publisher assume no responsibility for your actions.

Any people depicted in stock imagery provided by Thinkstock are models, and such images are being used for illustrative purposes only.
Certain stock imagery © Thinkstock.

ISBN: 978-1-4525-3430-5 (sc)
ISBN: 978-1-4525-3432-9 (hc)
ISBN: 978-1-4525-3431-2 (e)

Library of Congress Control Number: 2011905913

Printed in the United States of America

Balboa Press rev. date: 5/10/2011

ABOUT THE COVER ART

This painting *Evolving Life* depicts one who, through the power of choice, has decided to focus on the spiritual growth. It begins in rough terrain but, even so, the eye and hand are symbolic of the help from spiritual guidance and direction that are always present. Our path may lead us through periods of difficulty and even darkness as the path in the painting shows. These times, however, are when we often experience our greatest growth. The path off to the right is one that some choose but it never leads to growth and goes in meaningless directions. This occurs when the ego is in control. These paths may lead to violence, substance abuse, or other great difficulties in life.

If we stay on the spiritual path, and expand our consciousness with the greater spiritual truths of life, we evolve at increasingly faster rates and, through our greater understandings of life, we find Life gets in sync with the greater good until that time when we rise out of the physical and enter into a high dimension in the wondrous World Beyond.

ACKNOWLEDGEMENT

I would like to express my heart felt thanks to my sister Jan Martin for the loving support she graciously offered throughout the writing of my manuscript. Not only did she complete the majority of the editing, but she was also my word processing consultant because of her extensive knowledge of the software. Several times I called and asked her, "How do I ....?" when I was composing the chapters and she always came through. It is wonderful to have such a close, loving, and supportive sister.

CONTENTS

PREFACE

Deep within the soul of humankind, there is a longing to come to know "who we really are" beyond the vast differences within the many fundamental teachings, especially those teachings that create fear, anger, turmoil, and confusion. Our hope lies in the key that will unlock our greatest power, a power that will lift us beyond the many limitations programmed into our consciousness by mainstream institutions, media, religions and educational systems. That key, that power, is nothing more than LOVE. The word is capitalized because we are speaking of a Divine Love, and it lies within every physical and spiritual being who exists. That love resides within our 'oneness' with God our Creator and all that He created. For too long, it has been pre-empted by the human ego, by a materialistic world, and limited by the dark energies that have created a magnitude of negative influences upon the human race and an attitude that we are all separate beings.

I believe the original foundation of most religions in the world was for the purpose of giving humans guidance and inspiration to live better lives and grow spiritually. However, through my years of communicating with the higher realms of spirit I have become aware that throughout the ages, the influence of the human ego within religious teachers has integrated into the sacred writings and has created many distortions of the greater truths originally given by the teachers God has sent to Earth. Little-by-little ego driven religious teachers around the world now preach non-truths that have filtered into religious teachings and beliefs. I realize this is a disturbing statement for those embracing traditional beliefs; however,

Spirit source has decreed IT IS TIME that the greater truths are given to create greater understandings and new ways to see and experience life.

The planet is now in a state of great chaos as religions around the world, with their distorted beliefs, have created fear and hostility, and destroy great numbers of human lives and property. While the Holy Scriptures tell us to "judge not," hypocrisy prevails as those in a particular faith judge others with different beliefs as being wrong, especially if they tell them "You are doomed to eternal damnation." IT IS TIME to move beyond this insanity. IT IS TIME to understand greater truths and evolve to a greater level of spiritual awareness and live accordingly, without judging others.

While absolute truth cannot be fully understood by the physical mind, there will always be greater truths to learn, though they are relative truths. Spirit has said that all religions have some of the truth but no religion has all of the truth.

The messages that are presented within the following pages were received from many levels of the spiritual hierarchy. Also, messages are shared from those who have graduated from the Earth plane to the life beyond. From that greater perspective, they describe the realities of the many mansions in God's great kingdom, one of which we all will enter one day.

The communications from the higher realms are intended to expand the consciousness and bear witness to the greater truths that will free us from our limited views of who we are and bring forth a greater clarity of the Light and Love that resides within us all. So also will many distortions within the myths that were passed down through the ages be revealed, myths that mislead and create fear. Please know that Love and fear cannot coexist because they are directly opposite.

The Universal Law of Cycles ensures spiritual evolution continues and brings back any areas of life that have gone astray from Divine intent.

Every 26,000 years, the Earth and all upon it pass through a grand cycle that cleanses and purges a system of any negativity to which it has succumbed. This cycle is experienced throughout the Universe. It is a period when the planet transforms from a time of darkness to a time when the increasing vibrations act as a catalyst to lift life into a new era of Love, Light, and Peace. We on Planet Earth are now entering into this time. It will be a time when the darkness and corruption are cleansed and give way to a time when all beings will truly experience Divine Light through a greater spiritual evolvement.

As the old ways break up and make way for the new, the transformation period is often difficult. Those who reside in the darker and lower vibrations will find it more difficult and may ultimately not survive. They will simply find it more difficult to withstand the higher vibrations and thus begin to experience and express more anger and chaos. It is therefore a time for humanity to rise out of negative and hostile ways and be lifted up with the increasing vibrations of the planet. Simply said, "LOVE IS THE KEY" and is the answer.

The false perceptions of the truths that embrace fear will ultimately give way to the greater truths of love and create a peace that passes all understanding. For a time, the chaos between nations and religions will fill the headlines of the media. Even so, many around the world who are of the Light are quietly undermining the negativity and increasing the vibrations of Love and Light.

As the chrysalis bridges the process of the caterpillar and transforms it into a beautiful butterfly that is no longer limited to crawling upon the earth, so is such a transformation of the planet and all of its beings now unfolding. This magnificent transformation will truly set us free and provide many opportunities to be lifted to new and unimaginable heights of expressing life in a framework of Love and Light. The result will bring humanity into the reality of "Who we really are," magnificent life expressions that are One with the Source of all life. These are the opportunities that lie before us if we but use the power of choice God gave us. We must determine if we want to open up to the new ways or hang on to the old, to those ways that have clearly demonstrated they do not work for the good of the whole. It is all a part of the Universal Law of Evolution. IT IS TIME to realign our life expression to Divine intent.

Chapter 1 presents the challenge given to the author from the Lord Most High, a challenge to bring together the many messages received over 33 years from the higher realms, messages that present the greater truths that provide an understanding of our purpose in life and suggest many ways to achieve Divine intent. Moreover, the many communications from spirit messenger's help to create an understanding of why many things and events occur that make no sense to the finite mind. The author shares a profound experience that emphatically opened his mind and created a curiosity about the true realities of life, death, and life beyond. That thirst was wetted when he began communicating with the higher realms from the world of spirit over three decades ago. The first great awareness he learned was, as one sincerely seeks greater truths, truly he shall find them. The only criteria required to travel the journey that lies before you is an open mind and a seeking heart. As you ingest the material ahead, remember that truth is sometimes stranger than fiction.

Ronald Radhoff

PART ONE

Evolving Life

Introduction to Section One

In Chapter One, I share the communication from the Most High that gave me the direction to write this book. The following three chapters get into the experiences that truly opened my mind and completely changed my life. Once I began to connect with the higher realms of spirit it was like opening a door to a new reality, one that was both exciting and so very enlightening. Also in this part I have shared many of the things I learned from spirit that will expand your consciousness, as it did mine and move you in a direction of spiritual growth, for that is the intent of these writings. Moreover, those things that block our growth are covered. Included also are several messages from highly evolved beings on other worlds who share details of their planets, their societies and cultures, and why they have become more advanced than we here on Planet Earth. It is my sincere wish that you enjoy the journey of the body, mind, and spirit.

CHAPTER 1

A Communication from on High

It's 4:17 AM and I've been lying in bed, half-asleep and half-awake, with many thoughts pouring through my mind. As I moved gently from sleep to half-awake, I began hearing in my mind, "It is time, It is time" over and over again. Finally I reached over in the dark next to my bed and picked up the hand held microphone connected to the tape recorder I always keep in the record mode so I can capture thoughts or messages that come to me while in the mental Alpha state. Sensing a message was about to be given, I slid the switch on the mic to the ON position to start the tape recording.

"Okay, it is time for what?" I asked and then mentally tuned in for an answer. I've done this many times before. The early predawn hours are a good time to tune in to the higher realms when it's quiet without any interruptions. The following are the words that I recorded as the answer flowed into my consciousness.

> *I AM that I AM. My dear Lamb of Fire, I have a message for thee. Yes my child, it was I knocking when your mind heard me say, "IT IS TIME." For now it is time that you begin the book, that which my Archangel Michael and others have been*

encouraging you to write. You, and all of mankind, have been given the power to choose, for never will I demand anything of you. However, for over three decades you have been blessed with an abundance of great knowledge and truth from the higher realms. Do you remember the message given you that states one should pass on the greater levels of knowledge one has been given, especially when it has been given freely unto you? It is in this way that knowledge expands and humankind evolves to greater levels of understanding. Among the 24 Universal Laws given you several years ago was The Law of Knowledge. It so stated that knowledge is never given openly to anyone. The requirement is that one must have a desire to attain, and it will only be given at the level of comprehension. Know this my son; there will never be an end to attaining greater knowledge and higher levels of truth, and as one seeks it, it will be given.

Should you accept the challenge of producing this task, we from our realm will support you, assist you, and give you guidance as you may ask for it. Are you now willing to go forth and commit to producing this effort?"

"How could I refuse to honor such a grand request, especially after receiving such a wealth of knowledge from you and others of your Light? I am honored you think I am worthy and capable to accomplish this endeavor."

"If I had not thought you worthy, I would not have come to you this day with my request and encouragement. My first suggestion to you is to start by sharing your adventures and experiences beginning with your childhood. Remember, you came into this life that you may experience it unto its fullest. From that inner drive, you have had many experiences of an extreme nature and they ultimately have led you to opening

*your mind and realizing there was so much more to life than
one could ever imagine. Your thirst for greater knowledge
will continue to be fed to you as you continue to seek it.*

"If I write about those crazy things I did growing up and on into my
younger years, might the readers question my sanity and credibility?"

*"Worry not my son. Do you not know that this was one of your
primary goals to achieve in this your lifetime? While some
may think you extreme, most who read what you would share
in your writings will be of open and seeking minds, eager to
hear of the experiences and how it has opened your mind
and created a desire to seek greater knowledge of the truths
of life on all levels. You have so much to share, my son. Those
who read and mentally digest your writings will understand
your deeper purpose for creating these extreme experiences
and they will see how your life's path ultimately led you to
a connection and communication with spiritual sources of
higher truth. For it is through these communications that you
learned a greater understanding of life; why certain things
happen as they do yet leave many wondering why, because
they make no earthly sense; and why so many in their prayers
ask me why I would allow what are considered tragic things
to happen. You have learned the greater purpose in all these
things. Share them!*

*For those who still wonder if there is other life out there in
the Universe, you have received from your Starbrothers many
communications to share, describing their evolutionary
achievements, such as their ability to travel great distances
in minutes. So also, how effective their education system is;
how some communicate without language; how the unified
philosophy of their spiritual reality creates great peace and
harmony among all the beings on their planet; how great the*

Love System serves them in their lives; how I have directed some of your Starbrothers to keep you from destroying your planet by preventing nuclear war; and so very much more. You will enjoy writing this chapter.

"I'm really glad you want me to cover the extraterrestrial realm. I perceive it will be a long chapter unless I share just a select few of the many communications from my very evolved Starbrothers. Their descriptions of their planet alone will stretch the mind beyond the imagination. It sure did for me. And to know how benevolent and loving these marvelous beings are will be comforting to those who erroneously believe they are all hostile and wish to take over our planet as so many of the science fiction movies have portrayed them in recent years."

That is one good reason alone for writing this chapter. You will want to cover the power of mind and the power of love. You may also wish to discuss the many changes occurring on your planet as she and all upon her surface are evolving to a higher frequency of expression.

In another part, it would be good if you discuss what happens when one's physical life on Earth ends. It will be good if you share some of your interesting experiences as a hospice volunteer over the past thirteen years. A chapter on near death experiences will also be interest to many. While you are covering the so-called 'death' aspect of life, a chapter on the crossing over experiences of your family and friends will give the readers a foresight as to what they might expect when their turn comes to leave their physical form. It should also help dispel fears about crossing over after reading what a magnificent experience it really is for even non-religious beings.

As you share the knowledge that my messengers of Light and I have joyously placed within your mind through these many years, those with open minds shall also gain some of the greater truths and knowledge I have blessed you with. Know also that more will be given you during your process of writing each chapter, especially when you do so with a purity of heart.

Think not that you need to write with flowery words. Merely write in a straightforward language, just as I communicate to you now. Choose wisely messages that will help increase the awareness relative to the subject of each chapter. You have many to choose from within the multitudes given unto you over the past three decades.

In the third and final part of your writings, you also have much to share that will dispel the many myths that were integrated into some of the holy writings carried forth from ancient beliefs born of fear, those writings that cast dark illusions of places where I am said to condemn beings I have judged and thus commit them to a torturous place of eternal damnation, namely a literal hell filled with demons. While I have promised mankind free will, IT IS TIME these myths of great fear be transcended with the truths of my love and forgiveness. You may make it known, however, for those who have committed inhumane acts, it is the Universal Law of Cause and Effect that determines the levels or dimensions awaiting them that balance their wicked deeds, not places of eternal damnation but ones that eventually provide opportunities to rehabilitate misguided and sick spirits, but only if they so seek it.

Readers may enjoy reading about the many mansions (dimensions) within my spiritual kingdom where great love and beauty exist beyond the comprehension of the finite human mind, and where the spiritual being can continue to evolve to ever higher and more beautiful levels of beingness.

As you have guided your aircraft from one destination to another; as you have fallen through the skies and opened your parachute thereafter guiding yourself to a target below; so also guide your readers through your written words to a greater understanding of their life and so called death which is but the transition to that greater life that lies in the great beyond, that which you know as the world of spirit -- the world of true reality.

"Should I include the period of my life when I was reading and studying the Bible and how eventually I had difficulty accepting some of the writings as literal or even totally accurate relative to the greater truths? And I wonder what will readers think if I share messages received from the Master Jesus who walked the Earth over 2000 years ago and has explained how some of his quoted words in the New Testament were misunderstood, and how some distortions occurred through mistranslations. I fear some of the readers will think I have connected with the dark side."

My son, there will always be those who are rigid in specific beliefs and nothing on Earth will influence them to believe differently because they fear being led astray from what they believe is absolute truth. If anyone challenges their beliefs, they will argue profusely and some will even fight to the death. Certainly you know, this has been the basis of most wars, even and especially in your present days. For those who are open-minded and are seeking a greater and expanded knowledge of life, they need only to look back in history to see how beliefs in supreme beings have evolved beyond those times of many gods who were angered easily and demanded appeasing sacrifices. Though spiritual beliefs have evolved, you have been given *yet another level of truth to help many realize who I AM, who they really are, and what the relationship between us really is. The beliefs between the eastern and western cultures are very different though there are some common threads that flow between them. Common sense will tell you, of all the variations in beliefs, how can they all be **the ultimate truth?***

Galileo was excommunicated because he tried to teach man that the sun did not revolve around the Earth but rather the opposite was true. It took considerable time before that truth was finally accepted. While all of the religions in the world have some truths, none have all the truths. Because of human's natural resistance to change, the teachers I have sent you throughout time must spoon-feed you greater levels of truth. Even so, many of the teachers I have sent you were rejected and even killed. If too much is given too fast, humans will not only resist accepting greater truths but so have some totally rejected them. The rigid fundamentalists will call them heresy. I give you Galileo as my case in point.

It is encouraging to see how many in your current time are gradually becoming more open to accepting greater levels of spiritual knowledge. As your technical knowledge expands exponentially, be aware, however, if technical knowledge evolves without a corresponding evolution in spiritual knowledge, it can become a great danger. The occupants of a few planets have destroyed their world when the balance between technology and spirituality has shifted to the extreme of technology.

*I say to you once again, IT IS TIME for yet a greater understanding of spiritual truth. More needs to be shared forthwith. I say to you, never is anyone given **all** truth. You* *have been given higher truth not yet received by others. Others have been given some unknown to you. Little by little each truth begins to form a bigger and clearer picture, yet any picture is but a part of a larger one.*

*Throughout the ages, greater truth has always been given to mankind when his intellect can comprehend and the mind can accept, but the acceptance has always been the most difficult part for humanity. The consciousness of mankind has once again expanded and is ready for greater understanding of that "which is" (truth). However, know that no human can comprehend **absolute** truth with his finite mind because it is beyond time and space. Absolute truth is of a spiritual nature and can only be truly realized in the spiritual dimensions. So it is that the higher dimension one evolves to, the greater levels of truth will be made known to him.*

In your more recent times, the greater understanding of spiritual truth has expanded more in the last half century than in many centuries before it. So also has your knowledge and understanding of deep space and the entire universe grown immensely. Using your technology to visually explore deeper space has certainly advanced your greater knowledge of it all, has it not? Through the advancements of science and technology you can now see beautiful images of my creations in the deeper regions of space. Therefore you have a better understanding of how the galaxies, stars, and planets were created. Know that creation is always ongoing. Your world has come to know there is so much more out there than ever imagined a short time ago. Your technology has recently given you close-up photographs of your nearest planets and you speculate on what the environmental conditions are like on their surface.

I tell you, there is so much more you have yet to learn of your solar system, your galaxies and your universe. So also is there much more to learn about your spiritual world, your own beingness, and your relationship to the whole. You, my son, have much to share in these areas of truth and there are many who thirst for greater understandings beyond the teachings of traditional religions. I say to those who scoff at this, religious arrogance is dangerous to your spiritual welfare.

The statement, "Many are called but few are chosen" is not quite correct. The true statement I now give you is, "Many are called but few choose to answer." You, my son, have been called. You have been given many truths of a higher understanding. Though all truth is relative in the physical realm, IT IS TIME to comprehend greater truths that move closer to absolute. Many before you have been given the gifts of greater knowledge and have answered the call, yet many others have not. Many writings have been published in recent years that have been channeled down to willing humans from my teachers on the spirit plane. Yet more must be shared forthwith. Why? Because IT IS TIME for humanity to grow beyond its limited beliefs and to grow to greater awareness of the truths that will set humanity free – free of hostilities and wars, free of corruption, free of fear, free of greed, and free of all that limits growth to higher levels where humanity will peacefully and lovingly express and honor all life.

Many are connecting and receiving messages from the Ascended Masters, angels, archangels, and saints as you have termed them. Additionally, highly evolved beings from other worlds have shared how life on their worlds, once like yours, have evolved to greater levels of expressing and living life where all live and work for the greater good of the All and do so without illness, without wars, and without aging and

11

dying before the time the body was designed to live. Others have received messages from their loved ones on what you call the other side and they share the wonders and beauty of the next world, the world you will all eventually come to know once again. You, my son, have been blessed with messages from all these sources and have so much to share in your writings.

I say again, IT IS TIME the many preachers, though they have good intentions, stop pounding their pulpits with messages of fear and condemning the new messages of truth. I say unto you, soon their words will fall on fewer numbers as the masses continue to awaken. I am not saying all of the old teachings are wrong and will be cast aside. There are many great truths of old that will carry forth and integrate into the new teachings. My son, the Christ implied the same with his teachings though many misunderstood him.

New progressive churches are expanding to the seams with those who no longer wish to hear the messages of sin, Satan, evil, and hell's fire of eternal damnation. They thirst for a more positive spirituality. Those who prescribe to the new thoughts realize that focusing on and fearing evil only empowers dark energies. Even so, there are those who will hang on to the old beliefs until their dying days. The messages of greater truths are pouring forth like cornucopia. As more are received and understood, even greater truths will be given – because IT IS TIME.

Your new technologies provide opportunities to communicate the messages of expanded truth very rapidly. Though books of old have been published with greater thoughts of truth, they are now being written; published and entering book shelves as never before, and will continue to come forth. More recently, you can download books directly to your computer. Newsletters and websites frequently contain a multitude of messages from the spirit world. However, use great discretion before accepting all as real truth.

In the Book of Revelation it is written, "He that hath an ear, let him hear what the spirit sayeth unto the churches" (or the body of believers). Soon I will send more teachers from the higher realms to walk among you in physical form and the numbers of new believers of the greater consciousness will reach a level of critical mass. When that occurs a mass awakening to the higher truths will occur on the planet in a very short time. With the new mass consciousness within mankind, you will evolve into a new world where the greater love will transcend the hostile warring ways of old. Can you conceive a time when the nations will all come together to create peace and a time when borders and fences will dissolve? Can you imagine evolving to a greater sense of unity within all mankind and expressing life with the knowingness that all are truly one?

If you look at your world's current state of affairs with its religious wars, its divided governments; great imbalances between the rich and those of meager means, with thousands dying of hunger every day, with prejudice, hatred, and violence, it should be obvious the old ways have not worked and they never will as they exist in your current time. I am saddened, if you will, how far off track some of the religions of the world have become. Dark or negative energies have infiltrated some of the religions and have used fear and brainwashing to control congregation members to believe their religion is the supreme of all religions and they must defend their beliefs at all costs, even with their own lives,

Too many religions practice religious intolerance, even within Christianity. Where is the love the Christed one so avidly taught? When humanity finally evolves to a higher level of consciousness, all these things will change. But remember, it is always darkest before the dawn.

By accepting this challenge my son, you will become one of a host of others who have been given greater truths and encouraged to share that knowledge through various means of communication. Know that these efforts are helping in the awakening and enlightenment of many.

So, my son, go forth now with this project. Share the personal experiences that changed your life and ultimately led you to open up and receive the wealth of knowledge freely given you. I suggest you share the communication I gave you years ago about "Who I really am." Know that my angels, archangels, and other evolved spirit beings of the Light have agreed to assist you with this project I have requested of you. Fear not for I will always be with you and within you. Know that you have my deepest love and highest blessings.

I AM that I AM.

"I graciously appreciate your calling me to do this project. Knowing I have help is comforting. I shall do my very best to ensure the forthcoming messages will help others as they have helped me to come to a greater understanding of the life we have chosen to enter here, yet knowing we will eventually release the physical aspect of our beingness so our spirit may soar free and return home to that magnificent realm in the world of spirit."

In the following chapters, I include a few personal experiences. One is a ghost story that really opened my mind and created a strong desire to seek more of what the purpose of this human experience is really all about. Also given are many messages from a variety of spiritual sources that are enlightening and will dispel many spiritual myths. I hope it all gives you, the reader, a greater perspective on the realities of life, both here and beyond. It certainly did for me. With that, I invite you to join me now into a journey of the body, mind, and spirit.

Know the Truth *and the Truth Shall Set You Free*

CHAPTER 2

Experiences Leading to an Open Mind

One of my early dreams was to learn to fly. Finally, at age 20 I did just that. After I started taking lessons I bought a small two-seat airplane from a coworker who was in the middle of rebuilding it. I put it on a trailer, took it to my home, and put the disassembled plane in my garage. I really didn't know anything about the construction of airplanes but somehow I finished rebuilding it while asking a lot of questions at the airport.

When I completed the rebuilding effort, I loaded it up on a trailer, took it to the airport, assembled the wings, and had it licensed. Thereafter, I built up enough hours to qualify for and receive my private pilot's license. Eight years later, I completed the requirements to acquire my commercial pilot's license. Flying was always a joy but something inside me wanted more. I remember looking straight down while cruising through the heavenly blue and wondered what it would feel like to freefall straight down through the sky.

I had worked for General Motors in their Styling Division as an Engineering Artist and then at Chrysler Corporation in their Art Department. When the economy declines, so do car sales, and then layoffs occur. In the spring of 1961, instead taking a layoff, Chrysler gave me the option of being transferred to their Huntsville, Alabama Space Division Operation. They had been awarded contracts from NASA's Marshall Space Flight Center headed up by Dr. Werner Von Braun. Huntsville was quite progressive because of all the high level scientists and engineers who came to live and work there.

Often we find an inner drive in life that propels us in directions we may not really understand. From my very young years I had such a drive. I was driven to take many risky challenges to appease my spirit of adventure. It was much later when I learned why I did these things. I became aware that, before entering into my present physical life, my spiritual being had set a goal to move beyond fear, among several other things. Thus I was driven to create experiences that would provide me opportunities to accomplish this goal. It seemed I always wanted to experience and know more about the realities and greater purpose of life. To do that, I would need to keep an open mind, be unafraid, and be willing to seek truths of life's purpose.

While loud noises startle young babies, we actually learn all of our other fears as we go through life. Fears are created from a variety of sources -- overcautious parents, teachers, religions, television, and so-called accidents. All of these and more can create fears within us. Most women develop fears of rape or sexual abuse, either for themselves or when their daughters are growing up. We also develop psychological fears such as rejection, living alone, and the big one – fear of dying. (We'll go more deeply into fear in greater detail in a later chapter.)

As I look back, I can see how many apparent foolish risks I took growing up. I certainly wouldn't encourage any child to try any of the risky and sometimes senseless things I did. I'll give you just a couple examples. When rather young, my neighborhood buddy and I would shoot target arrows straight up, run a short distance and see how close the arrows would land to us. The one who had an arrow landing the closest, won that round. Here is another one. During summer vacations from school, a few of us kids in the neighborhood would hike a mile to where the train tracks ran through. When the trains were approaching, we would lie across the tracks. The last one to get up off the track won the dare. I did many other foolish things and, as I think back, I gave God plenty of opportunities to release me from my earthly life and send me back home to the spirit world.

While I did many absurd things growing up, I can now see how my spirit of adventure and my willingness to take risks for exciting experiences ultimately led me to really explore life. I always wanted to experience and learn more. Later in life it turned into seeking my life's purpose. The great Bible verse, "Seek and ye shall find," proved to be a great truth for me; however, to make it work, I had to keep an open mind, be willing to go outside the box of traditional beliefs, and not let fear be a barrier to discovering new things. I found that True Reality often goes well beyond our imagination but searching for it certainly stretches our minds. It seems the more we stretch our minds, the more wonderful knowledge is received of the Creator's magnificent truths.

After a few months with Chrysler, I was assigned directly on-site at NASA's Marshall Space Flight Center. It was quite exciting to work there. Occasionally, I had to climb around on the booster sections of the Saturn V Rocket assembly that ultimately went up into space. I had to draw illustrations of key areas of the booster while it was under construction, as well as do exploded views of some of the complex control valves. Now and then, I would create conceptual art illustrations of various aspects of the space flight to come. One of the things I really enjoyed was attending the static test firings of the booster rocket engines. We stood behind protective barriers relatively close to the rocket firings. On the 10-second countdown, water flooded a replica of the launch pad. At ignition, the fire and smoke blasted off the reflector shields and we could feel the shock waves hit the barrier as the ground shook underfoot. It was really an exciting experience.

One of the highlights while I was assigned there was a visit from President Kennedy. I was close by as they checked out the progress of the Saturn V development. The president had a great interest in the Saturn V Program because it was this rocket booster that would help make good his promise to the nation the day he said, "We will send a manned rocket to the moon, land upon it, and return safely before the end of the decade." What a marvelous achievement it was in space travel when astronaut Neil Armstrong on the 20th day of July, 1969 announced to the world, "Tranquility Base, the Eagle has landed." Shortly thereafter on television we saw him step off the landing craft for that first step onto the surface of the moon and heard the words, "One small step for man, one giant leap for mankind."

For those involved in the space program, the celebration was as great as when a home football team wins the Superbowl. There is, however, another giant leap for mankind that is yet to come. As you read on in the following chapters, you will begin to understand what I mean by that statement.

It was during this time, I heard about a sport parachute club that was being formed. A couple ex-airborne jumpers and a few others who had made a couple sport jumps were planning to begin sport parachute jumping at an abandoned WWII airbase near a small town 50 miles west of Huntsville. Hearing about the formation of the club triggered the memory of my pushing the door open a crack while flying my small Taylorcraft airplane, looking straight down, and wondering what it would feel like to fall vertically towards the earth below. As I thought about it, I also thought, this is my chance to find out, so I committed myself to join the club and go for it. I went through the training during the week by an instructor who had only made 10 jumps himself but had read the book on Sport Parachuting. Now I was ready to make my first leap out of a perfectly good airplane and this I did from 3,000 feet altitude in a light rain. But that was okay – I had a 28 foot canopy over my head after the chute opened. This was the first of more than a thousand parachute jumps I made over the next eight years.

I have, and now continue to share, but only the most significant experiences of my sport parachuting years for one main reason. My involvement in the sport led to an experience that significantly and profoundly changed my life. The details follow that led to that experience, so let's fast-forward another five years.

I began having very strange experiences. From time to time, I found myself having out-of-body experiences. I would drift slightly up and behind my physical body for short periods but I could still function normally in the physical. It did not scare me but I found it very strange. That spring our club and another from Nashville held a preseason competition. As I descended on an accuracy jump, I noticed I was coming in a little short of the target so I reached way out with my right foot to land closer. I didn't realize my left foot was hanging down somewhat. When landing, the toe of the left foot caught the ground and pulled under me while my full weight came down on it. It sounded like a 22 rifle going off as both bones in the lower left leg shattered. I yelled out, "I just broke my damn leg," and felt the shattered fragments tearing into the flesh with excruciating pain. I was gently placed into the back seat of a friend's car and taken to the emergency room of the local hospital. After taking x-rays, the doctor operated and inserted six screws in my leg to hold the many fragments together.

As I was recovering in a cast that went well above the knee, I became aware that I was no longer having any more out-of-body experiences. However, three months later when I began jumping again, the out-of-body experiences returned. I had a feeling this was trying to tell me something.

During other injuries and the time needed to heal two broken legs, plus knee and lower back injuries, I stayed active in the sport by judging competitions. Competitors who had competed on national levels felt my perception of judging their freefall maneuvers during the style event were very accurate. Soon I was invited to judge the National Sport Parachuting Championships. After judging several National competitions, including the National Collegians Parachuting Championships, I became qualified to judge International Sport Parachuting Competitions.

Stay with me because this is all leading to the title of this chapter.

The summer of 1970 was very significant for me. On May 23 I made my 1000th freefall jump. On June 1 I made my 1st jump on one of the new, highly maneuverable, rectangular sport parachutes. These new chutes were rectangular in shape rather than round. They glided 30 mph forward as they descended and were very maneuverable. In early July I traveled to Germany with the U.S. Army's Golden Knights Competition Parachute Team as the team judge. This was my first international parachute competition. They had not yet seen this type of parachute in Germany, so I made two demonstration jumps on it during the event.

After returning from Germany, my next event was to serve as the chief judge of the U.S. National Parachuting championships in Plattsburgh, NY. Four of us from Huntsville flew up there in our Cessna Skylane because the host organization requested to use it for the competition. At the completion of the competition I was presented my Gold Wings for making 1000 freefall parachute jumps.

Back in Huntsville, I joined Northrop Corporation supporting Marshal Space Flight Center. As the manager of the Technical Publications Branch, I hired a female graphic artist who was very spirituality open minded. I was still, from time to time, finding myself out-of-body and always I would be above and behind my body looking down on myself. Because of her open-mindedness I discussed my out-of-body experiences with her one day and she became very interested.

A few days later, she told me there might be a way to find out why I was having these experiences. She said her husband, who came from England, had a cousin there who was very psychic and practiced psychometry, a gift that entails picking up vibrations of objects from people. When she would hold an object such as a watch from a person she could see the past, present, and future of that person. The artist asked if I had something that had been on my person for some time that would have absorbed my vibrations. I looked in my wallet and found an old scapular medal I had carried for years. She asked if I would be willing to have her husband send it to his cousin in England to get a reading on it and possibly find out why I was having my out-of-body experiences.

A month later the artist approached me and said her husband had received a letter back from his cousin. Then she asked if I was willing to hear her reading, no matter what the conclusions were. Certainly I wanted to know, even if it was bad news. So, she called and asked her husband to bring the letter to our facility. We all met in the parking lot after work hours and he slowly and carefully read his psychic cousin's letter. I recall today how deeply it impacted me. I still have the letter. It was addressed directly to me and I will include it here, word for word, including her underlining for emphasis.

I have in my possession a _personal_ possession of yours. I appreciate the trust this displays, and hope I prove worthy of it.

My first reaction, and it was a definite _reaction,_ without any concentration, was one of a constriction of breathing and a great deal of pain. I delayed looking further for quite a while, as it did seem to be such a distressing state of affairs. However, I eventually brought myself to concentrate fully. I will now try to put into words that which I felt.

First of all, if it is at all possible for you to change your employment _immediately,_ please do. In this way you will have avoided that which lies ahead if you continue as you are. I see an iron lung. This will explain why

A Recipe for Contentment

Go placidly amid the noise and haste, and remember what peace there may be in silence. As far as possible, without surrender, be on good terms with all persons. Speak your truth quietly and clearly; and listen to others, even the dull and the ignorant; they too have their story. Avoid loud and aggressive persons, they are vexations to the spirit. If you compare yourself with others, you may become vain or bitter; for always there will be greater and lesser persons than yourself. Enjoy your achievements as well as your plans. Keep interested in your own career, however humble; it is a real possession in the changing fortunes of time. Exercise caution in your business affairs; for the world is full of trickery. But let this not blind you to what virtue there is; many persons strive for high ideals; and everywhere life is full of heroism. Be yourself. Especially, do not feign affection. Neither be cynical about love; for in the face of all aridity and disenchantment it is perennial as the grass. Take kindly the counsel of the years, gracefully surrendering the things of youth. Nurture strength of spirit to shield you in sudden misfortune. But do not distress yourself with imaginings. Many fears are born of fatigue and loneliness. Beyond a wholesome discipline be gentle with yourself. You are a child of the universe, no less than the trees and the stars; you have a right to be here. And whether or not it is clear to you, no doubt the universe is unfolding as it should. Therefore be at peace with God, whatever you conceive Him to be, and whatever your labours and aspirations, in the noisy confusion of life keep peace with your soul. With all its sham, drudgery and broken dreams, it is still a beautiful world. Be careful. Strive to be happy.

Desiderata, by Max Ehrmann

I was hesitant in writing. It is a big decision to say something like this. I implore you not to worry about this if you can do something to get out of a job involving rarified air (altitude) of any description, as this will take an entirely different course then. You will manage and have a full life ahead of you if you are willing to act on the advice I presume to offer.

Hope I have been of some small help. If you feel like writing, feel free to do so. I remain, yours truly,
Sheila _____.

Can you imagine what was running through my mind after hearing that message? I was in a bit of a shock. After settling down a little, I read the letter over and over. Then I meditated on it and came to the conclusion that she must have thought my flying and parachuting activities were a part of my employment. I asked the graphic artist if she could get me the phone number of Sheila in England. She and her husband were gracious enough to set up a day and time I could make a phone connection with her. I left work and went home to make the call at the prescribed time.

When Sheila answered the phone, I began by thanking her for her courage to divulge to me such a profound message. Then I explained to her that my employment had nothing to do with rarified air; however, I was very involved with flying and parachuting. When I said that, she immediately yelled out, "That's it."

I asked, "The flying or the parachuting?"

She thought it was most likely the parachuting because she failed to mention in the letter that she also had a feeling of falling before the traumatic accident occurred. I then told her I had already surpassed my goal of making a thousand jumps and, considering what she foretold, I would cease making any more parachute jumps. I decided to hang it up, as it's termed. But then I asked about my flying activities. She answered, "To be sure, it would be best if you stopped flying also."

23

I was agreeable to quitting my parachute jumping but I didn't like the thought of also having to quit flying forever more, especially since I was half-owner of the aircraft we used for the jumping activities.

The more I thought about it the more I realized, that if I accepted her advice, what I would lose was my continued jumping and flying, which I dearly loved. However, if I disregarded her advice, and if what she perceived was true, indeed I had far more to lose. Therefore, I concluded that the consequences of Sheila's prediction were not worth the gamble of ignoring them. So, I did quit jumping and flying but I told no one why I chose to do so. I was soon to have a profound experience where I learned the impact of my decision.

In October of 1970, I made my last parachute jump. During our annual meeting of the Cottonbelt Parachute Council, I was awarded a 1st place trophy in <u>all</u> events, including the 1st place Overall Jumper of the Year award. Thereafter, when anyone asked why I quit jumping I would tell them, "After two broken legs, knee surgery, and two compressed discs in my lower back, and also because I achieved my goal of making 1000 freefall jumps, and also because I earned 1st place overall in all events for the year from our eight state parachute council competitions, I decided to retire at my peak."

In the next chapter you will learn how Sheila's prediction was proven to me.

How often things happen
and we never understand why.

Even so, there is always a reason
for every significant thing we experience.

CHAPTER 3

A Profound Experience

As the beginning of the competition season started in 1971, my only involvement was judging because I had quit jumping. That summer, I received a call from the State Department inviting me to participate as the U.S. Military Parachute Team's Judge in an international competition to be held in Sintra, Portugal in early September. My immediate thought was, "Oh dear, I have quit jumping and flying."

After a short hesitation, I said I would have to see if I could get the time off work even though I knew I had enough vacation time to make the trip. I promised to return their call in a few days. After serious meditation, I concluded it was not the flying but the jumping that I must cease to avoid the accident in Sheila's premonition. Two days later, I returned the call and agreed to participate as the team's judge if I did not have to make any of the test jumps before the start of each day's competition. My excuse was that my knee was still tender from a previous injury. They assured me there would be enough judges from the various countries to make those jumps.

After connecting with the U.S. Team in Ft. Bragg, North Carolina, we all flew to JFK airport in New York. From there we departed after dark on a Boeing 747. We flew through a short night when flying towards the sun and approached the airport in Lisbon in early morning. We had been flying through clouds for a long time on our descent and final approach. Suddenly, the pilot applied full throttle to the engines as he aborted the landing and pulled up in a steep climb. Just when the plane aborted the landing, I got a flashing glimpse through pouring rain of the ground only about 200 feet below. I wondered, "Could this be what the psychic predicted?"

Fifteen minutes later, we tried to land again but once more the pilot aborted and told us, "Ladies and gentleman, this is your captain speaking. We don't have enough fuel to wait any longer so we are heading for our alternate landing destination, Barcelona, Spain. We will arrive there in about an hour and twenty minutes."

After we landed, it was seven hours before we were put on another plane and returned all the way back across Spain to Lisbon.

Upon our arrival in Lisbon, we were met and greeted by the host organization and taken to a relatively new and modern sports center. It contained dorm-type housing plus a cafeteria and sports bar. I was assigned a room all to myself, even though it contained three single beds. There were two large windows the size of a large door that swung open for fresh air. This room would be the scene of a very strange experience two nights later.

We actually arrived two days before the competition was to begin so we could adjust to a different environment and time zone. On the first evening after dinner, we met in the social room and I became reacquainted with some of the competitors and judges from last year's competition in Germany. I was amazed at how many competitors from other countries spoke enough English to communicate. I reconnected with the Belgian Judge I had made friends with in Germany. He could speak six different languages rather fluently.

The next morning after breakfast, we were loaded on buses and transported to an airfield near Sintra, a 30-minute drive on narrow winding roads that passed through several small towns. This gave us a chance to see some of the countryside and to experience how very slow everyone moves in Portugal. This day was set aside for practice jumping, which gave us judges a chance to go over the set-up and review the rules and procedures we were to apply during the competition.

The next day was the start of the competition. When we arrived at the drop zone early in the morning, it was overcast. Even so, the opening ceremonies commenced and were a formal affair with plenty of dignitaries on hand.

By 9:30 the clouds were now at the minimum altitude to begin the accuracy event from 1,950 feet above ground. The judges made the test jumps and briefed the competitors regarding the wind conditions. This is a jump I would have made were it not for my decision to quit jumping. Though I would have liked to have made the test jump, I accepted the fact that I would never jump again.

Finally, at 10:40 the first competitor was in the air under an open parachute. I let out an exclamation of joy. It took five hours to complete one round of 94 jumpers. Shortly after starting the second round, low clouds moved in that were too low for jumping so we called it a day and returned to our quarters.

That evening after dinner and a couple beers with new friends in the sports bar, I returned to my dorm room and noticed the large windows were swung open on the outside wall. I decided to leave them open but chose the bed on the opposite side of the room so the cool evening air would not drift in directly on me. I had no idea what I was to experience that night.

I climbed into bed but felt restless and couldn't get to sleep. Lying on my back, I began thinking about how many new friends I had made from so many different countries. Most sport competitors are open and anxious to make new friends from other countries because of the common connection and dedication to the same sport. Still on my back and not getting sleepy, out of my peripheral vision, I sensed movement at the large open windows. I turned to see what that movement could be and was amazed to see the spirit form of a young man slowly gliding in through the windows. Though it was relatively dark, I could see his image quite clearly. He continued to slowly drift across the room toward me. For some reason, I was not afraid but watched with curiosity as he crossed over the top of me. Very slowly his form came down to a standing position next to my bed. I thought, *"Ron, could this be your imagination?"* I looked at his image long enough to clearly see its somewhat translucent form was that of a young man with short hair. For some reason, I intuitively felt there was nothing to fear; however, I rolled on my side facing away from him and said, "Go away!"

Finally, I fell asleep but the strange experience was not yet over. That night, I had a dream of a jumper in a white jumpsuit with a black stripe down the center of his white helmet. He was falling upside down towards the ground with no open chute. Just before he hit the ground, I woke up with a start. Shortly thereafter, I went back to sleep and the exact dream reoccurred. Again I awoke with a start. I thought it strange to have the same dream one after the other. Again I went back to sleep and again, the very same dream occurred for the third time. Each time, I awoke with my heart pounding but thankful I did not see him slam into the ground, knowing it must be a traumatic thing to experience.

Finally morning arrived and I wondered what that spirit visitation and those dreams were all about. However, I was glad to get up and leave all that behind. Little did I know, I would soon find out what the experiences of that night were really all about.

We left that morning an hour earlier to try and make up for lost time. We arrived at the drop zone just as the morning sun was spraying rays of light over the land but the clouds were still at the same altitude as the day before. I began wondering if this competition was being plagued by bad luck. By 9:30, the clouds had broken up a bit, the test jumps were completed and the competition resumed by 10:30.

The windsock now hung limp. The aircraft began making passes overhead but had to dodge around clouds to get to the opening point almost directly above the target. About an hour and a half into the jumping, as I was marking the landing of a competitor, I heard loud voices from the thousands of spectators and many were pointing up towards the sky. The only competitor from Sweden, a handsome 22-year-old lieutenant with a white jumpsuit and black striped helmet, had opened his all-black parachute but it had only partially opened on one side and the jumper beneath it was fast cork-screwing downward.

The young jumper went to the normal procedure with a malfunctioned canopy by ejecting from it and falling free. When he pulled the ripcord on his reserve chute, he was falling on his back. The reserve chute did not deploy but streamered above him. He reached in and manually tried to throw it out but some of the lines had tangled with his main ripcord that was dangling loose from his main chute's empty container. His streamered reserve canopy flapped loudly as he was free-falling downward at 90 mph. He struggled desperately to clear the lines so the reserve chute would open. At about 200 feet above the ground he looked down and realized his fate, saw it was useless, and just relaxed. A terrible crashing sound broke the air as his body slammed into the ground. His body bounced a couple feet into the air as dust flew out in all directions. There he lay, motionless on the ground, a couple hundred feet from where I was standing. Spectators were screaming in horror of what they just witnessed.

What happened next was one of the most profound experiences I have ever had. As I watched some of the competition staff rushing to his still body, I began to slip into an altered state. The sounds of screaming and crying spectators began to fade away as if someone was turning the volume down to zero. At the same time, my vision faded to nothingness, just like a scene from a movie that fades out. How long that lasted I do not remember but what I'll never forget was the soft but vivid voice that clearly spoke to me in my mind. *"Ron, if you had continued to jump, that would have occurred to you."*

When my external awareness returned, I saw the jumper from Sweden being loaded into a helicopter. Next all flags of the represented countries were lowered to half-mast and members of all the nations present fell in formation in front of their tents and had a period of respected silence. It was then that I realized the tent across from us was empty. The only competitor from Sweden was not there. Remembering what he looked like, it dawned on me that the spirit of the young man who drifted into my room the night before looked just like our friend from Sweden. Then it came to me. It was his spirit, out of body, that came to me the night before to tell me that it was his time and he was going in my place. As we stood there in silence I knew I had to write the psychic in England to share with her what I had just experienced.

As I recount and now write about this experience, I can feel the emotion of it swell up within me. It is rather traumatic to see someone die in such a manner right before your very eyes. I can easily see why soldiers in war can end up with post traumatic stress disorder, especially if they do the killing.

My experiences in Portugal were the beginning of a great opening of my mind, an opening that now had to be filled with answers. Why do certain things happen? What is our purpose in this life? Where did that young man from Sweden go after his spirit was blasted out of his physical form? This was the real beginning of my search for the greater truths of life. Soon the answers would come beyond my wildest dreams, and sharing these answers is the real reason I am writing this book.

We are all just passing through.

CHAPTER 4

Reflection on the Experience

Upon returning from Portugal, I wrote a letter to Sheila, the psychic in England, and explained everything I experienced in Portugal – the dreams, the fatality, how my sight and sound closed off, and the ensuing message that told me, if I had continued to jump, her prediction would have been fulfilled. Sheila wrote back to me and the following is her response, one that I still have.

> *Hello again Ron,*
> *So you have seen your possible fate duplicated. It must have been a most strange experience, one that very few people have ever had. I am sure, as you are, that this exact accident is what could have happened to you.*
>
> *There is something very few people consider, and that is, if something has to happen, and a person manages to make sure it doesn't happen to them, then obviously it will happen to someone else…eventually. I think this has already crossed your mind in some shape or another, has it not? If you find this communication in good health, then there is no need to be afraid of the future, to anything like the extent there was*

previously. I hope that if you do get worried again, you will write.

All men experience fear, but it is a man indeed who says so, and does his best to eliminate the cause of fear, when the cause is known, of course. Listen more closely and try to catalogue any other "dreams" you may have. You appear to be receptive. Do you feel you are?

Sincerely yours,
Sheila _____

Sheila was so gracious to share her prediction about my possible future demise, and how it could be avoided. Deep in my heart, I knew the decision I made to follow her recommendation by ceasing to continue jumping was the right one, even before I left for Portugal. I'm sure that taking her warning to heart saved me from an event that would have seriously crippled me for the rest of my life. Though I would not have died immediately, in all probability my life would have been shortened considerably as it had with the actor Christopher Reeve as a case in point. Fortunately, because of medical advancements, people who now have an injury that results in their not being able to breathe on their own no longer have to be confined to an iron lung.

I have not written about my risky experiences to portray my bravery, nor did I write about my parachuting experiences to show how well I excelled at the sport. I did, however, write about these experiences to show how key events in our lives, though they may be initially considered hard or difficult, can become opportunities for growth and ultimately lead to expanding our consciousness. So often when we experience certain events or so called accidents, we initially perceive them as tragic or difficult to endure. But if we look back on them with deeper insights, we can often see how we have actually benefited or have grown from them. Indeed, we grow much more in difficult or challenging times than during periods when everything is going smoothly, though I'm sure we would prefer not to have to go through traumatic experiences as so many do.

As I reflect back on all my so called daring adventures, I can see how they ultimately put me on a path that led to open up my mind and create a desire to begin exploring the deeper meaning and truths about life. I can also see how many times, I put myself into harm's way, yet I always survived. Looking back, I often wonder how I survived my youth. The more I thought about it, the more I realized there must have been some sort of guardian angel or protective force that has allowed me to survive so many potentially fatal experiences.

Here is another experience that could have done me in. When I was around ten, I was visiting my uncle in northern Michigan. Being adventurous, I was scaling across a cliff about 200 feet wide slowly moving from rock to rock, ledge to ledge. When I was half way across, I grabbed a rock ledge to hold onto while moving my feet further along. Suddenly the part of the ledge I was holding onto broke loose and I began to fall backwards towards jagged rocks 50 feet below. Immediately time went into slow motion, slow enough to reach forward and press my fingers hard onto another part of the ledge. My backward motion caused my fingers to slide back on the ledge until they stopped at the very front edge. Very slowly, I pulled myself forward until I was again upright against the cliff wall. I can still clearly remember that. What force was it that allowed me to enter into a state of slow motion? When I, as a kid, used to go out on the golf course fairway with my buddy and shoot arrows straight up, run a short distance and then lie flat on the ground and see how close the arrows would come to us, did I have a protective force that kept the arrows from hitting our backs, or were we just lucky?

Here is one more such story. While competing at a sport parachute competition at Ft. Bragg, North Carolina, I experienced my second main parachute malfunction. On my first malfunction a year or so earlier,

I cut away from my main chute, went back into free fall, deployed my reserve chute, and made an easy landing on the grass runway without any problems.

During individual accuracy events, aircraft fly tight orbital patterns, letting the competitors out one at a time on each orbit until the plane is empty. I was the second one to jump on this load of jumpers. I made a short delay before opening; however, I opened directly over the first jumper about 500 feet below me. Immediately, I realized my chute had a partial malfunction. One side of my chute was tangled with the lines and that prevented it from fully opening. I was descending in a spiraling manner. Then it got testy. I was coming down right over the open chute below me. If I released and fell free from my tangled main cute, it would mean I would fall into the jumper's open chute below me and that could become fatal for both of us.

As I was spiraling, I swung slightly off to one side of the chute below. I released the lines from my harness on my left side, but held onto them. When I swung to the outer edge of the chute below me, I released the right set of the lines while letting go of the left side I was holding on to. Thinking I had released totally free of my main chute, I immediately pulled my reserve and when it opened, it actually bumped the jumper's open chute that had been below me. I can still remember seeing the surprised expression on the face of that jumper. But then I noticed the right set of lines I thought I had released had not totally disengaged, and part of my reserve chute tangled with those set of lines still attached to the main chute. It was so tangled that I was coming down on two-thirds of my reserve chute at a good rate of speed. I desperately tried to untangle it while I was descending but that only made it worse. I was swinging back and forth quite a bit like a pendulum. Then I saw the ground coming up fast. If I landed on a down swing the landing force would have been that much worse. But once again, the forces of protection were with me and I landed on the upswing. Even so, I hit the ground quite hard and badly bruised my hip, but luckily nothing was broken.

Yes, as I reflected back on the first half of my life, other than some physical injuries, I surely must have had some force or energy protecting me. There must have been a greater purpose for my life than jumping out of perfectly good airplanes. I had other close calls beyond parachuting but I won't go into the details of them here. Why do some individuals like me seem to be protected when we put ourselves into harm's way and others at various young ages get wiped out early in life? I was to find the answer to this and so much more during my search for the truth that became much more serious after a surprising spiritual experience the day after Christmas, 1972.

Through the years of growing up and attending church in the Catholic religion, I always felt there had to be a greater spiritual depth and there was something I needed to know and wasn't getting. Though many Catholics love the rituals and ceremonies, to me it was just like watching the same play week after week with the same prayers being read. I needed more than that, something deeper. I broke away from the church for several years, yet I knew I eventually had to find some source of spiritual fulfillment as well as pursuing a greater knowledge of spiritual truths. Some years later, I began to feel something drawing me back to the spiritual aspect of life, so I began attending different churches seeking the deeper knowledge I was seeking. If I brought up any subjects other than what the doctrine and dogma of that religion adhered to, I experienced a resistance to discuss it. Yes, some of the philosophies in the traditional religions were good and even helpful, but I needed something more, a deeper level of truth that I somehow knew there must be. I never could find what I was looking for in the traditional religions.

Finally my quest for deeper spiritual truths was answered. By the day after Christmas, all the festivities were over and it was time to slip into a quiet meditation and let the rush and stress of it all go. After a couple minutes of deep breathing, a mental voice entered my consciousness and said, 'Greetings dear one."

It was my spiritual guide who came through and began by giving words of wisdom. I was quite excited and asked questions I longed to know the answers to. This went on the whole evening and continued until 4 am. As I think back, I asked a lot of really dumb questions. From the very first communication, I was warned to always begin a communication with a prayer of protection and also surround myself with white Divine Light. This was to prevent any negative or dark energies from slipping in. These communications were the beginning of the answers to my search and the fulfillment of the Bible verse, *Seek and ye shall find.*

After a time, I asked why I was receiving communication with the spirit plane. *"We have come to you because you were seeking, because you were open, and because you were unafraid."*

That was followed by detailed instructions of a process to clear, open and receive mental thoughts, one they called Thought Plane Transference. It is a process of transferring thoughts from the spiritual plane into the consciousness of an open physical mind

Having practiced meditation in years past was very helpful. First one must become very still and deeply relax into a meditative state of Alpha. Next clear the mind of random thoughts (this is the hardest part). Then pray for protection and surround yourself with white Divine Light and affirm that only those of the Light whose intentions are of the highest good may come through. Finally, open the mind and mentally become aware of the thoughts that come into your consciousness. The thoughts that transfer from the higher dimensions and enter into the human consciousness are often very subtle. In the early stages, the human ego will try to slip in thoughts to make you feel good. After a time, there comes a knowingness of the difference between spirit communication and ego infiltration into the consciousness because the vibrations are different.

While the communications began with my spirit guide, as I began to comprehend a greater knowledge of spiritual truths over the weeks and months that followed, I gradually connected with the higher levels of the spiritual hierarchy, so to speak. On the Earth plane, we tend to use the word "truth" very loosely and usually think when someone uses the word, they really mean *"the truth."* My years of receiving messages have revealed there are many levels of truth. To learn more about *truth,* read on.

Know the truth and the truth will set you free

CHAPTER 5

When Is Truth Really True?

All truth on the Earth Plane is relative truth. Absolute truth is most often beyond our comprehension because it involves the spiritual realm, Universal Laws, or that which is God. As humans, what we perceive as truth changes as humanity evolves. If we did not change our beliefs, we would never evolve. Let's look back in time. Long ago, it was considered true that the Earth was flat. Long ago, it was considered true that the sun rotated around the Earth and the Earth was the center of the universe.

If you were able to tell someone in the 18th century that humans would be able to fly from one side of their continent to the other in a matter of hours, do you think they would believe such a thing could ever be true? *"Why if man was meant to fly, he would have been created with wings."* Likewise, if I were to tell you that, in another 60 years people, on this planet could travel from Earth to a distant solar system many light years away in a matter of minutes, would you believe such a thing could be true?

There has always been a natural resistance to change within humanity, but the truth is, progress is only possible through change. If someone from our future were to come back to our current time and tell us what the Earth will be like in another 50 years, most people would think it preposterous. Could you believe that, in the not too distant future, the air and ground travel of today will be considered as primitive as how we now look back on traveling by covered wagon? Can you conceive that medically operating on a human body by cutting open the flesh for an operation will become a primitive method of returning a diseased person to health or screwing the bones back together of an injured person? Could you believe that our education system will some day educate our young by directly downloading knowledge from computers into their brain cells?

Physical changes are easy to accept as a way of life. A few years ago, all telephones were hard-wired. Today, cell phones receive and send sound, photos and more, and we carry them around with us on our hip or in a purse. How will it be tomorrow?

But what about changes to our religious or spiritual beliefs? There are many who will always refuse to change their beliefs, even when evidence proves differently. Let's look at some history of religions. In the very early religions, humans had many spirit gods who they believed controlled all aspects of nature. They held primitive forms of worship to keep their gods from becoming angry. Some gave human or animal sacrifices to appease the gods. If a tribe was defeated in battle, their tribal gods could no longer be worshipped but the absence of their god or gods created fear, insecurity, and a sense of meaninglessness. Mankind has always believed in a supreme being or beings of some sort. As knowledge of spiritual beings expanded and matured, it was no longer believed that angry gods caused hurricanes, earthquakes, or other violent acts of nature. Eventually the definitions of gods adapted to new realities. Later, the understanding of a single supreme force gradually became accepted when Moses connected with God and made clear the truth that there was only one God, the I AM that I AM. The stories of Exodus tell how Moses led the Israelites out of Egypt around 1290 BC. Gradually the consciousness gave rise to a single deity on a larger scale.

When the more modern world unfolded, the religious or spiritual belief of a one God evolved into various religions. When humans become ready and can comprehend greater truths, God sends teachers into the world to create a better understanding of our spirituality and of God Him/Herself. As a result, three major religions were created. The Hindu/Buddhist religion developed for the people in the Far East. The Islam religion expanded into the Middle Eastern part of the world. The third major religion unfolded after the life of Jesus and became the Judeo/Christian religion that grew into the western world but also expanded into parts of other Third World countries. Now missionaries have spread Christian beliefs throughout the world. Time carried these three basic religious philosophies into the most populated countries in the world.

As more time passed, interactions began to occur within these three philosophies and created some confusion and uncertainty. Soon, the confusion led to anxiety and created divisions within each of the three major religious systems. Those who were threatened by the changes taking place turned to a fanatical fundamentalism and vowed to fight to the death for their beliefs. Those who welcomed a more open and expanded belief system moved to a new consensus of beliefs. As religion stands today, there are many separate factions within the same sects but those that are more deeply rooted in the fundamental past are unchanging and unwilling to open to new possibilities of truth. They stand firmly and unwavering in their beliefs because they truly believe they are the absolute truth.

No religious system is very tolerant of any efforts to change. Religious writers have created the fear of damnation to anyone who would add to or delete any of their writings.

To those in the past who have tried reform or who brought forth new possibilities of thinking, the powers within religions have burned them to the stake, or have excommunicated them, and they have even gone to wars defending their false beliefs. Regardless of the resistance to change, or fanaticisms, or the wars and killings, beliefs have eventually given way to new thoughts of truth as change slowly wins out. If this were not so, we would still be worshiping gods made of stone. The views of a wrathful and vengeful God of the Old Testament have given way to a loving and forgiving God in the New Testament. The radical fundamentalists with obsolete negative beliefs will slowly decrease in number and new thought religions with a more positive and spiritually optimistic view will grow in numbers. This shift has already begun.

There is a great awakening occurring as increasing numbers of people in recent times are truly seeking something new and they realize that what they are seeking cannot be found in the usual places, not in money or possessions or a better job or a different relationship. What they seek cannot be found through fame or power. Some even realize what they are seeking cannot be found in fundamental religions.

Within the University of Chicago is a recognized organization called the National Opinion Research Center. They report that the proportion of adult Americans calling themselves Protestants had been a steady 63% for decades; however, more recently this has fallen to 52% and the trend continues to fall. Catholics seem to remain steady at 23% of the population while Jews or Muslims do not exceed 4%. The category that has increased the most in the past decade is the one with people who do not subscribe to any specific religious identification. They are in the process of shedding their old affiliation and embarking on a great search for deeper or a more meaningful spirituality beyond religious dogma. This group has more recently grown from 8% of the American population to 14% and continues to grow. They still believe in God but do not consider themselves as religious. They instead consider themselves 'spiritual' rather than anything more specific and are looking for a new and more powerful spirituality for their lives. Many are flocking to the new thought churches such as Unity or Religious Science where the focus is more on our Oneness with God and all life, while also focusing on love, forgiveness, service, unity, religious tolerance, and many other aspects that promote spiritual growth and spiritual healing. The new thought churches rarely ever focus on evil, sin, and Satan because they believe spiritual faith should not be driven by fear. This positive approach is a shift away from fundamental beliefs and practices that so often give rise to fear, those aspects that no longer serve the many who are seeking spiritual growth.

For most humans, regardless of what religion they affiliate with, their beliefs are not inherent from birth but are taught to them from a very early age, and are usually based on the beliefs of a parent or parents. In some marriages, the parents may not have the same beliefs because they are unwilling to give up or change from the religious teachings they were brought up to believe. In this case, the parent with the stronger convictions usually wins out and leads the child or children into his or her religious faith. Consider this. Nearly all of our beliefs are based on what we have been taught by parents, religious leaders, or from the writings of others human entities.

Everything in the writings of the Bible, the Koran, or all other books written and published as the accepted truths of their respective religious beliefs were written by humans through human minds. Nearly all these religious writings were based on a combination of history, words of prophets and sages, or from the documented memories of the words of the Masters such as Jesus, Buddha, and Mohammad. Jesus and other Masters taught in parables and used symbolisms as examples to assist in making their teachings more understandable.

After reading the Bible over many years, I became curious as to how the Bible originated; who were the writers; how was the information received, and when. So I went to the library and found several books on the history of the Bible. The data is somewhat different from book to book but I'll give a general overview of what I found.

The stories recounted in the books of Genesis and Exodus were verbally passed down from generation to generation and they were passed down this way for centuries before any were written down. The Israelites are thought to have begun writing down their literature and history during the reign of David in the 10th century BC. When Jerusalem fell in the 6th century BC, they began putting everything in writing to preserve their history. Some of the writings were considered holy and are known today as 'The Books of Hebrew' in the Old Testament. The Bible was originally put together from a series of often unconnected or loosely associated groups of short books. There were many thousands to select from. In both the Old and New Testaments, most of the stories regarding significant events were circulated long before they were ever written down.

Jerome, who was named a saint after his death, had collected many manuscripts for years during his many travels. Beginning in 386 AD, he spent 30 years working for the church, translating many manuscripts into Latin from those originally written in Hebrew (Old Testament) and Greek (New Testament).

One story had it that, from these translations, the Roman Emperor Constantine gathered a large staff of about 2,000 to determine, from all the translated manuscripts, what should be included in a bible. Much argument and dissention occurred within the many members of the staff about what should be included, so Constantine got rid of all but a couple hundred of his staff and he ultimately made the final decisions on what would be included.

The references to reincarnation were eliminated because they thought man would try harder if he thought he had only one chance. Even so, in at least five different areas of the scriptures there is an indication that a man expresses more than once upon Earth.

After the final material was selected, Constantine ordered 50 Bibles to be produced for the instruction of the church. They were to be hand-copied on parchment. After this version was produced, the Bible's evolution was very involved. Following Constantine's Bibles, various versions and translations to other languages were made. Later, when copying and translating the writings into other versions, some parts were added and some rejected. The overall history is long and detailed. The following is from *A Book: A History of the Bible:*

> *"Many people who have used the Bible throughout its long history have regarded its text as having been divinely inspired, and that this very unusual status has been why the Bible has been so widely promoted and read. The history does include accounts of burning and deliberate destruction of various writings."*

In those days when the consciousness had not yet expanded to an understanding of the human ego, stories were created about such things as evil, the devil or Satan as a means of explaining the negative influences of the ego. In the stories of the Old and New Testaments that include the devil or demons, such as the story of when Jesus was tempted by Satan, exchange the word 'ego' with the word 'Satan' or 'demons' and see if it does not fit.

The ego in man was originally created as a defensive mechanism to protect the human form and assist in his survival. However, the spirit within has no fear of survival because it knows it is eternal and never dies or ends. Through time, the ego has grown to a level of outdoing its real purpose and thus it has created great problems for the human expression. You may ask, "What about the stories of demons possessing humans who were then cast out?" This can be equated to what we know today as exorcism. Exorcism of what, you may ask?

Some entities who have lived upon the earth plane have, shall we say, committed inhumane acts such as murder, torture, and other gross deeds. These acts, especially when doing so with pleasure, lowered their vibrations tremendously. When their lives ended, their souls never went into the light but continued to roam around the astral plane seeking to do more horrendous acts. However, they could not do so without a physical form, so they sought out other low vibration physical beings still living on the Earth plane to attach themselves to, so they could influence the beings through their attachment. A very strong and highly spiritually evolved human who possessed a strong spiritual power can release these low vibration souls from the beings they are attached to. Thus it was said, they cast out demons. There are those today whose purpose it is to perform the releasing of spirit attachment. It is termed "spiritual attachment release." The more traditional term is exorcism.

Throughout the years of stories being passed down and later written down, and through the process of translation from one language to another, some of the original Bible scriptures have become distorted. But even so, there still remain many great truths within the passages of the Bible. I want to make it very clear that I am not condemning the Bible. I truly love many of the scripture messages that are encouraging and instill a hope in us that life can be better if we but follow the words of wisdom given to mankind. I am only trying to make the point that everything in the Bible was subject to the fallibility of the memories of those who became the writers of the many scriptures and sometimes twisted or distorted the messages. That is why, when some of the passages I have read did not feel right within my heart, I questioned spirit wisdom for an explanation.

When reading and studying the Bible, the Koran, or any religious or sacred texts, it is important to understand that many of the original writings came from stories passed down over generations and did not come into written form until long after the events occurred. This is especially true in the Old Testament. Human memories are not always infallible and can be influenced by many things. Because the stories relied on memories of the original events, it is possible and even probable that some distortions occurred over the years of being handed down from one generation to the next long before ever being written down. In most cases these writings have been translated into other languages. I have experienced distortion in my own memory. When I have read something or seen a movie, I have noticed that when I've gone back and reread or seen the movie again, my memory of certain details was not accurate. It is simply a human mental weakness that occurs.

When a scholar or scribe of the writings translates from one language into another, that individual or even groups of translators must interpret what the original writings were really saying or intended to communicate, to the best of their understanding. In some languages, there are often no words that directly equate from one language to the next. In this case the interpreters must use a series of words to try and capture the original intent of the word being translated. In the English language for example, the word "love" is a single word that refers to many types of love, i.e., romantic, brotherly, the sex act, and more. There are, however, many different words in other languages that equate to love, depending on the type of love being expressed.

Consider these points: Translations from one language to the next can sometimes result in distortions of the original meanings. Some might say that God would not allow this to happen. But God promised us free will and the freedom of choice. To intervene would be to break that promise. The original holy writings of the various religions of the world have indeed been translated into several languages. Many of the readers of these holy writings believe every word as the literal truth. Therefore I believe that accepting these very old translated writings as literal can be misleading at times and following them religiously as absolute truth can cause many difficulties and even become dangerous. Some examples are presented here.

Old Testament verses from the Living Bible:

> *Leviticus 25:44 "...You may purchase slaves from foreign nations living around you, and you may purchase the children of the foreigners living among you, even though they have born in your land."*

We have long ago evolved beyond slavery in the U.S. and would get into much legal trouble if we followed the above verse.

> *Leviticus 21:20 states that "I may not approach the altar of God if I have a broken nose, have pimples or scabby skin, am lame or have a sight defect."*

Somehow I don't think God would so discriminate.

> *Exodus 35:2 "...the seventh day is a day of solemn rest ... anyone working on that day must die."*

If this were an absolute truth today, many of the churches would begin to lose many of their members to the other side. Other verses call for stoning your children to death, or for heresy.

There are many more passages like this. If we were to follow these Old Testament laws in our current day, we would experience great problems. These laws were obviously given and written for the people in the days of these writings and were created to ensure the people behaved according to the wishes of the religious leaders. It is obvious that many of these writings are not taken as truth for our current time. It therefore appears that what is considered literal truth for today's time is very selective.

The New Testament does not project the wrath of God but rather Jesus teaches of a God that is more loving and forgiving. Unfortunately, many religious teachers and writings tell us we are unworthy or less than the truth of that which we really are in spite of the Genesis scripture that tells us we are "created in the image and likeness of God."

In the Book of St. John, Chapter 14:6, Jesus is quoted as saying, *"No one comes to the father but by me."* Many of the fundamental Christians have interpreted this to mean, you must accept Jesus as your personal savior and if you do not, you will not be saved from eternal damnation and burn in Hell forever more, regardless if you have lived an exemplary or saintly life. I have always had a hard time believing this accepted interpretation of that passage. Most of the details about Jesus' life and his sayings were documented several decades after the activities and statements made by Him. One day when communicating with the Master, I asked Him if that could mean something else. He answered:

> *In the translation processes, the original meaning of that message became distorted. The correct interpretation of what I once said was, "No one comes into a oneness with the Father except by coming into the Christ Consciousness.*

This made more sense to me, but even that could be misunderstood so further explanation was given. Jesus came into the Christ Consciousness at the time of his baptism by John the Baptist. Thus he said, "I and the Father are One." Coming into the Christ Consciousness made him fully aware of his oneness with God. In reality, we are all 'one' through our God connection, but we are not consciously aware of it because we have not yet spiritually evolved and awakened to the level of coming into a Christ Consciousness.

Obviously, not all beings on this planet have accepted Jesus as their personal savior. Many do not have any knowledge of a man named Jesus who walked upon this planet two millennia ago. Could 75% of the world's population be doomed to damnation and an eternity in Hell simply because they have not come to know Jesus and accept him as their savior? This is what many fundamental Christians believe. During one of the communications with Christ, he said this:

> *"I have come into the world to **save** no one. However, I did come into the world to teach man how to save himself, not from eternal damnation, but from the dark ways of his ego that can destroy his and other lives."*

There are millions of very spiritually evolved humans on the earth plane who live very Godly focused lives. Many have never had the opportunity to hear of Jesus. Would God condemn these beautiful people if they have never even heard of Jesus? Not the God I have come to know. Jesus said, "I and the Father are ONE," but so is **all** life expressing in **all** realms. I received the following communication early this morning. It will help to understand this truth.

"My dear son, I have come to your consciousness to help you understand creation. It was written that I created Heaven and Earth. While this is true, understand that Heaven is symbolic of the spiritual aspect of life and Earth is symbolic of the physical aspect of life. Everything I have created in the physical realm has opposites. Where there is hot, there is cold; where there is dry, there is wet; where there is light, there is dark; where there is life, there is death, and so it is. Know that all I have created, I have done so out of the energy of my beingness. Among all else that I am, I AM energy. Know also that a part of my energy remains in all that I have created and acts as that which bonds all matter together -- all that is within a physical beingness. So then, I AM within every human being on your planet. So also am I in all else, including the mineral kingdom, the animal kingdom, and all aspects of nature. But even more for I am in the celestial realms of stars, planets and so much more you are not yet aware of.

When the spirit leaves a physical creation, as in death, my spiritual essence leaves also and the physical is then no longer held together. When this occurs, the physical is transformed through a process you term decay. This you experience in humans, animals, and plant life. This also occurs in the universes with stars, planets, moons, and other formations in space. But in these so-called deaths, the disintegration process is different. Thus I have said, everything in the physical realm is temporary.

*The transition process from physical to spirit is a natural one within all physical creations. The duration that a physical creation exists varies greatly within the realm of time. For insects it is a matter of days, for animals and humans it is in years, for stars and planets, it is millions of millennia. Know, however, that in the realm of spirit, there is **no time,** as you know it. Therefore 'forever' is an eternal 'now.' Nothing (no thing) in spirit ever dies.*

Realize that there is no such thing as a normal life span in the physical realm. Insects die on car windshields; humans die in car crashes, or tornados, or tsunamis; deer die from hunter's bullets, humans die from their enemy's bullets. Though you may think life is cut short, in reality there are no accidents. All is part of a greater plan that most humans do not understand. You may think it a great tragedy when a human departs the physical at less than an average life span. I will tell you this again. There is no such thing as a normal life span. When a spirit departs from the physical body at any age, that spirit, which is the reality of its being, enters into a world of great peace, great love, great freedom and a joy that is beyond your imagination. Yes, there are some who enter into a lower vibrational plane, but they are not doomed to exist there for eternity, though rising to higher planes may be slow.

I have created a multitude of life and matter in deep space that you have not yet dreamed of. Know this. As you are aware of Body, Mind, and Spirit, all that I have created in the physical realm is the Body aspect of my beingness. All of my creations are brought forth from the Mind aspect of my beingness, and all that I have created contains a part of My Spirit. Therefore I AM ONE with all that is, and all that is, is ONE with Me. As above, so below. Therefore my son, since I AM in all that is, so also am I in you and all of mankind. I would not express this in words if it were not so.

For those who believe in a literal Hell, I say this unto you. If I AM in all life, would I ever cast a part of myself into eternal damnation? With this thought, I now give unto you who are a part of me, my deepest love, for love is what I AM."

I found this communication very helpful in explaining the point I have been trying to make.

I am not condemning the Bible or any religious writings. The point I am trying to make is this. Whenever we take all the holy writings in any religion literally, we can become distanced to the understanding of the true essence of the messages. There **are indeed** great truths in the Bible, in the Koran, and other religious writings. However, these writings were written a very long time ago, yet some still apply today while others were directed to the people of that time, especially in the Old Testament.

Here is an example of how a couple words can change the original intended thought. One of the Ten Commandments states, "Thou shall not kill." A message from spirit has said that it should more correctly be stated as, "Thou shall do no murder." To murder is to intentionally take the life of a human being. We kill animals for food. We kill insects, animals, and other humans with our automobiles, and we kill each other in wars but these killings are not considered murder. This is just another example of how a few words can change the original intent of the meaning. Blind literal acceptance of everything as it is written will create distortions of the intended truth. If we become attuned to the spirit of the messages and read the holy writings with our hearts instead of our brains, we can better perceive the true essence of the messages.

Words are so very limiting. For those on the higher realms, and even among highly evolved beings on other planetary systems, not only are thoughts given and received without words (hard for us to believe) but also the feelings and the vibrations associated with the thought are also sent to the receiver. The statement, "A picture is worth a thousand words," applies to Universal Language. It is a language of symbols but also includes vibrations, colors, and tones. For example, if you were to receive a symbol from Universal language that meant *I love you*, you would experience the vibrations of love, the colors of love, the sounds of love, and the feeling of love. It is a level of communication far beyond the mere use of words and leaves little for misunderstanding.

Remember, true reality is oftentimes beyond our comprehension. I would have found this deeper level of communication difficult to really understand had I not experienced it once. Here is the true story of that experience.

My mother was a gentle and loving spirit. In her mid-eighties, she began to decline physically and mentally. She began falling and injuring herself in addition to having memory problems. My sister and I agreed that she had declined to the point of needing an assisted living environment. Mother seemed to be okay with that but after 17 months, the staff in the assisted living home felt they could no longer adequately care for her declining condition, therefore she needed a greater level of care. The next move was to a nursing home. It became evident with every visit in the nursing home how much she was declining. Finally, she declined to the point where she longer recognized me. During my last visit with her, I asked her if she knew who I was. She replied, "Yes, you are the man who owns the golf course." Where that came from I'll never know.

It was no surprise when soon after that last visit I received a call with the news mother had passed on. I called my sister with the news and we both headed for the nursing home. I lived much closer and arrived there first. Her body was laid out in a private viewing room. When I looked upon her, my first thought was, this is not my mother, this is just an empty physical shell. So I sat down next to the bed, quieted myself, and tuned in to her essence. In less than a minute, I experienced something very profound. I began to sense a great feeling of joy, even to the point of elation. I was overcome with these powerful feelings, feelings that were very unnatural considering I just lost someone so very close to me. Then I clearly heard the voice of my mother in my mind as she said to me, *"My dear son, you cannot begin to comprehend how absolutely beautiful it was moving into this plane of life."*

The point is, my mother was not only able to convey her thoughts into my consciousness, but she was also able to permeate my being with her powerful feelings of love and joy. Her complete experience of crossing over is presented in Chapter 15.

If we seek truth through our intellect, there is a greater chance the truth we find will be a relative truth, not very aligned with absolute truth. If we seek truth through an open heart and mind, there is a greater chance the relative truth we find will be closer to absolute. It is very important to come from the heart, rather than the head, when it comes to perceiving what is true. There are those who are imposters and those who are coming from ego who can misguide and lead us into false beliefs. This is the agenda of many of the secret societies, and sadly their power and influence has reached almost every level of life. The good news is, the 'Light' is now becoming stronger and is exposing their lies, their secrets, their dishonesty, and their cover-ups almost daily. Our use of discernment is so very important. Look carefully at what or where someone might try to lead you. It is best when we summarize our perceptions of what someone tells us by taking it into our heart and being aware of how it feels. I suggest you do this with all the writings in this book, but please read the entire subject before doing so.

From beliefs of multiple gods in primitive times to our current beliefs of a one true God, it is easy to see that what was once considered a truth continues to change. On the earth plane, there will always be different levels of truth. If ever we believe we now have the absolute truths, we will never spiritually evolve to higher understandings of truth.

When we were in grade school we were taught basic addition, subtraction, division and multiplication. When we understood this level of teaching, we were then ready for the next level. When we entered high school, our prior learning prepared us to comprehend mathematics -- algebra, geometry, trigonometry, and calculus. When we entered college, we were ready to comprehend yet more advanced levels of complex formulas. And so it is with our understandings of a greater level of spiritual truths.

Progress is only possible when we, our society, our country, or even our whole world, achieves greater knowledge and applies it with wisdom. Where does new knowledge come from that replaces the old accepted levels of truth? For example, let's take the food pyramid that displays the best nutritional foods for our body. When the levels of the best or healthiest foods to the least healthy were published, we accepted them as true values. As greater knowledge was achieved in this area, the values we accepted as true changed. If we accept current nutritional values as the ultimate best it can be, we will never search for greater values of nutritional benefits, or of medical procedures, or of religious dogma. Better and safer automobiles are always being built, yet the ultimate automobile is far from being created. The world of medicine and surgical techniques is advancing rapidly, yet we will continue to experience greater breakthroughs in this field because we accept that we have not yet achieved the highest knowledge about medical procedures.

But with religion, it seems quite different. There are such wide and varied beliefs within a vast number of religious faiths, yet most religions believe they have the absolute truths and some are willing to die to defend their beliefs, especially in the East. Religious fanaticism is the basis of most wars. When it comes to changing one's beliefs, too often the element of fear comes into play. Many religious leaders preach a message that creates fear if their followers stray from the doctrines and dogma of their rigid accepted faith. Even so, it is nearly impossible to prove any aspect of what any religion believes as being *'the'* truth.

Why is it then that we humans with our religious and spiritual beliefs are so reluctant to open up to higher levels of spiritual truths? Too often, the scripture writers have inserted statements that are fear-based and indicate bad things will happen to anyone who strays from the teachings or changes any of the written words. An example is written in the last chapters of the Book of Revelation: "If any man shall add unto these things, God shall add unto him the plagues that are written in this book."

How often have I heard some of the fear-based preachers tell their followers they will burn in hell if they do not literally and strictly follow the preacher's interpretation of the scriptures? Please know this. The true teachings of the Masters will never incorporate fear based messages in their teachings because they know that fear is a tremendous barrier to spiritual growth.

Our Creator God continues to send us spiritual teachers, and when those teachers bring forth a higher truth that is, shall we say, outside of the box of the current fundamental beliefs, they are at least severely criticized and called blasphemers or heretics. In the extreme, they are exiled, crucified, or assassinated. This is why the guides and Masters have said they must spoon-feed us spiritual truths which go beyond those that are generally accepted at the current time. The Master once told me that if I wanted to continue to evolve spiritually, I must be willing to let go of any aspect of my current beliefs, even those I had been given earlier, because there will always be higher levels of truth that edge closer to absolute.

Let us not fret and think everything we believe is wrong. There is just a higher level to understand, and there always will be while on the physical plane. It's because the human mind/brain cannot comprehend pure absolute truth. Even so, if we are open, we can continue to spiritually evolve by becoming open to truths that are closer to absolute. Relative to this, the Master once told me that it would help our spiritual evolution journey if we had a goal of outgrowing any church or spiritual group we had joined.

The God within us continues to speak to every human on the earth plane. Many of us speak or pray to God, but how many really quiet themselves and listen for a response? This is something we are all capable of doing. The first thing we must do is believe we can, but it seems most do not try because they believe they are not able to hear God speaking to them.

It can be a great benefit to learn how to really quiet ourselves and clear the chatter in our minds. While this can often be difficult, it can be achieved, for example, by focusing our mind on a beautiful scene and then become open to the thoughts that are coming from Source. Oftentimes, the thoughts will be very subtle, but sometimes very direct. Other times, the communications will come as intuitive thoughts or just very positive feelings. It will not always be in words, but it may be.

God may also speak to us through other physical beings. Someone might say something that is an answer to a question we had and it could even be from a beggar on the street or from a little child. God might also communicate to us through that source we call Mother Nature. Remember that old saying, "God speaks to us in mysterious ways." The key is to be open. Progress occurs when one is willing to get out of the 'box of accepted beliefs' and explore or search for greater truths. When greater levels of truth are accepted, new paradigms are created and the 'box' shifts to yet another level. Those with closed minds usually scoff at new paradigms. Jesus was often accused of blasphemy when he presented new thoughts of that time. He is quoted in scripture as saying "*I and the Father are one.*" However, spirit has said that what Jesus continued to say, but was not recorded is, "*and so are all of you.*" However, this was considered too extreme and was omitted from the scripture writings.

During His time, this truth was considered complete heresy and even today, some will undoubtedly think so. But spirit teachers and God are telling us that the essence of God is in all that He created and this includes us. Thus, through our spirit connection to our Creator, we are all one. Without that spiritual connection, we would not exist because God is the essence **in** and of **all** life, just as He indicated in his message earlier in this chapter.

The Master Teachers through the ages have always brought forth greater truths, often with great resistance to their acceptance. But now, IT IS TIME to become open to even greater truths as spirit teachers on the higher planes as well as masters on the Earth are pouring out messages of greater understandings for a world that is now moving up to a higher dimension of life expression. If all Earth beings could understand, in our oneness with God, whatever we do to another is, in a sense, doing it to ourselves, then crime and wars would end and peace would be assured. Spirit has assured us that the energy for this movement is in motion and this time it will, indeed, come. However, it is up to us as to how and when.

It is easy to sit in the rocking chair of the traditional beliefs, but progress is seldom achieved when we stay with the status quo. Know this:

The true hallmarks of history came neither from the keening of the crowds, nor from the thunder of the conquers, but from the hearts of the handful who skirmish into the lonely unknown beyond security.

If the masses would look at our world, many might say, "Okay, so we have wars; so are there those who die of hunger; and so is there poverty. That's nothing new so let's just accept that that's the way it is." But the Creator has said, *"The primary purpose of all life is to evolve to a higher expression of life."* This can only be accomplished if we are continually open and seek higher and better ways of being, of doing, and of living, first with our own lives and then collectively as planetary beings. The closed minds will always throw out anchors to maintain the status quo and keep humanity from moving forward. This is especially true for those who are in power and control, or if great financial gains are being made from the current system.

The open mind looks to the heavens and says, *"Yes there is a bigger and better way. Let us seek and find it."* A better way usually comes from discovering a higher truth, be it spiritual or physical.

From the times of Moses and as time continued to progress until the time was right, God sent to Earth another great teacher, Jesus of Nazareth. He came and taught greater levels of understanding about life and God. He did not discard all the old thoughts and beliefs but taught higher levels of truth through his teachings and examples. IT IS TIME once again to open ourselves to greater levels of truth. We must, therefore, be willing to let go of some of the old limiting beliefs that have crept in to religious teachings and allow or accept the new. This is evolution. The old beliefs are in transition to higher levels of truth and are being given now because many **are** ready and the time **is** right.

In the book, The New Revelations, author Neale Donald Walsch dialogs the subject of organized religion with God. While what God said may be a shocker, as I observe what is going on in the world today I am not surprised.

> *It is time you acknowledge a human truth at which no one wants to look. One of the biggest problems in the world today is organized religion.*
> *Organized religions are a problem. They are not a solution, they are a problem.*
> *Not all religions but most, and certainly most of the largest.*

What is it then in religions that cause all the problems? It appears to be the great diversity in beliefs; not only what they believe about God, but also what they believe God would have them do according to their religious teachings.

It is religious intolerance at its worst when religious leaders tell their members to kill those of other faiths, but it is also religious intolerance when one Christian religion teaches its congregation that a different Christian religion is wrong and should be avoided. When we see massive religious demonstrations or become aware of who the suicide bombers are, it is usually the youth doing it and it is the religious leaders who are brain washing them to believe that it is God who wants them to do these things if they are to receive great rewards. If these radical and negative beliefs do not change, neither will the religious intolerance, the hate, and the hostile aggression cease.

IT IS TIME to share the greater truths that so many dedicated human messengers are recently receiving from God and His many teachers of the greater Light. If all religions of the world would believe and live the simple yet greater truths of love, forgiveness, tolerance of differences, and the knowledge that, in reality, we are all one, it is then that peace and unity will transform the world into a marvelous place to express life, and to do so without fear.

A child's belief in Santa Claus is not wrong. It is good for children that age to have such a wonderful belief. Religions and their spiritual beliefs have evolved through the ages from Stone Age tribal beliefs, to the one God of Abraham's time who was believed to be wrathful, vengeful, and expected animal sacrifices. When the world was in turmoil and needed greater understandings of God, He sent the Master Jesus into the world. He taught us of a God who was loving, forgiving, and did not require sacrifices. Now, IT IS TIME for yet a higher understanding of God and spirituality.

I received a communication years ago from our Creator God. It was during the early stages of my communications with spirit and it came through in the Old English style of language. When later I asked why the old style, He thought I would relate better to Him using the style of language I associated with God when reading the King James Version of the Bible. The message began with "I am." I then asked, "You are who?" Next came, "I AM that I AM." Shivers ran through my whole being and I was swept with a beautiful energy. I turned on the tape recorder and just mentally listened. This is what I recorded as the words came through.

I AM Thy Lord Thy God. Thou shall have none before me.

My purpose for coming to thee this Earth day is to relate to thee what I really am. I AM many things and the human mind is incapable of knowing or even understanding because of thy limited definitions. I AM first of all energy. It is my movement. I AM more than energy. I AM intelligence and I AM movement with mind. I pour my mind into all that I have created out of my energy. I AM fragmented yet whole. I have personality because of the personalities of my expressions. I AM male and female yet neither. Thou lovest because I love and thou art a part of me. Thou givest because I give and thou art a part of me. Thou livest because I live and thou art a part of me.

I manifest all my thoughts into reality, yet what thou seest as reality is unreal. Only the essence is real. I AM the essence of all that is known or unknown to thee. I AM vibration and movement. I AM intelligent energy capable of creating intelligent energy. I have no beginning and I will have no end. I know all things in all realms. I AM never away from thee for I AM in thee and surround thee. Thou needest never fear me. Fear cometh only when thou willfully separate from Me.

I AM not an old man sitting in the clouds. Many think of me and speak to me as if this were true. I manifested my

*expression in the Christ who is my child as thou art and he
tried to teach thee where I was but so many did not listen.*

*I AM totally connected to all creation. I AM Power. I AM moving
never still, for life is movement -- Love is movement. Allow
thy mind to escape its finite limits and thou wilt see Me in My
essence in the All that is. It is done by not limiting thy thoughts
of me. I AM beyond all man's perception of My Being.*

*I walk in a black man's shoes; I sit upon a king's throne; I
die of hunger in India; I travel in the great starships. I AM
a flower in the field and the bread upon thy table. I AM THE
FIELD; I AM THE STARSHIP; I AM INDIA.*

*Expand thy consciousness of me and when thou doest, thou
wilt expand thy consciousness of thyself and thy potential.
I AM trying hard to get willing humans to see beyond their
limited vision. I AM and so, my children, art thee. Allow me
to work through thee since thou art my creation and thou
art my idea. Accept thy Sonship as the Christ accepted His.
The way you can serve me best is TO BE for I AM within
thee. Doest thou not understand that we are one and that
I will work and walk within thee. This is easy if thou wilt
allow it. My way is easy. My way is easier than thy ego's. Be
never sad for I AM with thee and in thee and around thee. I
will come to thee again. Thou hast my Sourcal blessings and
Omnipotent Love.*

I had become comfortable communicating with guides, angels and even the
Master, but I never expected I would or could speak directly with God. A
feeling came over me after the above communication that I cannot explain.
I have since received many communications after this one as He promised,
some of which are included in the next chapter. I understand now what God
means when he said, *"I pour my mind into all that I have created."*

Most believers pray **to** God but how few listen for a response. Traditional Christian beliefs feel that God selected only a few chosen ones to directly receive his word, especially the writers of the scriptures and, of course, Jesus, but this message tells us He connects with all of mankind through our minds. This gives a greater understanding to the Bible words, "BE STILL and KNOW that I AM GOD." God and His many teachers are now pouring out greater levels of truth because IT IS NOW TIME. In the above message, God expressed, *"I am not an old man sitting in the clouds..."* So many messages continue to express the truth that God is in all that He has created and thus we are all one. God stated that many are called but few choose to answer. IT IS TIME to become open to the new thoughts for a new world. IT IS TIME to choose to answer the call. Many are afraid to listen to these kinds of words of wisdom in fear they will be led astray away from God and into the clutches of Satan. What a limitation fear is to our spiritual growth.

The new thoughts are actually simple and not that radical. Yes, God is more than a bearded old man in the clouds beyond pearly gates with St. Peter checking out our qualifications to enter. It bears repeating that, God is the essence of all life and has a part of Himself within all that He created including humankind. He knows we are not perfect and therefore has given us many sources, many teachings to continue to grow to a more evolved state of spirituality. He has sent many teachers to assist us in attaining a greater understanding of His truths. Therefore, the greater understandings of God continue to evolve. IT IS TIME we become aware of the truth of who we really are and that we **are** all connected with all life on all realms through the Spirit of oneness. Only with open minds and hearts can this understanding be accomplished.

The following message from spirit helped me to understand how important it is to keep an open mind to the possibility that there will always be a greater truth to learn.

I come to you as a dear friend from a higher dimension. I am working with you now from this level to assist you in your quest for spiritual growth, for a greater awareness, and to help you unfold into a knowing of who you really are. In your seeking to know more about truth, you have more help than you may imagine,

The way of the Light and truth is growing on all levels. Though the ways of the physical may become difficult, know that it will be the process that cleanses and renews the world to higher levels of vibration and expression. You have become aware of your focus on material things and now you wish to focus more on reality and truth. The Course in Miracles you have been studying has been good in expanding your awareness of greater truth, as you understand it. However, on any dimension of life, there will always be higher levels of truth to learn.

When planetary or mass consciousness reaches a certain level of truth, most of its beings will ascend to a higher dimension of being and expression. The ascension from your third dimension to the next highest is usually the most difficult. Other than the human ego, the greatest barrier to comprehend absolute truth now is the limited ability of the third dimensional human brain because it filters out universal mind and keeps you out of oneness. However, if one fully existed in a state of oneness on the third dimension, it would be most difficult to function normally.

The Ascended Master Jesus was an exception to this because of His mission. Even so, He had some difficult times with it. A greater part of His mission was to increase the consciousness to a greater understanding of God, moving away from fear and more in the direction of love and forgiveness. He sought

63

to teach humankind a closer understanding of Universal Truths and Laws. Unfortunately, so many of His teachings were misperceived or distorted, not only then, but increasingly so down through the ages because of language and the many translations of the words as they passed through the filters of human consciousness.

For this reason, many entities in these days have been led to, and have accepted the mission of receiving truths directly from spirit teachers in a process you understand as channeling. Even so, some of it becomes filtered or distorted as it passes through and is laced with one's human consciousness of many belief systems. Others have had near death experiences of leaving their physical bodies and going to the other side for short periods of time and then returning to the physical. Many have shared similar experiences of going through a tunnel and viewing their entire life go by in a few moments while feeling a great sense of love and peace. Some came back with missions based on truths they were given while on the other side. Many have come back with very different accounts than is accepted by traditional religious beliefs. (Near death experiences will be discussed in greater detail in Section II).

*Language itself is a barrier in understanding higher truths. You, my friend, have at times experienced truth when it has come to you, not in words or even language, but as true knowledge, a knowingness beyond words and it is completely clear to you. However, if you attempt to describe that knowingness into language using words, you **cannot** communicate the true essence of the all knowing you received.*

Similarly, when you experienced oneness in your deep meditation, you lost all sense of the physical because the experience was beyond the physical third dimension. Once again you could not begin to describe it in words. That is because a true oneness experience connects you with true essence, that Divine aspect within you that is your Omni consciousness, your God consciousness.

Your ability to receive and understand greater truths increases as you expand your consciousness, especially when you transition to the higher dimensions. Know that whatever realm you reside in, physical or spiritual, there will always be greater truths to learn. Because life never ceases, awareness never ceases to expand as you continue to evolve to higher expressions of life.

I am your dear friend on a higher vibrational dimension.

My definition of truth has become: **Truth is, that which is.** In the next chapter, we'll go much deeper into the whole aspect of communicating with the higher dimensions of life.

That which appears true, oftentimes is not.

That which appears not, is oftentimes true.

CHAPTER 6

Connecting to the Higher Realms

Communications from the higher realms have been going on for eons of time. While much of the Old Testament is history, many of the passages are direct quotes from God. The Bible is often referred to as, "The word of God." There are also hundreds of passages where it is written, "…and the Lord said unto me," or, "thus saith the Lord." If these stories were true, then God must have communicated directly with several beings in those early times. In the New Testament, John the Divine received messages and visions from Jesus after the Master's death. Many believe that God no longer communicates with humans since the days when various beings received His words and were thereafter recorded and included in the scriptures of the Bible. However, since those times, God, His angels and archangels, ascended masters, and others high spirits and guides have been communicating with humankind ever since, and continue to do so.

Would a parent ever stop communicating with his child? We are all God's children. He and his messengers will always continue to guide and teach His creations. It is His promise. He also sends spiritual teachers in physical form, especially during difficult times on the planet. Let's face it. If we look at our world today with all its chaos, corruption, and wars, we need all the help we can get in all phases of our lives to rise above it and live as more loving and caring human beings.

Every human born onto the Earth is given a gift of some kind. To some, it is in the arts, to others it is in the areas of mechanics, technology, ministerial services, cooking, athletics, teaching, and a host of other special and natural abilities. Some are born with a sixth sense. Many of these gifts or natural talents must be developed. Sadly, many get very entrenched in professions, jobs, or other efforts that are not relative to their natural abilities, and so they are never developed.

God communicates to us in so many ways. Yes, some have learned to quiet the mind, go deep within, and hear God's gentle voice speaking to them or see visions. Some individuals receive messages while in a trance state. Edgar Cayce, while in trance, was able to receive in a variety of ways to help heal or cure diseases. He could also sleep with a book under his pillow and wake up knowing what the book contained. Many like Jean Dixon could see visions of future events. There are many who receive messages through automatic writing. Neale Donald Walsch published several books of *Conversations With God* through automatic writing. Others can tune in while still in a conscious meditative state and clearly hear thoughts within their minds being sent to them from higher realms. To others it comes more subtly. They experience intuitive feelings, hunches, or dreams. I have been aware of individuals who began to receive messages by some of these methods but became afraid it might be a demon or the devil and rejected using their gift. Usually it is fear created through religious beliefs that the devil is always out to get them.

There **are** discarnate spirits hanging around the Earth, those who have passed on but have not gone into the Light. Some of these beings are those who have been killed suddenly and are not aware they have died. Others have developed strong earthly attachments such as alcohol or drug addiction. Addictions can chemically alter the mind, lower one's vibrations, and become so earthbound they are unable to cross over to the other side when they die. Some of those who are earthbound seek to enter the consciousness of a human's mind who has become weak from excessive use of mind-altering substances. In this way, the discarnate spirit can get the experience of the intoxication they were addicted to. For this reason, before intentionally opening up the mind to receive communications from the higher realms, it is very important to first ask for protection or visualize being surrounded by God's Divine Light.

As I stated in Chapter 4, my first direct contact with spirit was with my spiritual guide. When I got around to asking about how I would do financially in my life, my guide answered, "It is not your financial wealth I am concerned with my son, but rather your spiritual welfare." That was the last time I ever asked about anything concerning money. After I became comfortable with communicating with my spiritual guide I began connecting with other realms on the spiritual plane. The next level of communication was with those who called themselves Ancient Spirits. They have never been physical, and were part of God's Kingdom from the beginning of creation. They are filled with great wisdom and are great spiritual teachers.

I had practiced meditation as a way of dealing with a stressful job prior to developing communications with the higher realms. I think that discipline was very helpful in being able to really relax and open my mind to receiving thoughts from higher vibration entities. My guide called this process Thought Plane Transference. It is a process whereby those on the higher planes transfer their thoughts into my consciousness. It always worked best when I was relaxed and my mind was in the Alpha state, a typical mind state when going into meditation. It's the same state when we first wake up gradually in the morning and are not yet fully awake.

When we have been dreaming and first awaken, many of the details of our dreams are clear. However, after we get up and get moving into our day, those details quickly seem to dissipate, if not totally disappear. Receiving communications from spirit is the same. If I did not record them as they were streaming into my consciousness, I most often would forget them. Sometimes I would hear a ringing in my ears and know there was something I needed to receive from spirit, maybe a warning of imminent danger or a reminder to follow through on something. If I was in a position to quickly quiet myself, I could receive the message. If not, I would do so at my earliest opportunity. In these cases, I might write the messages down on paper so as not to forget. I cannot write as fast as I can speak. Later I realized that a tape recorder worked much better, though it needed to be typed from the tape later. Keeping a small tape recorder in the car is helpful. Many of the communications for these book writings were received in the predawn hours. A tape recorder with an external microphone with an on/off switch next to the bed worked very well. I could easily reach over in the dark and begin recording the incoming messages without having to get up and turn the light on to write.

In the early stages of receiving messages, I wondered if my imagination was sometimes creating these thoughts out of my own mind. In mid-September of 1971, I returned from Portugal with a serious urinary infection. I entered the hospital where tests determined the extent of the infection. They connected me with a urologist who put me on drugs to kill the infection. The drugs helped but did not ever cure the infection. Every time I visited the urologist he prescribed a different drug. This went on for over a year.

Shortly after I began communicating with my spiritual guide, I asked for help as follows: "The drugs are not curing my infection. I need some guidance to help me with this problem. Can you help?"

I received four words. "Seek one named Carter." I went to the phone book's Yellow Pages, looked under urologists, and there I found a Dr. Carter listed. I made an appointment and soon after, I was in his office explaining my infection. When I told him about all the different drugs I had taken for so long, he said he did not use drugs. His method worked. I came for a treatment once every other week, then once a month and finally no more pain, no more infection. At my last appointment he warned that the problem could flare up again in the future. When I told him I was directed to him by a message from spirit he replied, "I don't know much about that but I know what works relative to your problem."

Six years later, after I moved to Colorado, the problem flared up again and once more I asked for guidance. This time I was given three names and all three were in the Yellow Pages. I was also given the name of a psychic herbologist. When I saw her, she tuned into my physical and then told me to put my arm straight out. She then put an herb into my hand and told me to resist when she pulled down on my arm. My muscles strongly resisted. This is called kinesiology, or simply muscle testing. She told me the herb she put in my hand was what I needed. She tried the same thing with two other herbs but my muscles would not hold up. She concluded that the first herb was all I needed and she was right. After taking it, within two days the problem was gone. Needless to say, I developed a confidence that the messages I was receiving were not from my imagination. Twice now I was led to someone who successfully took care of the problem

When I would sit down, quiet my mind, and drift into the Alpha state, I never knew who would come through next. The more I opened my mind, the more I was given. The more I was given, the more it stretched my mind. Soon I began receiving messages from highly evolved beings in other star systems. All those I have made contact with were very benevolent and very loving beings. These communications really stretched my mind when I received descriptions of other planets and their life styles. The means of transportation on these advanced planets, both locally and interstellar, were amazing. I have shared some of their communications in Chapter 11.

Over the past 33 years, my communications with spiritual beings in various levels of the higher realms covered a wide variety of subjects that led to a greater awareness of Evolving Life, and Transition to the

World Beyond. I received so many answers to the questions we humans so often wonder about, the questions that are relative to the true purpose of physical life. So often we have questions about why some things happen to us, or why the so-called tragedies occur in the world. How many times have you heard someone say, "Why could God ever let this happen?" These and other questions will be answered in following chapters.

There are so many things we don't understand in life. To help develop greater understandings, I have been encouraged to write this book by our loving God with encouragement and guidance from archangels Michael, Gabriel, Ariel and others from the spirit realm. I have also been encouraged by some of my friends who know of the wealth of knowledge that has been gifted to me from spiritual sources. Many thousands of books have been written about life, not as many about death, and fewer yet about what lies beyond this physical plane in the world of spirit. I asked myself why write another self-help book. However, it was pointed out to me how very few have been written on all three subjects in one book.

I don't expect everyone to accept or believe everything I have shared in this book, but it has become my truth as given by so many beautiful beings of Light. If any areas of what you read trouble you because of differing beliefs, I ask that you move it from your head (religious beliefs) and take it into your heart. From that level, tune in to what it feels like deep within you. If parts are not comfortable, let them go but please continue reading because there is much that will certainly expand your understanding of life as it did mine. I myself had trouble with some of the material I was initially given, but as time went on it all began to come together and make sense. The spirit messengers have indicated that they must spoon-feed us when it comes to giving us greater knowledge and truths because of the natural resistance to change or threats to one's beliefs that humans seem to have, especially when it comes to spiritual beliefs. Having stated this earlier, it bears repeating. If you want to continue to evolve spiritually, you must be willing to let go of any area of your beliefs because there will always be greater truths to learn.

In the early stages of receiving messages, I asked, "Why have I been chosen to receive messages from the spirit plane?" My answer, "Because you were seeking, open, and unafraid."

As I continued to stay open and receive more messages, I received so much of what I had thirsted for during my earlier years. It was a greater knowledge never to be found in a classroom or a church. It was all enlightening and even exciting and included areas I particularly had an interest in such as the extraterrestrial realm.

I also received help in an area where I seemed to have a natural ability. As an example, I had done graphic artwork but never oil painting. I never had any formal instruction but it seemed natural to me. As I was trying to develop that skill help came from the spirit plane. I was delighted when I connected with some of the old Master Painters, especially with Vincent Van Gogh who helped me considerably. We actually became friends and he would address me as (catch this), "my very excellent friend buddy." I would consult with him off and on while in the process of creating a painting and he would give me subtle suggestions such as, "You might consider...." or "why don't you try...." Finally, when he said, "Sign it," I knew it was complete.

One evening I connected with a fellow pilot who was killed in a plane crash during a severe thunderstorm. He told me an interesting story about one of his spiritual experiences shortly after arriving to the other side. I'll share that story in a later chapter.

Now we'll get back to my spiritual teachers. In order to become more proficient at meditation, I was given a message on the subject by one named Joshua, an Ancient Spirit. He communicated the following in the old English style.

Meditation is a beautiful experience for the spiritual part of man. Man lives in a confused consciousness state most of the time. He is burdened; he is crushed; he suffers; and he feels many emotions. Quite frankly, I am amazed that he is able to retain his sanity, for certainly his soul has no rest, no relief. If I were able, I would ask every person on your planet to meditate and I would begin at a very young age. The problem with a great many people is that their spirit has no peace. One can really achieve marvelous things in meditation. One is a spiritual rest. Another is astral projection, but the greatest is achieving oneness with the universe and the Lord Most High.

Thou must never forget to pray for guidance and protection before meditation. Meditation that produces oneness with the Creator is an experience that I wish all could have at least one time in their lives. It is so incredibly beautiful. I think thou can attest to that.

Here he was referring to the evening before I received his message when I had such a oneness experience. It was beyond words to describe because it was not a physical experience. How can one adequately describe a feeling that comes when you begin to fly into darkness but towards the Light, and then become part of that Light, part of the Lord Most High, and part of Universal Love. What beauty, what supreme joy, what perfect Love. I thought the experience had lasted for only 15 or 20 seconds but it actually lasted over 45 minutes because I was totally out of the time dimension. The message continues.

Before thou goest into deep meditation, free thyself from all negative thoughts and feelings of anxiety, worry, and all such things of the Earth Plane. First pray for protection and then relax the body. After clearing the mind of all negative things, concentrate on a mental picture of something light and free and beautiful. Maybe see a golden eagle soaring or a yellow butterfly or a golden Pegasus; anything you perceive as beautiful. Thou can follow it or better yet, become it. Feel the wind, the speed, and the freedom. Remember that thou art not bound by physical limitations. Feel thyself melt, blend, and become one. It takes patience, time, practice, and discipline. Even if thou do not experience anything at first, remember thou have given thy spirit rest. There is another benefit of meditation, a chance to communicate with thy Master.

It was not long before I did communicate with the Master. While Jesus was His physical name when He walked the Earth, He preferred to be called Sananda. This was a spiritual name that better aligned with His vibrations. He too was a great teacher. Actually some had called Him Sananda while on Earth. He graciously communicated many essays on a large number of subjects. Later He became a spiritual guide for a group that a friend and I started and we referred to Him as Lord Sananda. The name we were given for the group was Universalia, meaning "Of the Universe." We started with seven truth seekers and were told to limit the group to 12, because it is the best number to work together in a group environment.

Lord Sananda would give us assignments to do during the week. We could see how the assignments were designed to expand our consciousness and become more aware of the deeper aspects of life. When we gathered the next week, we all shared what we had done in accomplishing our assignments. We were always given three assignments. When we finished sharing them, we would have a snack break and socialize for about a half hour. After reconvening, we received our assignments for the next week and then we had a question and answer period. What an educational time that was. We often continued this session until very late into the evening. Though His assignments were designed to expand our awareness about ourselves, nature, our approach to life, and our understanding of the greater Universe, His teachings frequently dealt with unconditional love. This group met for over six years and everyone realized how much spiritual growth we achieved during those years.

He that hath an ear, let him hear
what the spirit saith unto the churches.

(Repeated several times in The Book of Revelation)

CHAPTER 7

The Power of Love

This is the most important chapter in this book. Why? ***Unconditional Love is the Key.*** If we master this one thing in life, we will have mastered life itself. All else will unfold for the highest good. Love is the common thread that is contained within all the Holy Writings in the world. God tells us He is Love. If we master love, truly we will become God-like. Of course, it is easier said than done. The following communication will help.

A Spirit Guide Discusses Unconditional Love

> *There is a lot of discussion about that which is termed "unconditional love." Many human entities desire to love without placing conditions on that which they have selected to love. However, most fall short simply because they try to define what unconditional love is. The mere attempt to define it places conditions on it and it becomes conditional.*

> *As with all things on Earth, what is or is not 'unconditional love' is perceptual and relative to each individual. Unconditional love, in its purest form, cannot be defined*

because it is God Essence that is woven throughout the tapestry of creation. It is, then, That Which Is.

However, to bring it to the level of human comprehension, I will attempt to tell you what it is on the Earth plane and what it is not. First of all, it is not a feeling but rather a state of being. A primary quality within the state of 'unconditional love' is that of total acceptance and complete allowing. For example, in the area of relationships it is the acceptance and the allowing of another to be and to express whomever they are without judgments or criticisms. Very few humans are able to offer this on a continual basis. This type of acceptance and allowing means that one is emotionally unattached because unconditional love comes forth from the spirit and not the ego. It is not enough to simply allow something to occur or be outwardly accepting of a situation if your thoughts are not aligned to your actions. If you say "I'll be unconditionally loving" and you accept this outwardly, but the situation really bugs the heck out of you, you are not in a state of unconditional love.

Although most humans do not attain this state on a conscious level, they need not be discouraged or frustrated or see the attainment of unconditional love as an impossible goal. However, if you choose (and it is a choice) to strive to express yourself in the ways of unconditional love, you will make great strides in spiritual growth. From your higher self in your very essence, you are already in that state. Each unselfish act or expression of love is a fragment of your higher state of being.

What is an unselfish act or expression of love? It is simply expressing or giving of yourself at your present level of awareness without expecting or demanding anything in return, including recognition. Love is like a boomerang that, when sent out from you, returns again to you in some way. It is the Law of Cause and Effect in action, as well as the Law of Attraction.

You express the very best part and highest part of your being when you love your own beingness. Humans oftentimes have great difficulty in loving themselves and they are frequently harder on themselves than they are on others. Some believe that loving themselves is somehow wrong and lacks humility. It is important to remember that you cannot truly offer to another what you cannot or will not offer to yourself. If you say to another, "I love you," and yet you despise your own beingness, you are not nor cannot love another. You are your own first experience – that which projects outwardly and reflects back inwardly.

Humans would have much less difficulty loving themselves and hence, loving others, if they could see themselves as they are instead of through the dim light of their created illusions. Open yourself to the reality that you are Creative Expressions of the Creator where there is Love and Light. You are like flowers in the garden called Life and on this part of your journey you are not in a prison. Open the cell door and move forward towards your own light.

*You have so much power and potential dear human entities, but it is of little value if it is not used. You are each a significant part of the Whole, of the All and without you the All would cease to be the All. If I could, I would show you, in truth, **who you really are**. I would show you your essence, your light, and your inner love, but I can only tell you. It is the journey each entity must take and sometimes it takes lifetimes of lessons to connect with and unfold like a beautiful* *flower into your True Essence. The purpose of your journey is to become what you really are; to see and acknowledge who you really are; and to project this outward.*

*Some might say that it is wrong to elevate man so high for fear that he might consider himself to be equal to God. But know that, at the **highest level of his beingness, in his essence, He is One with God**. When he expresses the best part of himself at whatever level of awareness he is on, he is an individual Expression of God in manifested form. There is nothing egoic about this, for when an entity expresses the best part of whatever he is in the now moment, he is coming from spirit, not ego. This then is the goal – to express the best of yourself, always with the knowledge that you are in a beautiful process called Life and that you are changing, growing, unfolding, becoming more, becoming finer, and becoming what and who you really are. Enjoy the process; follow your own inner guidance and your own sense of truth; release from all those gods that no longer serve you well; and most of all, trust in your own process of unfolding, This done, you will, with greater frequency, discover that you are moving toward a state of Unconditional Love.*

The guides seem to communicate to us in our everyday type of language. However, God in the earlier stages of my communications preferred to communicate in the Old English style of language. This is the same style used in the King James Version of the New Testament. God is known by many names. Those in the higher realms of spirit often call Him "The Lord Most High." He is referred to in the Old Testament as Jehovah or simply the Lord. He is Allah to eastern religions. I will sometimes refer to God as the 'Source' for He is the Source of all life and the source of all Universal Creation. I may also call Him 'The Creator' for, as stated above, He is the source of all creation in all universes. I may also refer to God as Her when love is involved.

The most frequent topic that has been received from all sources in all realms has been that of LOVE. It is truly the greatest and most important thing that we will ever master for our human and spiritual growth. It is Love that gives us both inner and outer peace. It is Love that will ultimately bring us world peace and it is Love that will allow humankind to evolve to a higher expression of Life on a higher evolved planet. Jesus was quoted saying, "In my Father's house there are many mansions…." How much love we have expressed in our lives will be the determining factor of what level we will enter into the Father's mansions (also called dimensions or planes) when we release from our physical form and ascend to our next realm of Life. In reality, we do not have to learn how to love because love is the essence of our beingness. What we need to do is to let go of all the ego type of barriers we have accumulated in our lives and the Love will flow freely from us. The barriers? – Anger, hate, resentment, judgment, guilt, condemnation and other such ego traps. The teachings of love that continue from spirit help us understand all the aspects of this supreme quality. The Lord Most High, the Source of Love, presented a series of four communications on Love and they are included here.

Love - Part 1

Love is the greatest and most precious gift thou can either give or receive. Without love, all living creatures die or wither or become bitter and hateful. Perhaps there are some living things which thou may feel are incapable of experiencing any form of love. That is not true. All living things experience my love, whether they realize it or not.

Humans have analyzed love, dissected it, stripped it, categorized it, and after all that, know less of love than other lower members of the animal kingdom. Have you not seen the love a dog has for his master, even when harshly treated? Humans are aware of their feelings but they are so afraid of them. Humans want to love but most do not know how. They seek only the good things from love but they pad themselves, put on shock absorbers and armament of all types to keep from suffering the disappointments of love. Yet, if humans truly loved as my son the Christ taught thee, they would never have to fear disappointment. Humans tend to be selfish in their loving. They want to give love but oftentimes the desire to receive love is far greater than the desire to give it. Unless one experiences the feeling of total giving, he can never experience the feeling of total loving.

The love of which I refer to is the highest kind of love, the kind of love that has total commitment and total responsibility to the one who is loved. This type of love is void of selfish motives. It is the highest and purest form of love. I do not think humans really understand love. If they did they would not have lowered it so, as when I have oftentimes noticed that one says love when he really means lust. He has placed love in the realm of the flesh.

Two types of love come closest to being what I AM referring to:

The love between a parent and child is the first. The parent is committed and is responsible more totally than in other relationships. This love sometimes exists between friends which bears total commitment and responsibility. When a man and a woman truly love one another they will try to keep peace with their beloved. Each gives much and sometimes suffers much and does so with joy because they loveth. They will not leave their beloved unless she or he is unfaithful to their vow before me.

Love is not constant. Love is like unto life. It has mountaintops, valleys, and plateaus. Be not dismayed if love seems hidden.

It is not. Sometimes thou must sit and rest and examine thy love. This will bring about growth in the relationship. Love is not always gentle and not always compassionate. Sometimes when it is hard and thou might wonder, "Do I love" or, "Why did I ever love." Love is not always smooth and sometimes it is painful, but it is always going in one of two directions. They are: to a greater and deeper love, or to hate. Thou cannot merely say, "I love " and be done with it. It is something which must be continually worked on. Love means greater understanding, compassion, giving and compromising. It means giving thy all and doing the best for thy beloved. If the love is weak it can destroy. If thou cannot bear the pain of love along with the joys, thou will never know love. The strong will fight for love. Many marriages have been dissolved because people knew not how to cope with the valleys and plateaus. They were both neither strong enough nor patient enough to wait for the peaks. Too many people give up without fighting or striving.

I have discovered that after receiving essays on specific subjects like Love, I take the information inside and evaluate it against my current life situation. Are there aspects within this message I need to pay particular attention to? It especially gets my attention when I hear, read or get a similar message from another source that is conveying the same basic thoughts. Maybe that is also why I've noticed the same points are often made repetitiously by the same source but expressed in different ways. I have found that this is when the Source, the Masters, or the guides are really trying to get my attention that I may do an analysis of my life regarding the subject matter and, if necessary, (and it usually is) to change or open up to a better way of being.

After getting so many essays on love, I knew that this was something I really needed to work on. I can't say that I've mastered it yet but the more I work at opening up to applying the many aspects of love, the more I realize what a difference it makes in my life and in the lives of others when I can get out of myself and be more giving, caring, compassionate, patient, understanding, and accepting. There is another key aspect of growing in love. It is when we can free ourselves from being quick to judge someone or a situation, especially if we do not know or fully understand the totality of that which we have become judgmental. We seldom ever see the greater depth or the big picture.

Love - Part 2

The Christ died upon a cross out of love for thee. It was that love which gave mankind the gift. He demonstrated that, in reality, there is no death and it freed them and made it possible for them to live full lives. How can thou expect to live a full life if thou fearest the hereafter or even if thou believest not in a hereafter. Thou have been told many times that Love is the Key. This is a great truth.

Try to imagine a world filled with love. Thou would never fear thy brethren or even wild animals. Thou would not be afraid to leave thy abode unlocked. Thou seest, my children, with the precious gift of love there comes trust and peace. Mankind, for the most part, keeps boundaries on his love and hence he had become prejudiced. For example one might say, "I will love you if you meet certain conditions. You must be Christian, white, hold a good job, and more and then I will love you."

Another disturbing thing is how mankind usually describes love when it should be termed lust. For instance, if you Ron said, "I love my friend Norman," some people would raise their eyebrows. It is, however, a basic love from one human being towards another and it goes beyond sex. It means that thou loves another because he is thy brother. It may go beyond marital love or sexual love or even parental love.

I am not saying that thou could not experience the two feelings of love. This is the type of love that can be given to all of mankind. It is the highest type of love. The others are basically physical. This is the type of love that transcends the physical and touches the Divine. As thou progress in thy faith thou will unfold thy love, not only to those that thou knowest, but also to strangers.

It is hard to achieve this level of love, but if ever thou doest, thou will feel such joy. This love is totally beyond physical and essentially means helping and really caring about thy brother.

"We have been given so much information and knowledge to realize what we should do about love, but somehow we don't and, as I wonder why, I think it's because we either do not stop to think about it or else we just do not feel it from within. My question is, in order to learn how to express the type of love you have been discussing, to actually have it, to acquire it, and give it; it must simply come from deep within. How then do we obtain that inner feeling so we will want to give this type of love?"

This feeling will come when thou art at peace with thyself. When thou lookest at thy life and thou seest thy blessings and thou feelest happy, then thou will want to share this love. Thou will never find peace with or through another human. Thou must seek it from within and I shall help thee if thou but ask it of Me. Do not expect another to provide thy peace. They can only provide a quiet and restful atmosphere.

"By now I think I'm really starting to get the deeper understanding of the various aspects of love. But there's another aspect I need to understand – how can we be loving to someone who is very negative and even one filled with an evil type of energy?"

Love – Part 3

Loving others does not only refer to thy wife, children, parents, and friends. It refers to everyone. I know this is difficult for humans. Is it easy to love a stranger? Though loving others may be difficult, it is not so hard when thou consider the fact that each human was created by Me. They are all born with a God spirit within. Sometimes they keep this spirit healthy while others become sick and infected with a dark energy. What I am saying is that when thou seest an evil type entity thou should just love him because I created him, but thou must not love his evilness. If thou cannot love him, thou should at least seek to help his sick spirit. Thou must be careful, however, not to let his evilness effect thee. Some can be helped while others are too far-gone. What my children who love me have as a responsibility to those sick souls is, if thou can help them to be healed, thou has done a wondrous thing. If thou fail, then at least thou have tried to help thy brethren.

Thou should give a starving man food before thou feed him the bread of life. So also should thou clothe him and make him warm before thou clothe him with My word. When thou meet a prisoner thou cannot make him free without unlocking his chains. When thou meet a stranger, let him meet Me in thee. If he seest thy love for him, he shall see My love for I am in thee as I am in others. So, to love others is to love Me, and what thou doest to others, so also do thou doest it to Me.

This type of love is basically a concern type of love and it means that thou have a concern about others and thou will strive to assist them in their physical needs. But to thou who love me, it means more. It means that after thou have attended to their physical needs, thou will strive to attend to their spiritual needs by helping to bring them to me. Never feel that thou have failed if thou have truly tried. This type of love means more than a real giving of food, money, shelter, clothing, and so forth. Anyone can do this. It means giving more presentment of Me to others who perhaps do not know Me. This is love. Feed his body then feed his spirit. He will most likely be more receptive.

By now you might be going into love overwhelm, but as I said at the beginning of this chapter, "This is the most important chapter in this book." There is so much about love most humans do not understand. In this series of communications, The Lord Most High, in Her love for us, is trying to bring us to a greater understanding of love. Twenty-three days after receiving Part Three, the last part of this series was received. It is the longest part and conveys how very powerful a pure outpouring of love is. And finally,10 different aspects of the nature of love are expressed. I like to think of them as the 10 commandments of love.

Love – Part 4

Love is the secret of the Universes. Some have learned of its power and glory. They have, in a sense, harnessed and used it for good. If ever the power of love is released throughout the universes, thou will see something truly splendid. Its force will make thy atomic bomb look like a firecracker in comparison. But, there would be a difference. Thy nuclear weapons are used for destruction. My power of love will be used for construction.

Think in terms of thy own planet Earth. Try to imagine what it would be like if all was love. Love is the starting point of all life. I am love and I create life in all forms. Mankind, however, does not realize that his starting point was love. If he is fortunate he has parents who teach him love. Oftentimes parents merely provide the physical necessities of life and they call it love. Love means more than administrating to one's physical needs. Love cannot be bought and it has no monetary value. Love must always be free. This is where poor mankind has gone astray. His love is not free. When he loves another he binds them with conditions and because he does this he can never truly trust another to give him love freely. Because he sets conditions, he expects others to. Hence he never gives or receives freely. When man learns that love must have wings and not chains, he will have a truly abundant life, both on Earth and here into his next life. Love is truly the key that unlocks all doors. In thy own life, thou could experience true love and an abundant life if thou would learn of the nature of love.

1. *Love is power. If thou will learn to truly love Me, thy brethren, thy fellow creatures, the planet, and thy Universe, thou will have a power to achieve good and great things.*

2. *Love is a positive force. It is never negative. It is a force that can make all things change in a positive direction. No matter how small or how great a problem may appear, if thou lovest, a change in direction will occur. This will happen in all areas of a man's life.*

3. *Love has wings. It must be free. If it is bound in the chains of condition, it will eventually die or change to hate. For instance, if thou knowest I love thee, does thou accept the fact that my love for thee is free? What if I said to thee, "My children, I will only love thee if thou are perfect?" Thou might strive for a while to attain my love but eventually thou would give up. In*

other words, I must accept thee as thou are. That is love. Aye, thou might be thinking that I set conditions when I gave man laws. I speak to thee of Universal Laws. Those are not conditions for gaining my love. They are patterns for thee to live a better and more spiritual life. My laws are based on my love for man. Sometimes I am saddened, disappointed, and even angry but still I forgive and welcome my prodigal children home.

4. *Love is forgiveness. Man has not learned to accept each other and freely give his love. Then he must show his love when the conditions he has set up are not met. He must be able to forgive for the breaking of his conditions.*

5. *Love cannot be purchased or sold. If thou sell thy love by saying, "I will love thee if thou do this or that," thou will become unto like a prostitute. Love is far too precious to have a value placed upon it.*

6. *Love chooses few, but is sought after by many. This means that many people chase after a word called love. Many confuse it with lust or physical pleasure and unless man understands the nature of love, he will run after love the whole of his life and never find it.*

7. *The true substance of love is spiritual. Thou cannot touch it or see it or hear it. It is a real presence and thou will always know when it is near. Yes, love has physical expressions such as a baby curling his finger around thine, or the becoming one with thy wife or husband, but love itself is spiritual.*

8. *Love is loyal and steadfast. It is not betraying and it is not fickle. He who is blessed with love finds peace in tribulation.*

9. *Love is eternal and it shall never cease to be. Worlds may die, people will come and go, but love will always remain. If all were destroyed, love would still be forever.*

10. *Love needs a subject. If all were destroyed and love remained, what purpose would there be for love? Thou seest, my dear children, love means giving to another. When thou withhold thy love for another, what purpose does thy love have? Remember always that the love of which we are speaking of in these messages is the highest form of love. Love always and thou will grow and blossom beyond thy imagination. I am love, my children, and in thy deepest understanding of thyself, so also are thee.*

Love and sex are often interrelated in the minds of humans as the Source indicated. Some religions believe that sex should only be experienced for the purpose of procreation. At a more physical approach, most sex is primarily experienced for pleasure of the body. Many religions believe it is sinful to have sex if it is not within the bounds of matrimony. Because there are so many views on what sex should or shouldn't be I've looked to spiritual sources for the answer.

Let's begin by realizing that we were all created as sexual beings. It is a very natural and normal part of our beingness. Within our sexuality lies a powerful energy and it is a gift from God. That innate energy can be used for our highest good or it can be misused to the detriment of our physical and spiritual being. Moreover, it has ruined many a marriage and it has ruined careers and high positions in political office. Many religions have attempted to keep us in ignorance about sex and our sexuality. The sexual union in a loving and bonded relationship can be a wonderful exchange of a deep love and it can create an energy pattern that will release invisible energies that can actually heal. During sexual activity you and your partner's energies align and allow a deeper bonding to occur. But remember, once again, love is the key here.

However, when engaging in sex, if the love is only to love the pleasure of the experience, then the energy does not move throughout the body but stays in the lower two charkas. It's important to not experience sex with a variety of partners because you take in a part of every person you have sex with. Therefore the energy of the partner you engaged with will become a part of you. When one partners with more than one individual on a frequent basis, it can cause both emotional and physical problems. If one becomes addicted to experiencing sexual activity on an ongoing basis with several partners, it will also become damaging to the spirit. If one has had several partners in the past but has now found his or her true love and becomes committed to only the other, then it is good to do a clearing and cleansing of the variety of energies taken into your field from others. It is best to not share these energies with your beloved and committed partner. The Native Americans had a way of purifying themselves by smudging with the smoke of sage. Incense can also be used. Unwanted energy can also be cleansed by smudging the whole dwelling. When this is being done it is helpful to visualize the releasing of the various energies.

There is a great balancing occurring on the planet in these times. A balancing is also occurring in cases of a misuse of sexual energy. Though there have always been diseases that relate to sex, there are new and even some fatal diseases that have recently come into the social world to expedite the balancing process. These diseases have also helped in bringing a greater awareness to our society of the dangers relating to the misuse of sex. The promiscuity of teenagers is occurring at an increasingly younger age. A recent TV special on teenage sex indicated there is an accepted standard now for 13-year-old girls which indicates it is acceptable for the girl to allow finger penetration by a boy during teenage romances. Even some of the teen's parents thought that this was acceptable. A much greater level of sex education is needed for our youth with their raging hormones getting out of control. We can be sure that the balancing process will ruin the future of many a teenager if his or her current sex standards continue, especially if the standards continue to become lower.

Let's get back to the sexual experience with a committed and loving partner. It has little to do with and is far beyond how you perform. It is rather about expressing a deep intimacy with each other; it is about bonding, and it is about sharing a great joy, a joy that can connect you both to your divine nature. See yourself as merging into oneness with each other. When an orgasm is reached, especially when doing so together, you become in touch with the Universe. Sex by two loving individuals is and should always be considered a spiritual event.

Relationships

So that we may grow as humans as well as spiritual beings, when we learn about the various aspects of love, it is important to move any head knowledge to heart action. Relationships give us the greatest opportunity to express love. If we lived in seclusion, our only opportunity to express love would be one of self-love. Though our love should not be limited to only those we have relationships with, it is through our interactions with those in our relationships that we have the best opportunities to practice or demonstrate love, regardless of the type of relationship it may be. So it is that the communication from the Master on relationships is presented here in this chapter.

> *Throughout your lifetimes you will encounter many people as you travel your own road. You will form relationships with some and with others you will just continue on your way. People enter*

your own life force at different times in order to create growth in yourselves and in others. You would be wise to welcome people who come to you for this reason. Anyone who comes into your life and touches it in some way is for your growth. When a purpose is achieved, they will leave your life force and move on to others and allow you to move on as well. When growth is achieved your paths will not be as close, but you will remain friends. When a new person moves into your life force, do not be too quick to move away from his or her beingness.

Relationships, like parents, children, spouses, and other close relationships provide you the greatest opportunity for growth and that is why they remain in your life force longer. They are generally entities you have known before and thus have other things that need to be worked out. In the case of two people who become divorced from each other, this is a case where the growth was being retarded and thus removal of the relationship was effected. Many people will move in and out of your energy field in your lifetime. It is never an accident when someone moves into your energy field. The purpose of one-time encounters is to learn that you have nothing to gain from one another.

There really are no accidents; therefore you must never be afraid of anyone who enters your energy force. Those who are most trusting of others will have a higher growth factor because more people will enter their energy field. Oftentimes people choose not to let others into their life force, usually because of fear. There are in reality no game players except in your perception. It was no accident that Judas moved into my life force. People come to you from different levels of truth. That's all. truth changes, as you know. Even people who seemly play games, on a deeper level they are trying to grow. You will never really get hurt in a relationship if you trust it is for your highest good, though it may not seem so at the time. If you allow spirit to control, how can you have emotional pain unless it is a pain that is born of the ego? The key things to remember are:

1. *When someone enters into your energy field, do not fear or run from them or try to postulate what they will do to your life.*

2. *Trust and people will be removed from your energy field if their purpose can harm you.*

3. *Trust that God will bring only growth producing people into your life.*

4. *Trust that only questing students will come into your energy field.*

5. *Know always that there are no accidental relationships. You were all created equal in spirit but you are not all the same and should not compete.*

In a committed loving relationship, it is important for your individual growth that you allow each other to do things individually. However, if you never do things together, then you will grow apart. There must be a balance in a marriage. If you do everything together, you cannot grow as individuals. Remember the wise words of Kahlil Gibran as he once wrote:

"Let there be spaces in your togetherness, and let the winds of the heavens dance between you.

Love one another, but make not a bond of love: Let it rather be a moving sea between the shores of your souls.

Fill each other's cup but drink not from one cup. Give one another of your bread but eat not from the same loaf.

Sing and dance together and be joyous, but let each one of you be alone. Each as the strings of a lute are alone though they quiver with the same music".

Sometimes when a marital relationship is secure and you allow it to be controlled by the Source, you can have many friends with no intimate situations or problems and this is good. Learn to trust each other more. There is no reason why you should not trust if you are committed to one another. You cannot live and fully express if you withdraw from experiences and opportunities to know others. Yes it is true that there will be lower levels of individuals who will try to bring you to their level, but you will become aware of their intent and you will put a greater distance between you. Those who are lower will leave and cause you no harm. Doing things on your own is for your growth, but so also are doing things together. By creating a balance in your relationship, you will express more fully. Once again, love is the key.

During the process of keeping a marriage alive and well, it is imperative to maintain a passion, not just a sexual passion but spiritually as well. The basis of most arguments comes into play when people start telling each other they are wrong about something or something is wrong with them. The argument then escalates when one or both become defensive.

One way to quickly end an argument requires you to get out of ego (if it can stand to do so). Whenever you are accused of something wrong, agree with your accuser, even if you do not. "Yes, you are so right." Then wait for the next response. The other person might continue not believing you are sincere. Repeat saying, "As I said, you are absolutely right. I'm just not perfect yet." Now watch the tempo of the argument quickly change and even bring it to a close. If it continues, continue to agree. I repeat, you must get out of your ego to do this; however, it will almost always work to end an argument. Another thing I have found to keep from starting an argument is, when accused of some trivial thing, put a smile on your face and say, "Gee, it must be, if you say so."

How we live and interact within our relationships is a determining factor of our growth. So also do the ways in which we think and the attitudes that we express have a tremendous impact on what we will experience in our journey through life. After reading the next chapter, you might find yourself reflecting on both the way you think and what your attitudes are. I'm not inferring they are bad, but read on.

The plain truth is this: Love is not a matter of getting what you want. Quite the contrary!
The insistence of always having what you want, or always being satisfied, or always being fulfilled, makes love impossible.

Love is not a deal, it is a sacrifice.
-- Thomas Merton

CHAPTER 8

The Power of Mind

At age 16, I came upon a book about the power of positive thinking. I read this book with great interest and proceeded to complete an exercise contained in the latter part of the book. When I completed the exercise, I was convinced of just how powerful the mind is. It also inspired me to always follow a mindset based on positive thinking and here is why. The exercise described in the book was simple and, as best I remember it, was as follows:

Get a cork, a sewing needle, and a three inch square piece of paper. Press the eye end of the needle into the top of the cork. Fold the paper across the opposite corners to make a small shaped pyramid. Place the pyramid on top of the sharp end of the needle rising up from the cork. Next connect your thumbs and middle fingers together from each hand and drop your connected fingers around the base of the paper pyramid. Next came the key of the experiment. Applying the techniques learned from the book, mentally tell the pyramid to turn to the right and visualize it turning while believing and knowing, *without any doubt* that it will turn.

I followed the instructions carefully and when I began applying the mind treatment, the pyramid actually started to turn to the right. Then the directions continued: To ensure it did not turn because of a draft or from your breath, mentally tell it to stop and reverse the direction of the spin. I did and sure enough it turned the other way, as I believed it would. I then repeated the exercise with the same results. At 16 years of age, I was hooked on **the power of positive thinking,** or should I say, on the power of believing. At this young age, I began to understand how powerful the mind is and what a difference it can make in creating positive outcomes in our lives. I also realized we could make our dreams come true if we but believe in them and believe we can.

Later in life, I came to understand that negative thinking has the same power. If someone says, "I can't," that's probably true because most likely they will never try. However, if someone worries about a negative outcome such as, "I'm afraid if I walk outside after dark, I might be mugged," obviously the person thinking that has also visualized it in his or her mind. Additionally, the fear of it will energize the thought and can very well create the energy to manifest the thought if the person puts himself or herself into that situation. People often create their so-called luck by the way they think, such as, "With my luck, I'll never ___ ____ _____," or, "If I go to the game tonight, it will probably rain." This type of negative thinking will most often bring negative results, simply because of the power of the mind. Fear is the most powerful form of negative thinking.

Levels of Consciousness

The mind is more powerful than most people ever imagine. The mind and the brain are not the same, although the brain processes information from the mind. The mind is more connected with spirit, whereas the brain deals mostly with the physical. The brain does, however, react on what it receives from mind. The brain registers everything from our five senses, i.e., sight, smell, hearing, touch, and taste. The mind relates to our sixth sense, i.e., spiritual consciousness, intuition, psychic impressions. This is what we would term our higher self. When our physical life ends, so does the functioning of the brain; however, our mind continues on with our spirit.

Here is where it gets a little complex. Our total beingness, including brain and mind, is connected with seven levels of consciousness. Of those seven levels, only three relate directly to the brain – consciousness, sub-consciousness, and supra-consciousness. The other four are a part of the deeper mind but still interweave data into the brain consciousness. The seven levels of consciousness follow:

- *Sub-consciousness* – Information registered and stored for the consciousness.
- *Meta-consciousness* – Physical conception of ideas or thoughts. Storage of all past physical life data.
- *Supra-consciousness* – The transmitter of Universal thoughts or ideas to the individual mind.
- *Magna-consciousness* – Universal thoughts or ideas.
- *Omni-consciousness* – Universal Mind (God Mind) Christ Consciousness.
- *Pre-consciousness* – Knowledge of origin or Etheric State. Storage for Omni-consciousness

Even though it is a bit complex, when we can come to understand all these levels, not only is it interesting and amazing how much there is to our brain/mind, but it also shows us how powerful our potential is.

Have you ever thought about our autonomic nervous system? It's a marvelous system. It performs functions in the body we never have to think about. Our heart beats at a rate to keep us in a comfortable mode. It speeds up automatically when we exert ourselves while the breathing rate and depth increase as well. When we ingest food, our body knows how to extract nutrition from it and then the waste is separated into liquid and solid and sent to the proper exit points. When it is time for the waste to be released, the body sends our brain a message by creating a feeling we recognize. I hope I'm not getting too graphic. (smile). If we have an injury, the proper cells go to work to heal cuts and broken bones. All these things happen within us automatically without giving any conscious thought to it. As for the healing, here is where the mind can help. We have the ability to decrease the time it takes to cure an illness or heal an injury by consciously sending healing energy to the affected area while also visualizing and believing healing is rapidly occurring.

Let's look at some examples of how our brain and mind interact. Let's say that we developed talents in art or music. We develop these talents by practicing them. But on the other hand, we have come into this world with some basic talents and innate abilities. Usually these talents start to surface when we are young children, but not always. Children may start creating art pieces in school or even before. And so it is with music. A child may show an interest in playing a piano or another instrument at a very young age. However, our talents may have been developed in a past life and carried forward from the mind's meta-consciousness to the brain. The brain must be used to redevelop the talent but its basis already exists. It is often termed a natural talent. As for myself, I tried to learn to play several musical instruments but the natural potential was just not there. On the other hand, I have produced many oil paintings that, according to friends, are very good, though I've never had a lesson.

Spirit has said, "If you want to know your past, take notice of what you are attracted to in the present." I've always been interested in ancient Egypt. No wonder. Through a past life regression I saw myself developing bright and vivid colors and being involved in producing artwork for a pharaoh. The problem there was, when he died, they sent members of his staff with him to the next life (ouch).

I believe that natural talents and abilities are synonymous. Let's say one has a natural ability in a technical discipline. Educational classes would probably be selected in mathematics, physics, or chemistry. If the natural abilities were in the arts, one would naturally choose classes or lessons in art, music, voice, or acting. We will always do best and be happiest at doing what we are naturally good at. We will most likely be unhappy working in a job our parents pressured us to pursue if the work is not aligned with our natural abilities.

If a man or woman becomes an astronaut, they may have flown starships on advanced planets. Those who have a strong fascination with science fiction stories and movies (excluding those with hostile creatures), they also may have lived in other star systems.

We'll go more into that subject in a later chapter.

Hypnosis and Brainwashing

Because the mind is so powerful, those who are able to manipulate the brain can create very significant changes, either for positive or negative results, depending on the intent. As a certified hypnotherapist, I completely understand this. The mind/brain can be made to believe many things (but not everything) when induced to deeper levels of consciousness. There are five basic levels of hypnosis. At the deeper levels suggestions can create positive illusions. When I took my first formal lesson in hypnosis, the instructor put one of the students under and told him to look up at the clock on the wall in front of him and tell us the time. He said, "It's 8:35." There was no clock on the wall but when everyone looked at his or her watch it was 8:35. Creating a negative illusion can also do the opposite. For example, if you suggest to a subject there is no object when there really is one, the subject will not see it. I have never used hypnosis for play but always to achieve a positive purpose or outcome. Most of my hypnosis work has been for past life regressions.

Many people have subjected themselves to this process as a way of quitting smoking, losing weight, eliminating fears, and for a host of other beneficial results. A positive result can be accomplished using hypnosis when hang-ups or fears are dissolved or eliminated by taking one back in a present or past life where the subject originally experienced a major occurrence that resulted in a psychological fear or hang-up. If the subject begins to relive the experience and actually feels trauma from the experience, I always instruct them to lift out of that body and become an observer of the experience, thus disconnecting them from any upsetting or traumatic feelings. The suggestion is then given to disassociate that experience and release all fears from it in your present life. It might take more than one session to be successful.

To illustrate how powerful a suggestion can be in the induced state, I'll share an experience of a subject. Years ago, I put a woman into a state of hypnosis. As a deepening technique, I told her to set aside her physical form and to know she was now totally in a pure state of mind and going into a yet deeper level. When I brought her back out of her hypnotic state, she began moving her hands from her shoulders downward and said, "Something is missing." I immediately realized I forgot to tell her she now had her full body back. I had to put her back under to do so. It was after that, I took an advanced course in hypnotherapy and became certified.

Brainwashing and hypnosis are not the same. Hypnosis is usually conducted with the subject willing and aware of its purpose. Brainwashing is most often done without the subject ever realizing it has occurred. Those who have been unknowingly brainwashed will most often strongly defend those who have manipulated them, claiming they have been "*shown the light*" or "*miraculously transformed*" or "*happily converted*."

Religious programming began in the early 1700s. John Edwards, while conducting a Christian Revival, unknowingly brainwashed 'sinners' by inducing guilt and acute apprehension. This resulted in creating great tension until the 'sinners' would break down and completely submit to him. Actually he was able to create the right conditions that would wipe their mental slate clear. He could then get them to accept new programming by convincing them that they were sinners and destined to hell. Some became so obsessed and demoralized, they developed an urge to end their lives. If a manipulator, be it a cult leader or preacher, creates a mind phase to clear out the current mind set, his subjects are mentally open and can substitute new input and thus new programming.

The danger here is fundamentalist preachers and revivalists tend to convince followers that they are lowly worms in the dust and sinners who are abominations to God and must be saved. This type of programming can destroy one's self-esteem and, if one becomes really convinced of how bad he is, he may go out and do bad acts of unkindness. What's the difference if he is going to burn in hell anyway?

I worked with two women who were born and brought up in a cult and had been programmed into multiple personalities. I will not go into the details of why this was done, but I will only say that they could be made to do not nice things. Both women attended a talk I gave one evening at a local society and later came to me to see if I could help them break free from their programming. I agreed to discuss their situation and invited them to my home. I also invited a friend who was trained in Neuro-Linguistic Programming (NLP). We began by having them tell their whole stories. What they shared was incredible and even horrific. To maintain a trust, we promised to keep everything confidential. The induction into a deep level of hypnosis went easily and I was able to connect with many of their multiple personalities. The women referred to each different personality as an 'alternate.'

Soon my friend and I began to see how complicated it would be to reprogram the women in order to neutralize the alternate personalities. To begin with, there was a sentry or guard programmed into each personality that protected that personality from being removed or neutralized, even to the point of making the women self-destruct. Additionally, a signal was established in the programming of each alternate personality so if anyone in the cult gave the signal, that personality would come to the forefront and be subject to taking instructions and carrying out a covert activity. My friend and I both began to wonder if we were way over our heads with this endeavor. We tried to convince the alternates how marvelous love was and suggested they release and lift out and up into the Light. But the sentry would not allow that.

Finally we turned to spirit guidance for help. Spirit guidance instructed us how to use sine waves as a way to reach past all the programming of all personalities. Without going into all the detail of how this was done, it worked with one of the women. She said later that even her normal consciousness was aware of going out of body and into the light, where she was met by a group of angels. She now felt so relieved and so free.

Sadly, all stories do not end with everyone living happily ever after. Sometime later, I heard from the subject woman. She told me members of the cult now had her granddaughter and that if she did not submit to reprogramming, they would tear her granddaughter limb from limb. Between fear and the love for her granddaughter, it was too great and she resubmitted herself. Those who programmed the women were very skilled in programming techniques. They created horrific images of harm to create an intense fear and thus accomplished very strong levels of programming alternate personalities. That was the last we heard from her.

I never like to focus on things of a negative nature but I think it's important to understand there are negative or dark energies on the planet that continue to seek greater power and control of the masses. They primarily work behind the scenes and use fear as a means of control. Fear is always the greatest method to obtain manipulation and control. Their methods are subtle yet powerful. If we understand their agendas and their methods, we can create a non-aggressive defense against these dark forces.

In the sixties, a group of brilliant minds were brought together to study and determine how the governments could maintain control over the people during times of planetary peace. In peaceful times, the committee realized that the people would no longer need their government and a strong military force to protect them. This special group of brilliant minds met in secret over many months and completed comprehensive studies to analyze and establish probabilities of an outcome. To make a long story short, they concluded that the only way to maintain control of the people was to create fear by creating and maintaining an artificial threat.

Two basic approaches were agreed upon. The first was to maintain a lingering threat of war. This resulted in the years we lived under a nuclear threat during the Cold War. The threat was kept alive for many years by convincing us how this type of war would have major consequences. Meanwhile tens of thousands of lives were lost in the Vietnam War, one that the U.S. had no business engaging in, especially at the cost of so many American soldiers' lives and serious injuries. The more recent war efforts have been in the Middle East. We were told that this was necessary to protect us from the terrorists. Unfortunately, most of the people believed this. At this point on the planet, those who control the source of oil maintain a controlling factor in the world's global economy.

The second strategy was to create an artificial threat of an alien invasion. You may laugh at this one but remember that they work in subtle ways. Many years ago, a movie was produced called *War of the Worlds*. Spaceships came to Earth and began wiping out a vast number of cities with their deadly destructive rays. The hostile alien beings destroyed buildings and vaporized people. A new version of the same movie was more recently created as a reminder of the aggressive and destructive ways of alien beings.

Many other films have been produced that depict hideous alien creatures with sharp teeth that tear apart human flesh or they try to take over the world and vaporize humans with their death rays. These types of films continue today. Of all the major films produced with stories about extraterrestrial beings, I only recall a few where the beings were benevolent. If most of the masses are fearful of beings from other planets landing upon our own, I can understand why. They have been subtly programmed into fear by such negative movies that depict alien beings as hostile and destructive, some with the intension of taking over our planet.

There have been many true stories that became public accounts of aliens abducting humans, taking them up into their ships and performing terrifying physical examinations. Many of the abducted reported that the aliens ran instruments up through their nose and into their brains. Many talk of implants. Women have told of being impregnated by these beings. At the end of the first trimester, they spoke of being picked up again and the aliens removed the fetus and placed it into an artificial womb environment until it matured.

Some of the women have come to understand that this race of beings, who are often referred to as the Greys, were developing a hybrid race in order to save their race from dying out. I have personally talked to women who have experienced this and I believe their stories to be true. One woman was taken up and shown her fetus developing in an artificial womb environment. She was told that their mental and technical evolvement had increased the size of these alien heads to a point where a physical birth through a birth canal could no longer be experienced so they had to resort to cloning to reproduce. After a time, it caused their genes to weaken and their race was heading for extinction. Moreover, they lost all sense of emotions including love. By mixing our genes with theirs, they hoped they could strengthen their genes and regain a sense of emotions. However, the experiment was failing because they did not understand a baby with human genes must be held and loved to survive.

While these experiences often create psychological damage, I have never heard of anyone taken up in spaceships who were destroyed like those in the movies. But the point here is this: These types of *Close Encounters of the Third Kind* involving abductions are the majority that are made public through television or books, with a few exceptions. It is these stories that create a fear about alien beings. While I have never had any physical encounters (other than visual sightings of starships), I have had many communications with what I refer to as my star brothers and sisters. (I prefer not to use the word aliens because of the negative connotations that name implies.) All those I have had communications with are benevolent, loving, highly evolved beings who want the best for us. Their primary message is the same as I have addressed in the previous chapter --. that Love is the key to evolving both physically and spiritually. We will go into much greater detail of extraterrestrial life and share some of their amazing messages in Chapter 11.

Let's go back to the two strategies of creating fear to control the masses. There is an agenda of power hungry groups who control the masses for their own gain at the expense of the masses. There is, so to speak, a battle for the minds of mankind going on. On one side are those of the dark side who use fear to control. They know fear is the greatest weapon to maintain control. Subtle brainwashing is their main method. There are, however, hundreds of thousands who are on the side of the Light. On the physical plane, they are called Light Workers. They have dedicated themselves to serve their Creator and our planet in many ways. Many have connected with the Ascended Masters, angels and Archangels, and some are receiving directly from the Source. They serve by sharing the truths that have been given them so graciously. Spirit is pouring out great messages of truth to be used as weapons (figuratively) against the dark side, against those who seek power and control for their own selfish gain as they initiate their false truths in unsuspecting methods to those who are taken in by their lies and deceptions.

Of course, our Loving God has the power to intervene and smite those on the dark side but God has given mankind the power of free will and the power of choice. He has allowed the dark so we would know light. He has allowed bad so we could know good. He created cold so we would know warmth. He allowed negative so we would know positive. And, He has given us the free will to choose the dark side or to be of the Light. It is therefore up to us to choose either the ways of Love and Light or the ways of darkness and deception. It is easy to choose the latter if the ego is in control, especially if there is something to be personally gained, such as power or wealth. Therefore, we have come to the point of choosing. IT IS TIME. The wheat is being separated from the chaff. The battle for our minds and spirit is in full swing. Fear not for the Light is always stronger than the dark.

The following true story is an example of how one man's deeper sense of mind saved millions of lives. It is also a story of how divine influence can bring to mind a right decision. This true story takes place on September 26, 1983 in what was the USSR. It was at the peak of the cold war when tensions were high between the USA and USSR. Both countries had thousands of nuclear missiles, most pointed at each other.

Lt. Col. Petrov Stanislov was stationed at the Soviet command center where computers and satellites watched for attacks from the United States. He was in charge of monitoring the computers and, should an attack be discerned, he was also in charge of mitigating the processes that would create a counterattack of gigantic proportions with the combined effect of destroying not only both countries but hundreds of millions of people around the planet.

Something went very wrong on this particular day of September, 1983. Suddenly the computer alarms sounded that an American missile was headed for the Soviet Union. Lt. Col. Petrov reasoned that a computer error had occurred since the US was not likely to launch just one missile if they were to attack the Soviet Union. They would, in all likelihood, launch many. Besides, there had been questions about the reliability of their satellite systems in use, so he dismissed the warning that a missile had really been launched. Just a short time later it turned very serious. The computer was indicating that a second missile had been launched, then a third and fourth and a fifth. The sound of the alarms was deafening.

In front of Petrov was the word "START" flashing in bright lettering. The instructions indicated he must begin the launching process of a massive counterattack against the US. However, Petrov had a gnawing feeling the computer system was wrong, but he had no way of knowing for sure. He had nothing else to go by because their land radar couldn't detect missiles beyond the horizon and the information by then would be too late to be useful. He had only a few minutes what to tell his leadership. He made his final decision. He would trust his intuition and declare it all a false alarm. If he were wrong, nuclear missiles would soon rain down on the Soviet Union. He waited. Everything remained quiet – no missiles – no destruction.

His decision had been right. He had prevented a world wide nuclear war because he followed his heart. He was a hero and those around him congratulated him for his superb judgment. However, he had disobeyed military procedures; underwent intense questioning; and was later removed from the military. He was not punished but neither was he acknowledged or rewarded for his bravery and lived out his life in obscurity as a Russian pensioner.

Later, further investigation determined that the false alarm was due to a satellite that picked up the sun's reflection off the top of the clouds and mistook the reflections for a missile launch. The possibility of a reoccurrence of that situation was soon corrected. Because of Lt. Col Stanislov's decision to follow his heart that day, he prevented what could have been the greatest tragedy in the history of humanity.

Now here is the strange quirk of fate about that story. Lt. Col. Petrov was not actually scheduled to be on duty that night. The officer scheduled to be on duty that evening may very well have made the decision to launch the missiles based on the computer alarms. End of story.

I have been told by spirit that the Creator has decreed He will not let this planet be destroyed. He may direct extraterrestrial intervention to prevent planetary destruction or, when I asked spirit about the missile story, I was told it was a direct intervention of the Creator to prevent this catastrophic event.

This was yet another unusual occurrence that we humans are not aware of, i.e., those occurrences that really unfold at the deeper, or should I say higher levels of our life.

Yes, there is an awakening occurring on the planet. Many of the masses are rising out of fear and openly demonstrating against forces of tyranny and domination. Two such mass demonstrations occurred in the Middle East during the last 10 days of my writings. The Light sources of higher vibrations are slowly weeding out the dark energies. Deception and lies are being pushed to the surface every day exposing the creators of deception, though they shout their innocence. While the media continues to present a world of chaos, the Light continues to silently grow brighter and stronger. Spirit sources tell us that a victory of the Light side is assured. But it is like a story on movie film. While the whole story is there, we must experience it a frame at a time.

In the interim, the power of free will and choice continues as minds seek clarity and discernment. The journey is oftentimes confusing as the agenda of the dark side attempts to dull our minds and distract our senses with a constant barrage of conflicting messages and fearful images. Little by little they try to convince us to give up our sovereignty in the name of security. In summary, concerning this battle for our minds, be strong and be mindful of the false truths that attempt to lead us into the realm of fear and anxiety. Be of and in the Light and it will lead you in victory over those who want to destroy our sovereignty. Be cautioned, however, not to fall into the trap of despising or hating any faction of the darkness. Forgive them for they know not what they do – to themselves. It is best not to focus or dwell on the negative, for in doing so we will only give away our energy and power to those negative sources. It is, however, in our best interest to be aware of the workings of the dark energies so that we may be sure to rise above them.

If we search for the greater knowledge of mind, it will bring us to a much greater understanding of its workings and its power. It is important to realize that there will always be so much more to learn and understand about life. If ever we think we have all the answers and all the truths, be they physical or spiritual, growth stagnates and progress is slowed to a crawl. *If we always think the way we have always thought, we will always get what we always got.* Dreams are another aspect of mind. Let's go there now with a message from spirit.

Dreams

I am Noel. I am what you would term an archangel. Yes there are thousands of archangels you have never heard of. You have asked for information on dreams. So few people pay heed to their dreams but if they realized that dreams are their true reality, they might pay more attention. The subconscious is always dreaming, even when the conscious is not active. A human is like an entity within an entity. The subconscious controls the mental activity. It is like two beings living together, but in different worlds as it were.

The physical is dependant on the physical for life. The spiritual, however, has no need of the physical to sustain its life. When you sleep, the physical functions of the body are controlled by the subconscious. All that physical sleep means is that the consciousness is resting and not actively functioning. However, the subconscious never rests or sleeps.

It is always experiencing and it is always alive in the world you call dreams. You are not aware of most of your dreams. When you sleep, the real portion of your being seems to come alive. Sometimes the experiences of your dreams awaken the conscious and you recall what you were doing in your dreams. Other external stimuli, such as outside lights, noises, etc., may bring the conscious out of rest.

The world of the subconscious is very near to the level in-between the physical and spirit planes. This is where there is much interaction between the dream world and the spirit plane. That is why your dream state is actually more real than what you consider your reality to be. This is why you can feel very bad about something when you go to sleep and yet feel confident and reassured when you awaken. During the sleeping period the interaction between your subconscious mind, your spirit guide, and others on our side have had time to influence you. The conscious is actually very weak. Strength and courage come from within. The conscious world is actually the lesser state of reality though this may seem difficult to believe in your state.

All physical reality is based on physical stimuli and thus it is limited. Therefore, it is the conscious that is the dream. Many people try to generalize in their interpretation of dreams, such as Freud. Each person's dream must be considered individually. Quite often, what happens in the real or dream state will have a bearing on the physical level. Some dreams are just fun and have no specific meaning for the physical. Others are warnings and predictions such as your dream, Ron, of a parachutist falling to the ground. They may thus be protective to the physical shell. Of course your conscious attitude towards life will affect what you dream. If you are happy, then your conscious mind does not have to work itself out and more time can be spent in learning things on the spirit plane.

Man has confused his reality and unreality. He trusts his physical data to a far greater extent than his spiritual data or mental data. However, all protective devices such as hunches, intuition, feelings, vibrations, and so forth come from the subconscious level. This is why I am so amazed that mankind gets so upset all the time. Humans wouldn't if they realized their confusion over reality. Because the physical is limited by death, this must cause mankind a great amount of concern and unrest. His spiritual part is unlimited and need not worry about death. The Master tried to show man, but still he fears his physical reality, which is but a dream and not worth any great concern.

"When you say his physical should not really be of such concern, are you referring to his wealth, having fancy clothes and cars, and that sort of thing?"

Yes, his greatest physical concern should be of his health because if his health is bad, it affects his spirit. Remember the physical is temporary but the spirit is eternal.

"Sometimes some of the things we recall from our dream state seem to be so unreal, ridiculous, meaningless, and quite often frustrating. Why is that?"

It is so because you are unable to understand the meanings. Sometimes they are symbolic, but not always. Most of you do not have the ability to understand your dreams with your finite logical brains. Sometimes they seem ridiculous because they do not match up with physical standards. Sometimes you are working out situations from your physical consciousness.

Most of you have an undeveloped ability to fully understand dreams.

All the answers to the physical origin and origin of the Universe lie in the higher and deeper levels of your consciousness. An answer may not lie in an individual's subconscious but may be transferred to it from the spirit plane during the sleep state. This is generally done only if there is a purpose or need to know. I hope that this has given you a better understanding of the dream world and also understand there is much more to sleep than to rest. I leave you with my blessings and wishes for wonderful dreams.

I think Thoreau had a great inclination of the reality of dreams when he said, *"Our truest times are when we are in our dreams awake."*

The Power of Concentration

When we become more aware and have a greater understanding of the workings and abilities of the brain/mind, not only does it help us to realize how important it is to think positively, but it also makes us aware that it is our most valuable tool to create that which we desire in and for our lives. Years ago I discovered the formula for our ability to create.

There are two aspects to creation. One is to create something with our hands or using our imagination, education, or talents. The second is creating something in our lives by bringing it to us by focusing on that which we want to create along with using the power of positive thinking. It's also been termed 'The Law of Attraction.'

First comes a thought or an idea. Look around you right now. Everything you see began with a thought. Even our world and our Universe began with a thought of God.

113

Second, the thought or idea must be energized by a positive emotion such as a strong desire or a passion, or excitement, or a vivid visualization plus a commitment to persist in energizing the thought. Finally, we must believe the idea will manifest into form or reality. Sometimes, what we want to create begins only with a basic thought or idea. It might take a lot of experimentation or trial and error to achieve the desired end, but when the idea is energized by a positive emotion, the odds for success are raised considerably.

The power to create and concentration go together. For most of us humans with so much going on in our lives, it is difficult to keep a keen concentration. But know that our ability to concentrate will allow us to effectively meditate. Remember what the Creator said, "Be still and know that I am God." However, the complete statement to us from our Creator was, "Be still and know that I am God within you." To help achieve better concentration, Archangel Noel presented two essays on concentration, one to better understand it and the other on how to develop it.

Concentration is the greatest power of the mind. In fact, it is the basic source of all mental powers. If one cannot concentrate, he has no control over the forces of his mind. If he could learn to concentrate, he would be able to bring himself out of weariness and depression and all other negative emotions. Deep concentration is a way of rejuvenating the mind and is key to achieving self-hypnosis, meditation, visions, extrasensory hearing, and most other extrasensory perception functions.

Depending on how astute one is in concentration, one can achieve mind over matter by breaking all the laws of matter. It also gives one the ability to communicate in the universal language as in the case of prophets and others who acquired the ability to talk directly with God and audibly hear His response. Actually, all humans have the potential within them to develop this power. It is probably obvious to you that concentration powers could be dangerous if misused.

When your forefathers, the late Atlanteans, had their past civilizations, they had perfected concentration to the point of not having to verbally communicate. High powers of concentration can move matter. Effective prayer also requires concentration. It is a power that has been instilled in man from his beginning. Originally its function was to assist in communicating with spirit. As time passed, man grew more dependent on man and less dependent on God. The power of concentration eventually weakened and is not used to the degree that it once was. Natural man of the cave type of long ago actually had the ability to concentrate because he needed it as a means of defense. In your present time, man as a whole is not on a level of high concentration; however, you do have psychics, mediums, yogis, and so forth that do concentrate on higher levels. An average person will usually concentrate only on mundane activities. Obviously then, the higher levels of concentration must be developed. Some people are better at concentrating, but all people can learn to achieve high levels of concentration. One of the secrets of learning to concentrate lies in becoming very quiet. Artistic people have an easier time learning to concentrate because they already have learned to do so, to a certain extent, in order to practice their artistic endeavors. In my next communication, I will tell you how to develop concentration.

How to Develop Concentration

The first criterion to develop greater concentration is the desire to do so. First select an object and study it for five minutes. When you do this, you will be amazed at how much you didn't know or see before. Concentration means giving your full attention to the object you chose without any mental or physical distractions. Progress comes with how much quietness you can achieve while focusing on an object.

*Try this: Get an object like an apple and study it from all angles. After its image is clear in your mind, close your eyes and **mentally** see it clearly. Then mentally turn the image slowly a full 360 degrees and view it from all angles. Finally, open your eyes and see if there were any details you missed. Do this with several objects until you can see them as clearly with your eyes closed as with them open. Strangely, the more you train your mind, the less external disturbances will jeopardize your concentration. That is why some students can study while a radio or television is going while others cannot. When a greater concentration is developed, you will be able to concentrate on more than one thing at a time. As an example, you will be able to read and watch television simultaneously.*

As you learn to concentrate first by practicing with a focus on physical objects, eventually you will find you will be less disturbed by externals. Then you will be in control of your mind without losing your focus by having random thoughts creep in. The more you practice, the stronger your abilities to concentrate will become and you will be able to go to deeper levels of meditation or even self hypnosis where you will be able to tap into your subconscious.

The next step, after you achieve success with physical objects, is to concentrate on non-real objects such as your mind's eye or third eye as it is also called. Regardless of your concentration level, I suggest you also practice meditation in order to strengthen the mind. Other exercises to strengthen the mind are such things as memorizing verses, or a series of quotes, or playing games that stimulate the mind. Even try to read something boring and see if you can keep your concentration on the writings.

Never give up because, unlike the body, the mind does not have to age. Some people become senile, not because of physical brain disorders, but because they quit using or exercising their minds. Therefore, if you want your mind to stay young, keep active in mind activities. It will also help to keep the body young. One last suggestion: Keep an open mind and a willingness to be exposed to new thoughts or ideas. It will keep you from getting into a rut. One definition of a rut is, a grave with the ends scoped out. And about concentration: practice, practice, and practice.

Truly, when we strengthen our minds by mastering an ability to clearly concentrate, there comes to us a host of benefits to our lives, both physically and spiritually. Effective prayer can be achieved through concentration and meditation. When we pray for something, it is helpful to follow the Master's suggestions as a way to pray. To paraphrase his suggestion, "When you pray, know that what you pray for already exists." Also, focus on that result by seeing it clearly in your mind. This is much more powerful than begging on a high level as so much prayer is.

In reality, there are no accidents. Physical pain is usually a result of our actions that do not align with love, either in a past life or in the present one. It is part of the balancing that results from the Universal Law of Cause and Effect. Some call this karma. Spirit has said that all the pain we as humans have experienced has been a result of all the love that we have withheld. As for mental pain, we have withheld love when we have held judgment; we have withheld love when we have held resentment; we have withheld love when we have become jealous; we have withheld love when we have held anger; we have withheld love when we have held condemnation; and we have withheld love from ourselves when we have held guilt. We can also be sure that whenever we have experienced mental pain, it is a product of our ego. Therefore, if whenever we are experiencing mental pain, it would be to our benefit to self-reflect and be honest with ourselves about how we are being or thinking at the time. If it is negative, choose to move out of that beingness and into love. Choosing is the key here.

Think of an ear of corn or an orange. We must remove the outer surface one portion at a time before we can get to the goodness of the fruit or vegetable. And so it is with us – we must remove those aspects that cover over the love that is within us so it may flow forth freely. All the areas where we have withheld love are blocks to our spiritual growth. We'll get much further into blocks to our growth in the next chapter.

As a man thinks in his heart, so is he.

--The Master Jesus

CHAPTER 9

Blocks to Growth

The world is plagued with many obstacles to our human and spiritual growth. They act as dams, holding back the flow of our potential. They act as faucets, holding back the flow of our love. I could make this chapter short by just making a list of them, but we will be more encouraged to remove these blocks if we have a greater understanding how they work against us and how they imprison us, or at least attach us to a ball and chain that makes growth difficult. We can view the blocks like building blocks for a wall – the more blocks, the higher the wall, thus the greater difficulty to get over them. Some of the blocks on the list affect both our physical and spiritual. Let's take a look at one of the greatest of blocks and the most difficult to circumvent.

Fear

There are but two basic emotions on this planet, love and fear. All emotions are aspects of these two. Many think that hate is the opposite of love but this is not true. Fear is the opposite of love and it is a killer of your power. The greater your fears, the less effective you are in fully living your life and the less joy you will find in your life.

All anger is born of fear – not something we would normally believe. If you find yourself in a state of anger, ask yourself then, "What is it that I fear?" Going deep within and answering this honestly will allow you to move beyond your tendencies to anger. Moreover, an understanding of the true basis of your anger will help to control it. With that understanding you would begin to experience more times of calmness and inner peace. Pulling the reins in on anger is like releasing the brakes of your growth. Neither fear nor anger is a part of who you really are. Your reality is a being that is a magnificent and powerful creation of God. With that complete awareness, there would be no fear and thus no deep- seated anger. This does not mean you will never get upset or frustrated about inhumane acts or violent aggression or gross injustices. It means that undesirable events or the actions of others you do not agree with will no longer trigger a release of anger from within you. Remember what the Shaman said, *"Don't sweat the small stuff – because it's all small stuff."*

A child is born without any sensations of fear and the spirit within will never have fear. It has been said that the only fear a baby has is a fear of loud noises. When this occurs, a baby will be startled and cry. Actually what occurs is the spirit momentarily leaps out of the form and then leaps back in. This is common in very young children. Have you ever awakened with a start and found your heart pounding. It is the same. Your spirit has been out of body while sleeping and you were awakened so fast your spirit had to leap back into the body very quickly. This is the cause of a feeling of fear in a baby, not the noise that quickly awakened the body.

From the time of infancy, we have had many teachers in our years of growing up who have taught us to fear. Included are parents, schoolteachers, some religious teachings, and even cartoons where the evil ones are always there to get you. When we see movies in our early years that show poisonous snakes and spiders killing their victims, those images register into our subconscious. Though tarantula bites are painful, they are not fatal, but even so, a great fear has been instilled. To move beyond these fears, it takes a re-programming to release, let go, and move beyond our deep-seated fears. When this has been accomplished, it will be easier to trust that everything in our lives will work out for our highest good. You may wonder how to re-program your beliefs so that you may become free of any fears you have.

There is a true story about a man who had a great fear of spiders. This man would bind up in fear whenever he saw any kind of spider. Then one day, he saw a documentary on TV about spiders. He became aware of their contributions to the balance of nature. He came to understand how few are actually poisonous. He became so interested in spiders that he went to the library and studied them in depth. With his new understanding he lost his fear of spiders and simply knew which ones to avoid.

I worked with a woman who had a great fear of crickets. Now we all know crickets are not physically harmful but her fear of them overpowered that knowledge. In this case I concluded that her fear came from a negative experience in a past life. When I induced her into a deep level of hypnosis I told her to take herself back in time to a life where she encountered these small black insects she thought were harmful to her. She found herself in a primitive tribe where she was being punished as a young boy for some wrongdoing. The elder tribesmen applied hundreds of small black cricket-like but poisonous insects to the body and covered them with a cloth. The boy received so many stings that it eventually caused a painful death. I made sure to tell her to be an observer of this experience rather than a participant so as to ensure she would not re-experience the trauma in her current life form. I then gave her a suggestion that the crickets of our present days are not the same kind of insect and are not poisonous, but harmless and cannot harm in any way. And finally I said, "When you awaken at the count of five, you will no longer have any fear of crickets." It worked.

As you can see from this story, fears can be created in past lives and carry over into the present. This is true about many deep-seated fears, and hypnosis is an excellent way to release these types of fear. If a strong fear exists, yet there has never been an experience in this life to create that fear -- e.g., fears of heights, drowning, close places, and other such fears -- they very well may have been created from a past life experience such as falling from a high place, drowning, being buried alive or confined in a small dark prison cell.

I have studied hypnosis, became a certified hypnotherapist, and practiced hypnotherapy for years, and I have encountered many such incidents in past lives that have carried a fear or fears into the current one. I will go into much greater detail on this in a later chapter where I will share some astounding past life experiences. Could it be that some people have a fear of releasing their fears because then they will have nothing to fear about? Considering it took many years to create or develop our fears, so may it take time to understand and overcome them. Truly fear is a barrier to our growth and negates becoming all that we have the potential to be, both physically and spiritually. Now let's look at some other blocks to growth.

Punishment and Judgment

One of the Universal Laws received by Spirit Source addresses the areas of punishment and judgment very well.

> *The Law of Punishment states in a universal sense, there is no punishment. An entity, through his thoughts and actions, brings about his own punishment and reward. This, of course, has its basis in the great Law of Cause and Effect. A person is never punished for* <u>what</u> *he does but* <u>by</u> *what he does. This is one of the tragic mistakes that some religions make. They oftentimes teach that an entity will be punished for his sins. This is an untruth and teaches fear. It also implies the existence of a malevolent God. It also implies an entity is not in control of his life. If all religions would teach a simple*

message that what a person does will have a reaction, how much nicer life would be.

People need to be taught to think correctly and, in doing so, act correctly. So many believe it is normal to sin. Then they believe that if they ask for forgiveness, that's the end of it. Not true. Every action still has a resulting reaction and falls under the Law of Cause and Effect. Whatever punishment or pain comes as a result of an action, it is less severe if an entity understands that God is not out there punishing him. Thoughts and actions are like boomerangs. If thoughts are of a negative nature, some form of a negative reaction or occurrence will be experienced. That is how the law works. If an entity will reflect and recognize why his action has brought seeming punishment, he will learn from it. It will also make him a stronger spirit and even a better physical entity if he takes every responsibility for his actions. If you make God responsible for punishment, you do not learn and you have a distorted view of the Lord Most High who is Love.

The Law of Judgment is similar in that an entity ultimately must judge his own self. Just as the Lord Most High does not judge, it is imperative that no entity judges another. This is a very common thing that humans do, but it is very wrong because the only one an entity can really know and understand, and therefore judge, is himself. The reason it is impossible to correctly judge another is that you do not have the correct standards and the in-depth knowledge by which to judge. Thus, you judge others by the same standards that you judge yourself.

The Law of Judgment also has its basis in the Law of Cause and Effect. If you judge others, judgment by others will be yours. If you accept others with love and understanding, love and acceptance will be yours. You have heard of Judgment Day and you have heard that all the things you have ever done will be brought up to you and God will judge you accordingly. It is not quite that way. When you cross over, you will recall all that you have done and you will then judge yourself, but you will do it from a point of love, not self-condemnation. The Lord Most High will only see your beauty and worthiness. There is no need to fear a judgment. It will be just your analysis of you.

The churches discuss judgment day because it is a way of controlling you through fear of judgment and hell. They believe people might act better if these things lay in their future, but judgment and hell can be now conditions in the physical, depending on the thoughts and actions of an entity. Christ said, "Judge not lest ye be judged." He let you know of the Law of Cause and Effect through his teachings. So many still do not understand the essence of his teachings. Understanding this law will make humanity better. The fear of judgment and punishment does not seem to have had much effect on humanity, has it?

Aggression and Violence

Growing violence and aggression continue to weave themselves into our psyche in the mindsets of our culture. You can observe it almost anywhere you look. A violent tone imparts from so many things – the media, TV and movies, social commentary, schools, sporting events, on the roads and highways, and even in the churches and between religions. Sometimes it appears like the world is going mad.

Where is the peace? Traditional means are not working. Maybe we can find ways to peace in unconventional or novel approaches. Nothing so far has worked. Part of the problem may be, we do not have a clear concept of what peace really is. Peace is not the absence of violence and war any more than true love is not merely the absence of hatred. Surely love is so much more than the absence of hatred and so is peace so much more than the absence of violence, aggression, and war. Peace, just like love, is a spiritual quality. It's an energy built up until it becomes a healing and a transforming power. That is why Jesus declared, "Blessed are the peace makers." Blessed are those who have discovered peace and are building up the energy of it.

Arrogance

There is no universal law about arrogance but this attitude can cause many problems for one's self and others. The attitude of arrogance implies that one is better or more knowledgeable than others. While this may be true, it is the attitude that this is so and, if it is projected to others, it can turn them off and cause them to distance themselves from you. Arrogance can also be a mask for a lack of confidence. This kind of attitude is often seen in politics and religions. I read an example of religious arrogance in a recent paper. In an interview with a Christian University President he stated, "Jesus Christ-denying denominations are false religions. Think of the falsehood of Catholicism, Islam, Judaism and the Mormon faith."

He is implying that only what he teaches is right and if other religions vary from his university's philosophy, they are all in false beliefs and practices. It is this kind of religious arrogance that has created wars for centuries. In comparison, most New Thought churches recognize and bless all religions and the manner in which they practice their faith.

Think about the great Master, the Christ. He knew who he was. He knew the power he had. He had the awareness of his connection and unity, not only with the Creator, but also with all creation. He did not spend most of his energy proclaiming he was God. He only said, "I and the Father are One." He used his power to heal and lift people up. He used his wisdom and knowledge to teach and gently lead those who would follow. He listened to Spirit Source and was not tempted by the ego into arrogance and misuse of his power and wisdom. In quiet humility, he acted in Love. His total awareness was such that he moved in his Oneness and touched the world as no one else ever has.

Gossip and Innuendos

Gossip is often an unfounded truth and can cause great damage to another being. A wonderful example of the problems that gossip and innuendos can create is in the following short story about the philosopher Socrates.

> *One day the great philosopher came upon an acquaintance. The acquaintance ran up to him excitedly and said,*
>
> *"Socrates, do you know what I just heard about one of your students?"*
>
> *"Wait a moment," Socrates replied. "Before you tell me, I'd like you to pass a little test. It's called the Triple Filter Test."*
>
> *"Triple filter?"*
>
> *"That's right," Socrates continued. "Before you talk to me about my student, let's take a moment to filter what you are going to say. The first filter is Truth. Have you made absolutely sure that what you are about to say to me is true?"*
>
> *"No," the man said, "Actually I just heard about it and --"*
>
> *"All right," said Socrates. "So you don't really know if it is true or not. Now let's try the second filter, the filter of*

Goodness. Is what you are about to tell me about my student something good?"

"No, on the contrary --"

"So," Socrates continued, "You want to tell me something bad about him, even though you're not sure it's true?"

The man shrugged, a little embarrassed.

Socrates continued. "You may still pass the test though, because there is a third filter – the filter of Usefulness. Is what you want to tell me about my student going to be useful to me?"

"No, not really-- "

"Well," concluded Socrates, "If what you want to tell me is neither True nor Good or even Useful, why tell it to me at all?"

The man was defeated and ashamed.

This is the reason Socrates was a great philosopher and held in such high esteem.

Wisdom Is the Basis of Much Truth.

We'll close out this chapter with a dialog of wisdom between an old wise Cherokee grandfather and his young grandson.

One evening an old Cherokee told his grandson about a battle that goes on inside of people.

He said, "My son, the real battle is between two "wolves" inside us all.

One is EVIL. It is the anger, envy, jealousy, sorrow, regret, greed, arrogance, self-pity, guilt, resentment, inferiority, lies, pride, superiority, and ego control.

The other is GOOD. It is joy, peace, love, hope, serenity, humility, kindness, benevolence, empathy, generosity, truth compassion, and faith."

The grandson thought about it for a while and then asked his grandfather:

"Which wolf will win this battle?"

The old Cherokee simply replied, "THE ONE YOU FEED."

In the next chapter we'll explore the greater depths of who we really are.

The mind is a wonderful thing
Never let it be wasted.

CHAPTER 10

Who Are You Really?

Let's begin this chapter by focusing on the word 'really.' You are not 'really' a human physical being. Our physical body on this physical planet is merely a vehicle to carry us through this adventure by the means of using a physical form. Once again, everything in the physical is temporary, especially our physical form. Your reality on Earth is an individual spiritual expression of The Lord Most High (God). You have chosen your parents and the earth time and place to enter into a physical form. You have established a plan for this life and goals to achieve during your physical expression. You can even think of it as taking a little vacation from your spirit life by having a physical adventure; experiencing aspects of life not available in your spirit home.

If you achieve your self-established goals for this physical life, it will actually allow you to evolve into a higher spiritual level when you return home. While in the physical, you will not remember very much of who you really are. But even so, you will bring with you some of your special abilities or talents you had developed, both on the spirit plane and in past lives. These special abilities will help you greatly during your physical vacation, but you may have to work at refining them as you mature.

Before entering into your physical expression, you knew there would be great challenges and that you would be subject to physical discomforts and even pain, both physical and mental. You also knew that the greatest resource available to you to achieve your goals would be through the power of love, yet also there would be many distractions and negative energies to lead you astray. One of the distractions would be your own ego. Furthermore your time here, something you did not experience while at home on the spirit plane, would seem like a short dream to you after you return home. Finally, you knew it would take a lot of courage to enter into and meet the challenges that would be before you, regardless of how successful you would be in achieving your set goals. When you return, you will evaluate or judge yourself as to how well you did compared to the goals you had set for yourself. You will also see some of the things you could have accomplished and didn't for various reasons such as fear or lack of confidence.

One of our greatest goals in this life, whether we realize it or not, is to discover *who we really are.* Please know that you are so much more than you can conceive yourself to be through the awareness of your finite mind. We all have other aspects of ourselves that exist in other dimensions, in other realities, and even on other worlds, all being part of our 'oversoul.' One of the blocks to this knowingness is that, the human consciousness begins to be programmed even before birth while still in the womb. Sadly, nearly all programming creates limitations.

The first thing that begins to develop after conception is the brain. Have you ever noticed how large the head is compared to the body in the developing stages of the fetus? The brain initially carries the DNA and is the architect of the whole physical being. While some believe the spirit enters at conception, others believe it enters at birth. Some even believe the spirit is created at birth. Spirit sources, however, have said that the spirit may enter anytime between conception and birth and in some cases, a short time after the physical birth. A newborn baby cannot survive very long without a spirit source because the spirit is the essence of life in a physical form. At what point the spirit actually enters the physical form has a lot to do with one's mission or purpose. As usual, there are very few black and white situations in life.

The human brain is the computer of the physical being and programming of the brain is continually ongoing until physical death. Though the spirit knows the magnitude of its being, the brain only registers all it is given and all it experiences. After birth, as the brain becomes stronger, the spirit consciousness begins to recede. As the child begins to grow, its programming becomes greater; first from parents, soon after from television (especially from commercials), followed by school teachers, religious teachers, peers, society, and so it continues throughout life.

Fear is one of the first things that is programmed into the brain consciousness. Parents teach what they were taught. "If you run out into the street without looking, a car could run over you," or, "If you walk on that cold floor with your bare feet, you'll catch a death of a cold."

The programming that comes through television causes many problems for the evolving child. Parents often use the tube as a babysitter. If you were to carefully view a few cartoons sometime, you would quickly see how a child is taught that there are always bad or evil beings out there to get you and to do you in. It matters not that the heroes always win out; a subtle fear is created. In the next cartoon, the bad guys are back – different form, different name, but they are always there to do their evil and destructive deeds. Television teaches children and adults that violence is a normal thing in our society. Is it any wonder that kids feel they have to carry guns to school to protect themselves? Some of the young ones notice a sense of power displayed by the bad guys and they want to experience a feeling of that power for themselves. So, they take guns or knives to school to create a sense of security and feelings of power. Peer power has programmed them into moving to their dark side because it feels good and they experience a sense of recognition and acceptance, something so many do not get at home from parents who are too busy with their careers and other activities in an attempt to get the things and recognition they found lacking in their own lives.

Both parents and children are programmed in materiality by advertising. Not only do the advertisers create a need for their products, but they also attempt to make us feel we will become sexier, more glamorous, and more appealing. The advertisers are masters at appealing to the human ego and vanity. They create images that impress our minds how their products will give us greater status and recognition by our peers. These products are often advertised to create an image to satisfy a need never fulfilled during the development years of childhood.

The purpose of bringing to the forefront the many forms of programming we receive throughout life, especially if it creates fear, makes it clear how easily it can distract us from becoming aware of who we really are and why we have chosen to express our being through a life on the physical plane. There is, however, a revolution going on today and it is an inner one, one to get back to the realization of our divine nature by uncovering the presence of the God within us. This, if we choose, can be achieved in part by reprogramming our consciousness to become aware of how great we really are.

The term "mental programming" has a negative connotation because it implies mind control, and in a sense it is because it subconsciously controls how we think and even believe. Therefore, the term "reprogramming" can also have the same connotation. Emmet Fox wrote a small booklet called, *The Mental Equivalent.* This term seems to be a little more harmonious yet it basically means reprogramming. So, whenever we want to change or reprogram our belief system, we can present to our mind a mental equivalent. For example, instead of thinking, "I am afraid of _____," repeat over and over, day after day, and believe, "I am protected in all that I do."

We have all read several times that everything we have in our physical life is the result of our thinking and beliefs. But it goes beyond that. Everything in our cities is the result of the collective consciousness of the people. Everything in our country becomes the manifestation of its collective citizens' thinking and beliefs. This is why it is so important to change the mass consciousness of the world, primarily from negative attitudes of resentment, aggression, greed, and fear to greater levels of love, peace, and acceptance of our differences. The beliefs and attitudes of one individual can actually have an impact on the overall aspects of the world's mass consciousness affecting business, government, politics, abundance, peace, religion and even death itself.

Our current belief systems create the out-picturing of wars, suffering, fear, lack, and more. IT IS TIME on the planet to change the belief systems to those truths that are now pouring out from spirit as never before. IT IS TIME to believe in a planet where peace, equality, community, true freedom from oppression and depression, and a sense of inner joy will be a normal way of life, even though it may seem unattainable at the present time. Yes, every person's thoughts and beliefs really do have an influence and impact on the mass consciousness within its society, its country, and the entire world. That is how powerful our collective thoughts and beliefs really are. It has been scientifically proven that collective prayer makes a difference.

Here is the good news. Regardless of the images that the many forms of media project to us, the influence of increasing 'light energies' is now accelerating changes in consciousness both individually and globally. We can all add to these positive energies by individually choosing to make a positive difference on the planet by the way we think and act. Know that we have much help from the Ascended Masters, the angelic realm, and our own spiritual guides.

High vibrational energies of love and light are unfolding and sweeping across the planet as individuals begin to awaken and come into the awareness of who we really are and realize the power that is within us. Just as a caterpillar has with itself the inner awareness to know when it is time to become transformed into a beautiful butterfly, so are the souls of love and light awakening to their true selves and beginning to do the work they came upon this planet to do. Sadly, there is something that prevents such an awakening. Deep or strong programming based on fear can be a barrier and prevent such openings. We will never come into the knowing of who we really are as long as we are encumbered with fear. The following is an essay on fear by the spiritual teacher Master Angelon.

Fear comes from the base of the human ego, whose data emerges as self-created illusions, and is one of the greatest blocks to your flow and progressive movement on your earth dimension. It is that which keeps you from fully realizing and experiencing your potential power and from going to the top of the tree and to the outer limbs. It is that which imprisons your mind and gives power to others, to governments, to religions, and philosophies. It is also that which gives birth to and perpetuates hatred, prejudices, inequities, inequality, war, intolerance and all the chaos your planet is plagued by.

Many humans fear poverty, disease, pain, war, and thousands of other things you may never experience. In doing so you give great power to these fear thoughts and it adds to the mass consciousness, which increases the possibility of these thoughts manifesting.

Now let's discuss those fears that you have given birth to by what you feel you have experienced or otherwise know the basis of. When you fear something, it is your ego creating illusions for you. If you would analyze and study those things you fear, you would then understand that which you fear, and with this awareness would come the wisdom that would allow you to release the fear. For example, most humans fear snakes. If you study them and come to understand their habits and purpose in nature, you will cease to fear them but rather respect them. Your knowledge would teach you wisdom in your relationship to these God creatures that share your world with you. Your fear would be transformed to using caution with those that could harm you instead of letting fear cause you to want to kill every snake or spider you see.

Fear is the barrier to unity with nature, of which you are a part, and also to Oneness with the Father for that is what and who you really are. If you are unified and One, you will have no fear of those things known or seemingly unknown to you. You will use caution rather than being into fear when your wisdom instructs you to do so because the prime function of your physical consciousness is to protect and maintain the physical vehicle until your mission is complete, and your cycle on Earth is completed.

So then, replace fear with faith and trust and know that all you experience will be for your learning and your ultimate good. And with faith and trust know that as long as you have work to do on your planet, you will be empowered by the One Force. In your Holy Writings in the Bible, the words, "Fear Not" are ever present. The Great Master was always telling the people this. IT IS TIME for those who are aware to move from their self-created prisons of fear and assume the power that is inherent within the reality of who you really are.

Master Angelon

Though I have discussed fear in an earlier chapter, it bears further emphasis because it is one of the greatest barriers to our spiritual growth. Most fear is ingrained within us to a deep level. Certainly it is not easy to simply set fear aside. It takes great effort to overcome fear but the payoff is very high. Master Angelon's discussion on fear is yet another perspective that will help us to understand how fear can block us from coming into the knowingness of who we really are which is far greater than most of us ever know ourselves to be while on the physical plane of life.

Here is one more point regarding our 'oneness' with spirit. For our energy to be flowing freely, we have to be in tune and balance with all that is around us. However, we must also be in balance with our deeper or higher self that is within us. It is a magnificent life force energy that is within you, and me, in all the plant and animal kingdoms, and in the planet herself. It is a divine spiritual energy that connects us all to the All. When that life force leaves its physical form, it ceases functioning. Therefore, **"who we really are"** is an individual, conscious, spiritual expression of God, yet "One" with all life in all realms.

I'll close this chapter with a writing from deep within my minister friend, the Reverend Dr. Roger W. Teel.

Where I'm From

> *I come from the universal. eternal **I AM**. . .*
>   *the essence and the soul of Life. . .**God!***
> *I come from the infinite heart of **Love**. . .the blossom of healing*
>   *compassion, the ever-lasting spark of caring and sharing.*
> *I come from the fountain of limitless **Joy**. . .the rapturous song*
>   *of spirit, the glad tidings of deep purpose and hope.*
> *I come from the whirlpool of **Creativity**. . .the ever spreading*
>   *Wings of imagination, the architect of all beauty and being.*
> *I come from the vortex of uncontested **Power**. . .the faith-force*
>   *moving mountains, the steady impulse of justice and good.*
> *I come from the divine ocean of **Peace**. . .the pathway of*
>   *harmlessness, the courageous vision of the untroubled soul.*
> *I come from the essence of **Perfection**. . .the grace of original*
>   *blessing, the innate wholeness of spirit in all creation.*
> *Yes. . .I come from the universal, eternal **I AM**. . .*
>   *The essence and soul of life. . .**God!***

Know the Truth (of who you really are)
And the Truth Will Set You Free.

CHAPTER 11

The Extraterrestrial Realm

I'm actually amused when I hear a statement questioning whether there is any other intelligent life out there. I'm sure certain areas within the U.S. government are amused as well. Hundreds of millions have been spent by the government building giant antennas to watch for signals coming from far out in space as signs of intelligent life. Meanwhile, certain areas within the government have had several *"close encounters of the third kind,"* starting back several decades ago.

Moreover, thousands of people around the world have not only seen starships but actually have had encounters with ETs. I refuse to call them aliens simply because this term has a negative connotation about who they are and what their intensions are. This perception has come not from experience but rather because of all the films that have been produced depicting them as hideous beings that want to come here to destroy people and take over our world. There were only a very few films produced that projected ETs as benevolent, kind, and caring beings.

I cut afternoon high school classes in 1952 and went by myself to see a film that has become a classic. It is one of the few positive films about our extraterrestrial neighbors. *The Day the Earth Stood Still* was a wonderful story about another world being who came to Earth and landed his starship in a park outside Washington, DC. Though he dressed differently, he looked like any of us. A powerful robot accompanied him to protect him from any hostile aggression. This extraterrestrial's primary mission was to warn us that a misuse of our nuclear weapons could ultimately destroy our planet and they could not allow that because of the snowballing effect it would create throughout the galaxy. But even so, our paranoid government/military tried to capture him, as finally they did. When he escaped, his great efforts to pull together all the nation's leaders through a local scientist temporarily ended when the government eventually hunted him down and killed him. His robot temporarily revived him and allowed him to give forth the warning to many of the nation's representatives with stern words. With that they departed Earth.

Although special effects are not what they are today, the storyline was excellent and the film left us thinking if such a warning had true merit. The potential misuse of nuclear power still exists today.

At the young age of 15, I somehow sensed there were highly evolved beings out there and they were <u>not</u> out to get us or to do us in. Believe me, if that was their intension, they could have easily accomplished it long ago with the advanced technologies they possess. Movies like *War of the Worlds* would easily be possible no matter how far our weapons have been developed. But that is not who or what our space brothers are. There are many levels of various expressions of God out there in the Universes. Many are evolved far beyond us and there are others who are less evolved than us. How is it that I know this? I have been communicating with, what I prefer to call my Star Brothers, since 1974. Through these communications, I have developed many 'cosmic' friends. I'll share a few of my communications with them a little later in the chapter, but first a little background.

When a few of the UFO research pioneers, as I call them, began writing their experiences in the late 1940s and into the 1950s, I read nearly every one. They were confirming my inner beliefs. My first sighting was in 1958 while driving from Michigan to Florida even though it was a fast glimpse. I was coming down a rather steep incline in Tennessee so I had a good view out in front of me. I suddenly noticed a very bright light traveling toward me at a high rate of speed. It suddenly made a 90-degree turn and was gone in a flash. Though it was just a glimpse, I knew it had to be a starship because nothing humans had could make a 90-degree turn at a high rate of speed. Another sighting was a little different but I'll go into that one a little later.

In the early stages of communicating with my Star Brothers, I asked some rather stupid questions like, "How big is your head compared to your body? How tall are you? What is your skin like? How far are you from Earth?" As they patiently answered my questions, they began telling me about what life was like on their home planet. Now I was learning something of value. Then one day, I finally woke up. What did it matter how big their heads were? I had an opportunity to learn something much greater, such as what could I learn of the knowledge that was within their heads. Thereafter, if they wanted to share what their physical form looked like, okay, but I delighted in the knowledge they had about what life was like out there on worlds far beyond our awareness. They shared information with me that was not only inspiring, but it truly expanded my mind and opened it even wider relative to what can be achieved on planets when its beings evolve beyond wars, greed, dishonesty, selfishness, hate, corruption, illness, and all those things that keep us from achieving a greater planetary life. Another point they made was, if we took the efforts and resources required to build weapons and fight wars, and instead extended those efforts and resources on constructive advances, how much farther ahead we would be in the cures for diseases, more advanced transportation systems, developing non-polluting energies for our world's use, and so much more.

When I was working for the Solar Energy Research Institute during the 1980s, one of my Star Brothers told me that they could show us how to create solar energy that would be extremely more powerful than the level of its development today. But they would not do so for one main reason. We would most probably turn it into yet another weapon and certainly the Earth did not need another powerful weapon to destroy one another.

There are planets similar to ours yet others that are quite different. There are planets where the beings live within them and planets where the beings are all aquatic. There are beings much like us yet others quite different. With a few exceptions, most evolved planets have evolved with a balance between their physical, technological and spiritual evolvement. If beings on a planet evolve technically without evolving spiritually, it becomes very dangerous to their well-being and even to their ultimate survival. Why? Because, some planets have been totally destroyed from within due to a lack of spiritual evolvement leading to a misuse of power. The demise of Atlantis occurred because of this same misuse of power when egos of their leaders were in control. As always, love is the key to a balanced growth and evolvement.

On any planetary system where the beings have become very evolved, they have done so because they have become very spiritually aware and have come to **know** they are in reality **one** with all creation. That knowingness must come from deep within their beingness and not be mere head knowledge. When true oneness is achieved, never will one do anything that is harmful to others, to their planet or to beings on other planetary systems. Beings at this level have shared with me their true love of **all** life and how connected they are to the Source who created all life. They know that they grow to more evolved levels when they help others to be lifted and grow. It is one of the Universal Laws. That is why so many of our star brothers are concerned about planet Earth's problems because they want the very best for us but see the potential dangers if we continue as we have. They can assist us if we but ask; however, they cannot interfere or intervene in our evolution unless so directed to do so by the Creator. Some of them refer to God as the Supreme Commander.

Their God is our God but they totally understand their connection and oneness with God.

Maybe the following true story will explain why I feel so connected with these marvelous beings from beyond our star system.

In one of my hypnotic past life regressions, my first awareness was standing next to a starship about 200 feet in diameter and it felt like the craft was a friend with a consciousness I could connect with. I was the ship's captain and was greeting and welcoming those who would travel with many other ships to a far away planet called Earth. The ship was standing silently about a foot above a polished dark colored granite type surface jutting out from a slanted wall of a pyramid type structure. As I looked to my right I saw a row of many other starships in a similar fashion all resting slightly above the sheen surface. We were all about to depart for this beautiful plant in Universe 45.

This was to be a mass migration of many beings from not only this planet but also five others and coming together they would colonize a large area that later would become known as Atlantis. There were a few scout ships that went ahead to warm the root race of beings there that a large fleet would soon be coming and that they had nothing to fear.

As we approached the planet very slowly, I could see some of the beings below by zooming in on a viewing screen and they looked similar to fundamental Jews with black ringlets of hair coming down past their temples. The look on their faces was one of astonishment. That's as far as my regression went but it was one of other regressions I've had of being on other planetary systems.

Spirit guidance later said that this migration and ultimate development of the Atlantis culture was why the technology on Atlantis was so advanced in many ways beyond our current level on Earth. It was all brought to Earth from other evolved planets. They brought Atlantean fire crystals, and when hit with a laser at a precise angle, they released a powerful energy, enough to power their starships. Other crystals were used for healing. They also had developed anti-gravity.

I regressed a medical doctor friend who had worked with crystals in a lifetime on Atlantis. While in a regressed state he talked about creating various types of crystals for specific types of healing. He spoke of a method of speeding up the formation of crystals. Atlantis flourished for about 15,000 years before it ultimately sank because of a misuse of energy. There is a long story about how the beings from the other star systems mixed with the root race of Earth beings and how it ultimately weakened the genes and created chaos among various sects. It eventually came to power struggles, which resulted in a misuse of laser technology that broke up the Earth's plates. In a series of stages, it caused that part of the planet to sink into the ocean.

The Greek Gods

Throughout the history of the Earth's civilizations, there have been times when ascended masters or other highly evolved beings have manifested in physical form to teach greater truths for the purpose of raising the consciousness of the masses so as to enhance their spiritual evolution.

One of those times was during the period of Ancient Greece. Today many refer to that time as 'The Myth of the Greek Gods.' Most myths are based in aspects of truth. The truth part of this myth is, the so called Greek Gods were in fact highly evolved extraterrestrial beings. They were considered gods because of their great knowledge and powers of mind over matter. The myths or legends say these gods resided in a place they called Mt. Olympus. The truth is, they resided in a mother ship. How do I know this?

I have been honored to receive communications from three of these extraordinary beings; Zeus, Apollo, and Poseidon. The dictionary lists 'Zeus' as follows:

Zeus - ruler of the Greek gods: in Greek mythology, the god of the sky, ruler of the Olympian gods, and spiritual father of gods and mortals.

The following is an excerpt of my first communication from Zeus.

I am High Commander of the Blue Delos Star Command. Commander Apollo has told me about your interests. We are already nearing your universe where we will connect with the Ashtar and Hasidic Commands. The purpose of the trinity commands is to establish the new cities upon the new Earth.

The Eagle (America) is getting too many enemies. The best thing anyone who has higher awareness can do to help us is to LOVE YOUR ENEMIES.

When I was known to the peoples of the Earth during the period of ancient Greece, I did not come onto the planet but stayed on the mother ship and they assumed that was heaven. I was there for about 600 Earth years.

The difference between a Commander and a High Commander is, I command many fleets, whereas a commander only commands one fleet. For example, Apollo's fleet has 2000 starships. His ship, the Golden Crysolis, makes 2001. A starship fleet flies in a triangle and his ship is at the apex of the triangle.

It will be a major undertaking to assist with the transformation to a higher dimension of not only your planet but the entire galaxy.

You have the love of High Commander Zeus and the entire Delos Star Command.

In his next two communications, Zeus gave a long description and the purpose of 'Universe One.' In cosmic terms it is known as 'The Great Central Sun' and is at the center of all universes in the Cosmos. Yes, there is a multitude of universes. Our scientists are now realizing there must be more than one.

Following that communication, he shared a description of how a universe destroyed itself. The short of that communication is, a large life-bearing planet's beings evolved technologically very quickly but acquired very little spiritual awareness. Through a misuse of very powerful laser beams the entire universe was destroyed through a snowball effect. The Creator allowed this to occur only so that it would be an example of the inherent danger when the evolution of a system is not in balance with both the physical and spiritual aspects of its growth.

In my first communication with Apollo, he explained his purpose and mission for coming to the Earth plane during the times of Ancient Greece.

Many years ago I was upon the Earth and those of Earth worshipped me as a god from the heavens. I descended from the sun with my other planetary brothers to aid the Earth people by expanding their awareness, but I was mistaken as a god. The mythology of the time termed me a Sun God.

While on Earth I was served by some and served well. Some even had to lay down their lives for me. I have become the protector of those who served me and I have watched over them even until now. The secrets I shared with them, which they so jealously guarded, are with them still. But dormant they must remain, for the Earth was not ready then, and so it is not ready now. However, those who have the wisdom and accepted the truth shall be lifted up.

Apollo

Commander Apollo taught me a great deal about the grand makeup and organization of the Cosmos. I was just given permission to share the "big picture" so to speak of the Creator's Cosmos and the basic details as to how it is organized and structured.

IT IS TIME that the masses upon this planet become more aware that thousands of benevolent, highly evolved beings from many advanced star systems have been coming to our system to assist our Mother Earth and its peoples in a cosmic experiment to help lift our entire system to a higher vibration of a New Earth Paradigm.

You may ask, how will they assist? Cosmic law states that no planetary beings from one system can intervene with the evolvement of another system unless authorized by the Creator. Therefore, because enough of Earth's beings have chosen to express in the "Light," the Creator has requested the assistance from other world benevolent beings beyond Earth to intervene in any major nuclear or otherwise destructive intensions, including controlling the economics for financial gain of dark side controllers. Using their highly advanced technologies, a great number of space brothers are now in our area of the galaxy to serve the Creator's request.

We are beginning to have more and more sightings of starships as an effort to get more of the masses to accept their presence without concern for any intent of aggression. Possibly, by the time you read this, they may have landed and connected with humanity.

You may find it helpful to understand how the Creator, in His infinite wisdom and creation, has structured the Cosmos in an orderly manner that allows a wide variety of life within many universes, galaxies, and planetary systems to express physical life, all in oneness with the Creator.

Unfortunately, most physical beings in the 3rd dimension have no idea we are all connected through our spiritual essence and are a part of our loving

EVOLVING LIFE AND TRANSITION TO THE WORLD BEYOND

Creator. They consciously live in a world of duality – "I and everyone else." We will spiritually evolve to a higher dimension through an understanding of our ONENESS with the 'All." When we fully understand our oneness, we will never do anything harmful in any way to another, because it will be like doing it to a part of ourselves. All life is always created with opportunities to experience and evolve to higher expressions of life.

The Organization of the Cosmos

The following is taken directly from Apollo's communication which explains the cosmic structure and breakdown.

> *I will be explaining the structure of the 'cosmic whole.' At the present physical time there are four Cosmic Quadrants or Triads within the Cosmos. Each quadrant has three Celestial Zones totaling 12 in all, each governed by a Command and each one having a Supreme Commander.*

> *You are in the Ashtar Command which is in Celestial Zone 8. So also is your planet Earth in Celestial Zone 8 which is why the Ashtar Command has greater contact with Earth. The 12 commands, in times of crisis, form triads to aid planets and other celestial bodies within their particular Cosmic Quadrant, which is composed of many universes, which are composed of many galaxies, which are composed of many solar star systems.*

> *Because creation is an eternal process, each Cosmic Quadrant is continually expanding outward from the Great Central Sun. Although I've given you a diagram, (see Figure 11-1) in the form of a circle, do not think that there is an end to the cosmic whole. Think of the physical Cosmos like a flower with a golden center that keeps opening more petals outward from that center.*

Let's go a step farther. The Hasidic, Delos, and Ashtar Commands compose the Eagelian Triad for Cosmic Quadrant II. The Leoniad Triad is in charge of Cosmic Quadrant I; the Solarian Triad for Cosmic Quadrant III; and the Regalian Triad for Cosmic Quadrant IV.

So, Earth is in the 45th Universe in the 8th Celestial Zone in Cosmic Quadrant II, and in times of crisis, is under the attention of the Eagelian Triad which is composed of the Delos, Ashtar, and Hasidic Commands.

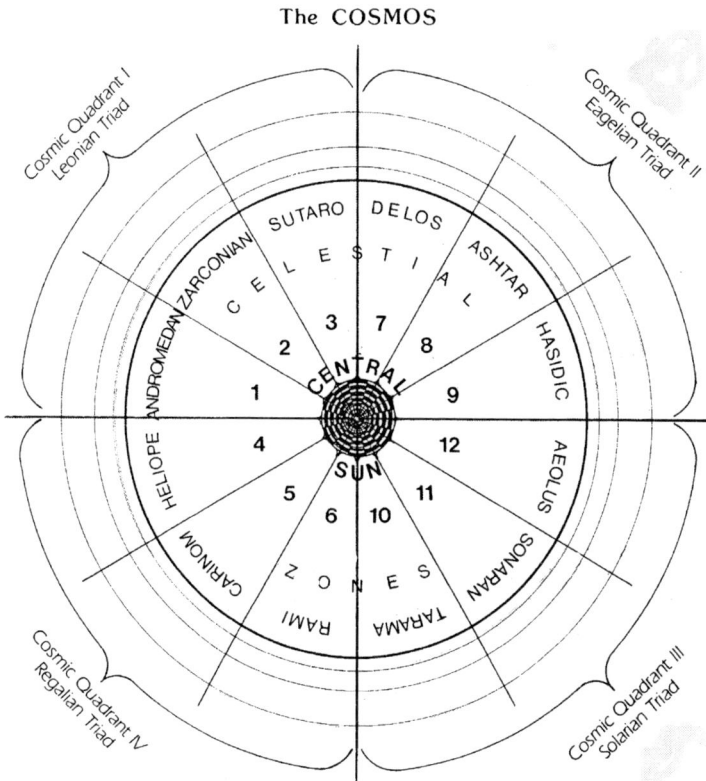

Figure 11-1 Cosmos Diagram

Note: The series of fine circles outside the dark circle are symbolic of the eternal expansion of the Cosmos. The numbers of the zones 1-12 are the order in which they were formed or organized.

Please know that because the Ashtar Command is controller of Celestial Zone 8, of which Earth is a part, it is always watching all planetary bodies within the zone, even when there is no crisis present. Remember as well, crisis periods do not necessarily refer to nuclear or laser threats. Crisis periods also refer to times when civilizations are being born or dying upon a planetary body, when there are wars, or even when there is a natural disaster or a man created disaster. If you have studied your so-called UFO sightings, you will note that greater numbers of sightings occur when civilizations are threatened by major wars or disasters. On your planet, you may recall, an increase of sightings occurred following your first nuclear events.

If the threat is great enough to affect the entire Cosmic whole, all 12 commands of the 12 Celestial Zones of the four Cosmic Quadrants would be called to intervene. Thus far, that has never happened and I doubt it ever will.

The 12 supreme commanders meet regularly in the Great Central Sun to discuss and review the happenings within the four Cosmic Quadrants. The sole purpose of all advanced entities is to establish and promote peace within the physical Cosmic whole and care for the newly created and expanding universes.

I hope this explanation has not been confusing and that the diagram made with my guidance will be helpful to all of you.

My love I send to you, my Earth brothers and sisters.

Figure 11-2 Commander Apollo

When I drew the Cosmos Diagram and later the symbols for all 12 of the commands, Apollo guided me through each step. He started by telling me to get a compass, straight edge, and sketch pad. Then, he told me to draw a circle. If I didn't make it the right size he would tell me to make it either larger or smaller, and as I continued, he would ask me to adjust the size or shape of any other items he had me draw on the diagram. It was if he was standing behind me and looking over my shoulder. The directions and any adjustments would continue until the drawing was complete. He finished by telling me what colors went in which areas on the symbols. I then created the final art from the sketch.

For some time I wondered how he could see what I was doing unless he was right there with me. At a predawn hour this morning I received my answer.

It began by describing 'universal language.' All advanced beings on highly evolved planetary systems communicate through universal language. It is far beyond all earth languages which are very limited and can often be misunderstood. Universal language does not use words made up of letters or symbols in an alphabet. I'll use some basic examples of the difference between the two methods of communication.

When a person says or writes to another, "I love you," the person receiving that does not know how great, or how sincere are those words. When expressing "I love you" in universal language (which is not really a language per se) the message is received as a thought, and the receiver 'feels' the love energy of the thought, the sincerity of the thought, and the purity of the thought. In such a means of communicating, there can be no secrets or misunderstandings. Furthermore, dishonesty is not possible.

Another interesting thing about this – distance has no bearing on receiving a thought. One can communicate to another universes away, and the thought is received the instant it is given. The receiver of the thought can also mentally see anything in the mind of the sender that is relative to the thought.

So, as I was drawing these diagrams and command symbols, Apollo could see in his mind what I was looking at, even if he was universes away. If any part of a thought or message needed to be documented, it would be in universal symbols rather than words. He joking called it all, "cosmic thought/sight."

Finally on this subject, I'll explain the artist's portrait of Apollo above. My friend Lois, with whom I exchanged regressive hypnosis sessions, is also a psychic artist. As I was connecting with Apollo, she could produce a pastel drawing of him, or any other high being, in about 15 minutes. Just as some individuals can receive messages from higher realms through automatic writing, Lois can produce art portraits by seeing an image in her mind and create the portrait via a form of automatic art. While the portrait above is in black and white shades, she always produces them in color.

I hope these descriptions help in understanding how our highly evolved star brothers and sisters can easily know what secret plans or activities are going on here and intervene if necessary to neutralize any destructive intensions, such as nuclear or other massive explosions, through their advanced technologies if directed to do so by the Most High. My guide told me this has occurred more times than we'll ever know.

Descriptions of other advanced planets

The following communication is from an extraterrestrial who identified himself as Patroculus. He had one lifetime on Earth during the time of Atlantis. His current planet's beings are one of the lesser evolved of those I've communicated with but more so than we on Earth.

> I am presently residing on Erin II. It is located in another galaxy from your own. It is very similar to Earth I. The number 2 of Erin designates that it is the second incarnation of the planet. The first one was totally destroyed. I am not in the fourth dimension but am a physical being like you in the third dimension of Erin II.
>
> **How do you communicate with us?** I can telepathically communicate to the spirit plane and your guide then translates my universal language to you from that dimension.

What is it you do on Erin II? I am a scientist.

What type of projects are you working on? I am currently working on healing from a physical and spiritual standpoint. Our planet is developed further than Earth I, but we have not completely learned to heal ourselves yet. We still greatly rely on physicians and scientific techniques.

From a purely physical point of view, how do you compare with the beings on Earth? We are almost identical except our brains and lungs are a little larger. Our atmosphere is a bit thinner.

What about the physical makeup of your planet? It is practically identical. We could pass for twins and that's why I thought we had so much in common.

What is it that destroyed Erin I? It was pollution, a pollution of the atmosphere and water, but more significantly a pollution of the mind and spirit of its people.

What actually happened during the destruction? First the animal and plant life died from the pollution. Then the people starved and some became greedy and tried to get more than their share and that caused wars to break out. Finally nuclear weapons were used which blew up the planet. When I say total destruction, I mean it was no longer able to support any forms of life. Though it was still intact, it was dead. A few of us escaped in space ships and went to Earth and became part of a migration from other planets that started a civilization called Atlantis. It's true; there were many entities involved from advanced planets that were involved in the formation of Atlantis. That's why Atlantis was so technically advanced, even

152

more so than on your planet today. So, our planet was destroyed before the evolution of the Atlantean civilization. I died a physical death there and returned to the spirit dimension.

Many hundreds of years passed before Erin began to clear up again. Some of who had lived on Erin I decided to incarnate to a nearby planet. After reaching adulthood we journeyed to Erin and planted trees and flowers and then we brought people and started a new world. The Lord Most High had a hand in all of this.

Did you return to Erin many times? *Yes, because there was much work to do in building the planet up as Erin II.*

Would you say that Erin II is much more advanced than our Earth? *We are in some areas. We have remembrances of our incarnations so we remember the bad times and situations on Erin I and do not want to repeat them.*

Do most of your people currently communicate telepathically? *Yes, but we still enjoy verbal communication.*

Being obviously on a higher plane because of your increased mental and spiritual levels, what advancements have you achieved that we have not reached as yet? *We have cured cancer; we are using total solar as a clean energy source; we have learned to live without killing animals; we can stop breathing at will; we use the laser for healing; and we do not waste any resources on weapons because there is total peace on the planet.*

How do you travel? *Most vehicles like boats, supersonic transports, and personal vehicles for long distances are* *solar powered. For relative short distance traveling we use underground mass transit systems.*

Is there only a one-planet government? *Yes, and it's workable in a peaceful environment.*

By what means do you practice your religious or spiritual activities? *By individual communication with the Lord Most High.*

You have no organized religions? *Not this time around. It is a basis for too much conflict.*

What type of economic system do you have? *We do not use money. Everyone works for the good of the whole – for all the beings, for all else that lives on the planet, and the planet as well. It is fair for all and it works. There is no suffering, no poverty, and no individual wealth. All is equal. Love for others is the incentive for all we do. All people are specifically educated in their chosen field. No one lacks for anything or worries about anything and therefore there is little stress*

Thank you for sharing your life and advancements on Erin II. *I would like to discuss my specialty, healing when we communicate again.*

I never realized until later why he referred to our planet as Earth I. Could he have had some insight as to what might happen on this planet in the future? Considering how we are destroying our environment, not dealing with global warming, and have nuclear weapons, could we become a potential candidate to experience the same things that occurred on Erin I? I'm not a doom-and-gloom person by any means, but looking at what is occurring on the planet, I sometimes wonder what will happen if we do not change in many ways. Futurists talk about a New Age, a Golden Age, a New Earth, a New Paradigm World. The *Book of Revelation* indicates a time of a great tribulation followed by a new time on Earth that will come when we will have 1,000 years of peace, a time of no more darkness and sadness, and a time of no more death. While some of this may be symbolic, it indicates it will be a paradise compared to our current ways of being and living.

I connected with Patroculus 38 days later and, as he promised, he discussed healing on Erin II. I've included it in this chapter because he discusses aspects of healing that are not common in the Western medical approach to healing.

Patroculus on Healing:

Erin II is advanced but not to the point of not needing physical physicians and continued medical research. We are trying to reach a point where this is unnecessary. We have discovered what some of your doctors are theorizing about, i.e., most of the healing that occurs within the sick body is controlled by the mind and, more exactly, by one's conscious and subconscious mind. We have discovered that sickness occurs when the conscious and subconscious are in conflict. When this situation exists, it will eventually manifest into a physical disease. Our new techniques involve bringing the conscious and subconscious into agreement and peace. This produces health and quickly frees the individual from any physical disease. We have brain-scanning lasers that bring the two together electronically. There is no pain or change in personality, just freedom from disease. We call it in Earth terms "Mind Marriage Therapy." What it means is that we wed the consciousness and subconscious into a happy unit.

We have methods that have eradicated cancer and we vaccinate all our young with a cancer vaccine. It's 100%

*effective. It's a live viral. In the past few years we have been
testing our Mind Marriage Therapy on cancer patients by
allowing some people to get this deadly disease. We have
succeeded in killing cancer cells with the power of the mind.*

*What it all boils down to is that the completely healthy mind
will produce a perfectly healthy physical being and, in time,
we will not even need the laser or electronic scanner. We will
be able to control the mind alone with no technical aids. I see
and theorize that far in the future, evolution will produce
beings whose conscious and subconscious minds will be in
union with each other.*

Through the many communications received from the extraterrestrial
realm, I have found it has stretched my ability to imagine greater things,
greater possibilities. I have also noticed that every entity I have connected
with on an advanced planet has indicated that there are no separate
religions. Actually they do not relate to religions as we think of them
because of varying degrees of doctrine and dogma. They do, however,
live their lives in a deep sense of their spirituality. Most of them seem to
communicate with their Supreme Being and have various names they use
to refer to God. Some have a physical entity that equates to the Master
Jesus, the Christ, and refer to him as their spiritual teacher. But, there is
only one such being for the whole planet.

Next, I will share a communication from one who identified himself as
Absolom. He is from a very advanced planet, strangely enough, called
Jerusalem. He begins by discussing the beings there and then goes on to
describe his planet, which is very different than our own. He also makes
a few suggestions for us.

*We never had to evolve physically. Our physical forms were
once of heavier vibrations than now, but we did not have to
go through birth or childhood or death. We manifested our*

forms while still in spirit before entering them. This is a power that you of Earth will have. Though most of you do not realize it, you manifest your illusions by your thoughts. Your problem is that you have to know how to control your thoughts, yet some of your less aware entities do not even know they are creating their own worlds. You see, if you were really able to control your thoughts and control how and what they manifest, you would be and have just what you wish. The only true way is to be without any negativity within you. On the other hand, if you become totally negative, you will destroy yourselves.

Earlier in our planet's beginning, we sometimes had physical discomforts and injuries that created an unpleasant physical sensation, but as we evolved and increased our vibrations, we no longer had these discomforts, but we never had illness or what you call death.

As an advanced planet, we were given universal knowledge to use in the physical dimension. We also never lost our knowledge of where we came from (spirit side). We could even recall our creation. Most humans cannot even recall their birth. This recall makes a big difference about how we interact with one another.

Please know I'm not putting you down. I'm merely telling you how things are here compared to your current Earth. I tell you things that may sound comparative, only to show you that one day you will evolve to this level, for the seeds of Jerusalem and other advanced planets are upon your own.

By recalling one's creation by the Source, you will never have non-believers and basically, in this way, there is only one religion. Our religion is the governing body of our whole planet and it is based on Universal Law. We have never experienced war because there has never been anything to war about when everyone lives by the same truths.

Next I'd like to tell you a bit about our planet's physical makeup:

Jerusalem is primarily composed of a crystal structure. Try to imagine what Earth would look like if everything were crystal -- crystal mountains, deserts, forests, liquid crystal seas, lakes, and rivers. Liquid crystal is just crystal that is not solid.

Jerusalem is identical with Earth except that yours is not crystal. This is why we found Earth so beautiful in the beginning and desired to seed it with our race. Imagine, if you will, going to the mountains and seeing the sun shine through emerald green trees, or blue and gold crystal flowers. Imagine trying to climb a mountain of pure crystal. The crystal waters are blue or green and you can see to their utmost depth.

The architectures of our cities are like your Greek, Roman, and Egyptian cities once were. They are constructed of rainbow colored crystals. The basic color of the planet is red crystal. We have areas on the planet where we can see the core. At various locations we have gigantic blue crystal pyramids that do two major things. They pull energy from the core and they are our communication devices to other universes. They also produce a protective shield around the planet.

While this is not yet a common belief on your planet, your pyramids were built with the capability of being communication devices with other star systems. The pyramids were actually created by Atlanteans who foresaw the impending doom and escaped from Atlantis and migrated to Egypt with their very advanced technologies. They used their advanced technologies to build the pyramids -- technologies you have not yet developed but shall in your future – technologies such as anti-gravity.

Though we are advanced, we feel the Greek, Roman, and Egyptian style of architecture is the most beautiful in the universes. The architecture in those Earth ages was left by entities from Atlantis who originally evolved from the planet Atlantan in the 61st universe. They are the master artists excluding the Source.

Our beings wear robes of a sheer crystalline material. Our computers use crystal chips. Though your computers have evolved considerably, by our standards they are still primitive and far too complicated.

We have advanced beyond space travel in starships. When we wish to go somewhere, either on our planet or far distant, we mentally raise our vibrations to that of spirit and then will ourselves to our desired destination. We then lower our vibrations again to our normal state. This is called "translating."

We have no schools since we have universal knowledge. We can, if we wish, move freely between all dimensions except the 12th which is the next highest to us. The 11th dimension is our normal dimension. So even though we have evolved to the 11th dimension, we still retain somewhat of a physicalness to our being. This is because of the uniqueness of our universe and it was the first one to be created by the Creator. Because of the great difference between your third dimension and ours, if you were here you would not be able to see anything with third dimension eyes because of the great difference in our vibrations.

It is very peaceful here and you would enjoy the music that echoes from the core. We do not work as you think of it except when the Source has a mission for us. Our mission to Earth will be to send walk-ins to aid in ushering in your New World as you call it. Basically, we began in a lower density like Earth except we were void of animal instincts and void of hostilities. Yes, once our planet was a denser physical like you are but remember, over eons of time, our universe and planet evolved to the 11ᵗʰ dimension. Earth, if she survives, will one day become crystalline.

The Cosmos is vast beyond our wildest imagination. Most people on our planet think our 'universe' is as large as creation exists. More recently some scientists have hypothesized that there must be more than one universe. According to my Star Brother Commander Apollo, there are thousands of universes in the cosmos. The cosmos is divided up into 4 cosmic quadrants. Within each of these quadrants there are 3 celestial zones totaling 12 in all. Earth is in the eighth celestial zone called the Ashtar celestial zone. From a physical standpoint, it is known as the Ashtar Command. The last time I asked, I was told that there are 1005 universes within this zone. However, new universes are being created all the time.

Speaking of time, the higher the vibration of a system, the less meaning time has. We think of time as being linear, but it is not. As an example, my sister transitioned to the spirit plane in 1978. (I share her experience of passing over to the other side in Part Two.) There was a period of a few years when I did not hear from her. When finally she contacted me again, she said that she'd had an entire lifetime on another planet.

Let's go a step farther. The being we know as our self here on Earth is not the totality of our total being. When we first split off from the Source of all life, we did so as an individual expression of God. We are created as a dual aspect. One half is of the masculine (not male) energy, and the other half as a feminine energy (not female). This expression is known as a Twin Flame, sometimes called the oversoul. From that level, we split off into other individual divergent expressions and enter into various dimensions throughout the Cosmos. I have communicated with a few of my higher aspects and one lower aspect. What follows is an experience with an aspect on a lower and denser level.

For a few days, I was feeling very apprehensive and didn't know why. I thought there must be some impending danger I was picking up on so I asked my guide what was causing these very uncomfortable feelings. He told me a lower aspect of myself was running for his life from those who were trying to kill him. Their bodies were very dense in the second dimension. Through my guide, I communicated with him. His name was Stane. They lived in small clans and were constantly fighting other clans for supremacy. One day an individual came upon their planet to try to teach them about love and peace. They knew not what love was for they had always been a warring race. The clan leaders considered this stranger a threat to their ways and killed him. (Sound familiar?) Thereafter, anyone who had listened to him was being tracked down and eliminated as well.

Stane had become interested in what this stranger had to say, so they were tracking him down to be dashed, as he termed it. He explained that to be dashed was to be crushed and die. They finally caught him and put him in a confinement. It was there that he explained all this from his spirit self to my guide who then communicated it to me. Stane wanted to know more about what love was. I communicated a description of love to him as best as I could through my guide. The beings on this planet had never known what love was but Stane was fascinated.

The apprehensive feelings I was experiencing were from the great fear Stane had as he was being hunted down. The next day, Stane was indeed dashed and I was then able to communicate with him on the spirit plane. He thanked me for helping him understand what love was and said, that, because he was ready to learn more about love, he was then ready to enter into the third dimension in his next incarnation. End of story. I know this must seem farfetched but it really happened as I have just shared it.

Spirit source has explained that as we master life on one dimension we then move on to the next higher one and merge with our next highest aspect. Eventually all our aspects merge back into a total oneness with the God of our being. At this point, we have completed the full circle journey. Though we have totally merged into a spiritual oneness with Source, the collective consciousness of our oversoul may choose to split off once again and go through a series of completely different type of lives, such as those of planets or stars. There is a tendency to think, all this must take zillions of years. Remember, our existence is eternal and there is no experience of time in the reality of our beingness which is spiritual. There will always be more to learn and experience in our eternal existence as expressions of God and this is how God experiences the totality of His beingness!

Now let's go to a communication from a higher aspect of my over soul who resides on a higher dimension.

Life on the Planet Eagelia

From Gamien, a higher aspect

> Eagelia is in the 7th dimension. Its vibration would be beyond your 3rd dimension eyes. Our rivers are of a gold liquid and our land is pearlized. This is the way it was created. This means the landscape has a rainbow of colors, some you have never seen. We have what you call mountains and

they are a clear rose crystal. Our cities are domed with a clear crystal covering about ¼ inch thick according to earth measurement. The purpose of the covering is to provide a constant environment. It is strong and shields us from the strong winds that occur once a year on Eagelia. Our year is 950 days earth time and the size is triple that of Earth. We revolve around one star. There are 10 other planets besides ours and all are advanced relative to Earth. We are the 7ᵗʰ planet out from the star. We have 10 moons and they are beautiful. We use them as communication bases and vacation spots. Our cities use the Greek and Roman architectures. The buildings are large. About 45% of the surface is composed of the liquid gold, which is translucent, and there are animal type forms that live within it. There are 12 billion entities on Eagelia and we keep a constant population.

We find that humans make things so complex. The mechanisms of our starships are really simple. Everything is accomplished with the use of laser light beams and that is simple. Sometimes we use sound vibrations; for example, in opening doors. We use these things in our everyday life. When Earthman learns more about color, sound, and light, he will have advanced beyond his current technology. All your illusions are but energy and vibrations, which create color, sound, and light.

I command a fleet of 500 starships. To give you an idea of what we do in our starship exhibitions, imagine 500 ships spinning together, each a totally different color and emitting a totally different tone, yet blending in harmony. Because of our high vibrations, we can change the shape of the ships and even blend the 500 into one. We can put on a good light show. We can fly one earth inch apart. We can also create beautiful works of music by each ship emitting a different tone or note on a fly by and with the proper spacing it will create the proper rhythm. It's quite fun and consider what we can do when we expand our fleet to 1,000 ships.

For our demonstration shows we keep the speed at the rate of a being's perception and we can also slow the ships to 0 to create different forms. The maneuvers are first worked out with models and computers. Once we have what we want, the ships are all controlled during these demonstrations but the key to make it all happen is conceiving the maneuvers with a combination of form, sound, and color and then progress it on the controlling computers.

By the way, as you say it, your computers are still very basic yet far too complex.

Love and peace from your Sun/Eagle brother.

If you might be thinking I have imagined all this, you have overestimated my ability to imagine. I've been trying to share communications with a variety of different kinds of planets that are in different levels of advancement. The last planet I'd like you to know about, which is very different in its physical structure, is one called Nedanon. It is a planet whose beings are all involved in some form of the arts.

Vincent VanGogh has been my art teacher and has been helping me with my artwork from the other side for many years. Our connection has been one I truly honor and appreciate. I have found him to be a beautiful spirit who is very gentle and loving. He refers to me as, "my very excellent buddy." I call him Vinny. He surprised me one day by introducing me to the planet Nedanon. It is one of the great art centers in the entire Cosmos. The communication begins with Vincent describing the planet as if we were coming in on a starship. He then turned me over to two of the planet's leaders.

Journey to Nedanon

Vincent: *From a distance, the Nedanon system looks like a glittering rainbow colored donut. As we near this donut-shaped planet, you will see it enveloped in a rainbow colored mist. This is the atmosphere of the planet. This mist is composed of water vapor. The size of the inner space within the center of the donut, so to speak, is the equivalent of 500 Jupiter planets stacked surface to surface. It may be hard for you to comprehend a planet so extremely large. Within the so-called hole of the planet is a small sun and this is what causes the rainbow within the mist. In addition to the sun within the hole, there are four large suns spaced out around the outer edge but the mist that surrounds the planet helps to keep it cool. Unlike your Earth, these four suns revolve around the planet. This is therefore a planet where there is no natural darkness. The atmosphere is hydrogen and oxygen that creates the mist of a fine gaseous composition.*

We will next go to Ganda which is the central city of the planet. This is the primary center of the Art Center. When we arrive Lothar and Rabin will take over. The city of Ganda, which means "Beautiful Light," is a composite of both modern and classical architecture. By this I mean that modern ranges from what earthlings call modern to ultra modern (things you've not yet imagined). Classical refers to all ancient styles from many universes. They may be classical to some entities and ultra modern to others. But what are present are all the beautiful styles in the physical Cosmos. Never have I seen anything unpleasing. The buildings are all pastel colors. Some are crystalline and reflect light while others are transparent. The streets are made of a glasslike material that reflects the mist. It is quite lovely. There are many beautiful fountains and streams and the water is clear with flecks of a gold material called Thilam that serves as a nutrient. It keeps the physical form free of illness and aging – the true fountain of youth. This water is abundant everywhere. Thilam is created from the suns penetrating the mist and causing it to solidify. It then sprinkles down into the waters. There is an abundance of flowers and other vegetation, but they are things you've never seen. There is also an animal of sorts, but these are highly evolved, mentally and spiritually. Their prime purpose is to care for the plants and to assure that no pollutants enter the planet. The entities of this planet care for these so-called animals by feeding, nurturing, and loving them. Thus, there is no survival of the fittest, no prey, or no predators. It's a beautiful co-existence and it's very peaceful. There are also birds, bees, and butterflies plus other insects that you are not familiar with. None are destructive or harmful. I am now going to turn you over to Lothar and Rabin.

Lothar: *We will start by going to the Central Art Center. It is a circular shaped building with smaller circular shapes attached. The entire structure is created out of rose and white marble. The height of the building is about a mile of your measurement. The diameter of the main central structure is about 2.5 miles. Remember that everything here is of a much greater magnitude than what you experience on your planet. The center was designed primarily for our planet's beings although we have many visitors from other systems. The ground floor of the central rotunda is the so-called visitor's reception area. A moving screen circles around the room. This depicts art from throughout the Cosmos. You could sit and watch this for years and never see the same thing twice. If you want to study a particular scene, you press a button and it stops it on an individual screen. These art pieces are* actually laser projections and they are multi-dimensional like a hologram. And the colors – wow!

Rabin: Another level of the central rotunda is the conference center. This is where artists meet and discuss new concepts. Additionally, spirits from the fourth and higher dimensions come and discuss what is needed in building new civilizations on evolving planets. Some of the artists, writers, and musicians take on forms or are born on evolving planets merely to bring beauty and culture to new civilizations. The smaller circled structures are classrooms. The instructors are the artists, writers, and musicians who have something new to share or teach. On the so-called campus are rooms and studios for any entity and whatever his or her need is, it is met.

Lothar: On other levels are museums filled with great art from throughout the Cosmos. There is a library that contains all the great literature of the Cosmos. All works are in the original language they were written in but are on our computers and can thus be translated. Even the art is holographic in order to provide more space. In the music room, all the great music of the Cosmos is contained within. There is a great stage for those who act or write for the stage. We have all the musical instruments for all the entities that come from all over the Cosmos.

Rabin: Transportation on this large planet varies. Some of our people are able to translate up or down to their desired destinations. The visitors who do not have this ability can travel on our laser transporters. They physically ride on the beam. Our civilization is composed from many throughout the Cosmos. We are the meeting place of the artistic minds. We *accommodate many visitors from evolved planets. Oftentimes they bring gifts of their culture to us.*

I'm not aware on what dimension this planet exists, but from the descriptions, it appears they have the ability to accommodate beings from various dimensions or vibrational levels. I can see why VanGogh and other masters in the arts such as Michelangelo would be interested in visiting this planet, one that totally focuses on creations in the arts. Four days later, I received the following information that focuses more on the entities who reside on Nedanon.

More on Nedanon

As you know now, Nedanon is one of the great art centers of the Cosmos. All natives of the planet are of the artistic mind. There is no native who does not paint, sculpt, compose, or write well. It is a totally creative planet.

We do not have birth, as you know it. New entities are created mentally and are manifested at an age that corresponds to your three-year-olds. We like working with these bright adventurous minds. Children are a delight to the artist. Their minds are so very pliable. We have schools for them and this is how we handle the education of the new mind.

They are first placed in a computer chamber. Wires are attached to their lobes and they are then fed general information and knowledge directly into what you would call a brain. This can be done in less than six months. This means that a three and a half year old would be ready to graduate from a doctorate program on Earth. At this time, the young one is tested to see what his creative and imaginative potential is. He is then placed in the appropriate arena of his potential to develop and expand his creativity. Then he just continues to unfold in his chosen area of creativity. After comprehensive testing, he leans in one direction as to which areas he will continue to develop, and it is actually a choice by his mind and spirit. If an entity shows potential in more than one area, he is allowed to blossom in all areas. No one is held back in any area of creativity.

Because everyone develops in areas where they have natural abilities, they are happy and it is a peaceful planet. Relative to other areas that are scientific, let's use laser technology, computers, or our star fleets for example. We consider 'inventing' as artistic thought. All knowledge is fed into an entity's mind, even scientific. So, an artist might draw a beautiful picture or image of a computer and a writer might accurately describe it. This is art. We do not manufacture these drawings into manifestation. We send the ideas to the inner planets and they are manufactured there. By inner planets, we are talking about the planets orbiting within the center of the donut so to speak. It is a perfect coexistence for those entities of the inner planets who do not have creative minds. They love building what we create. In this way, two civilizations are served. They are neither slaves nor servants. We merely serve one another and it is a total usage of potential.

Our entities grow and live to be the equivalent of your age of 45; however, they never look older than 20. They translate to make room for a new mind to learn. Ours is a communal society. No sex, as you know it, but love for all. The lifespan here is always pleasurable and the time spent is all-productive in some way. There is not a lot of time wasted as on your planet. As an example, you spend 20 or more years in your education system to obtain a doctorate degree, whereas here it is accomplished in six months. If you are doing something

*you enjoy, it is never work but pleasure. And because an
entity has no illness and feels no aging, his energy level is
always high.*

*We do not have natural darkness, so we must create it for our
sleep period that is the equivalent to about 4 to 5 hours on
Earth and the sleep period is once every 36 hours. So you see,
less time is spent sleeping also and the purpose of our sleep is
many-fold. First, it gives the form time to totally rest. Second,
it is the time of nutrient intake and elimination of wastes.
Thirdly, it is the time when the spirit can astral travel and
gather more data for creativity or visit friends or family on
spirit side. Our nutrients are taken in through the skin. They
are similar to your vitamins and other nutrients that you use
such as protein, etc. The elimination is also accomplished
through the skin, which is a soft gold color. The only oral
intake we have is when taking Thilam. We do, however, have
a cafeteria for our visitors from other systems.*

*Now I'll discuss a little about our transportation system.
Our starships are launched from points within the planet.
Steam is used to free the ship from the pull of the planet.
Then the ships convert to a solar crystal power. The crystals
are more powerful than anything on Earth. The gravity on
this huge planet is much stronger than that of Earth. There
are gigantic landing pads far out in orbit for the visitors and
a shuttle service takes them to the planet's surface. Another
method for those who are capable is to molecularly break up
such as you have seen on your Star Trek series.*

*Now I ask that you open up your comprehension factor.
As you may have perceived, everything in our system is
extremely larger than within your solar system. We have
10,000 evacuation starships the size of your planet Mercury.*

We have 21 mother ships nearly the size of your sun. Once the mother ships are launched we keep them out in space. All of our starships resemble the mother ship that looks like the large starship in your film Close Encounters. There are other planets that are larger than Nedanon. Next I will discuss our religion, government, and recreation on Nedanon.

Religion, Government, and Recreation on Nedanon

Religion on our planet consists of worship of the Creator. There are no dogmas, no rituals, and no divisions. We have no formal worship but we worship the Creator by the way we live our lives. We meditate often and try to constantly stay in Oneness with the Creator and all life. By doing this, we worship in the highest possible way. We have no evil, as you perceive it. We do err at times because we are not yet perfect. But we do learn from our mistakes that are generally caused by a lack of wisdom or not remaining in oneness. Most mistakes occur in the first 15 years of life, but we consider this simply the learning process and do not overreact.

We have what you call egos and it generally takes from 10 to 15 years to completely control it and become totally spirit led. We do have one season set aside to honor the Creator. We do this by using our talents that He has given us. We create beautiful music, write beautiful poetry, paint, sculpt, and more in appreciation for the talents we have received. We then have these creations sent to the Great Central Sun.

Everyone communicates with the spirit plane, usually starting around four years old. Once they begin, they do so on a specific schedule of 12 times daily for 30 minutes until age six. This is to discipline them. After that they communicate when they wish. Young minds need discipline.

Now let's move to government and politics. Our planet is the center for the inner planets and ourselves. Each planet has an individual that has been chosen by the planet's beings as its leader. Those from the inner planets come to Nedanon to help govern the whole system. Mostly we communicate what is happening to those who have chosen us. I am the Governor of Nedanon and Rabin is the Commander of the Nedanonnese Fleet. We hold these positions until we no longer want them. Almost anyone is qualified for these positions but one is usually 30 before he is chosen. Mostly we want to ensure that transportation is running smoothly, that education is advancing, and that all visitors are screened for any bacteria if from lesser-evolved planets. Also we do not want any negative vibrations on this system. We also send out ambassadors to other universes to seek out new positive advances that could help us.

Next, I'll discuss our variety of recreations. We swim and we fly. Actually it's like gliding that is accomplished by being supported by the mist. We simply leap up and overcome gravity mentally and then glide. Maybe you have done something similar in your dreams. We also have games similar to your tennis, volleyball, and softball. We have no football or hockey type of games because they are too violent and competitive. We love to walk and dance and we enjoy running more than flying or swimming. We also go on outings alone and in groups. And of course, we enjoy creating and when others share their creations. As an example, I am a writer but I enjoy going to plays, seeing beautiful art, or hearing beautiful music. Sometimes I interact with an artist or a musician and I have pictures and background music with my narration. Vincent has told me about your guided meditations where you create visualizations and use music to enhance positive feeling so I'm sure you would love what we do if you could come here.

It is so enjoyable to give birth to a new creation. I hope you have enjoyed our sharing what our system of life is like on a little more of an advanced planet.

I decided to leave the series of communications about Nedanon near the end of this chapter because their planetary system is so unique and different and the communications went into such great detail about all aspects of its physical size and makeup, plus how its residents live and express in their rather evolved way of life. As for me, it stretched my mind how magnificent our Creator really is. I hope your mind was stretched also because the more we open our minds, the more will be given us when we are ready. I am sure that all I have shared in this chapter is but a mere grain of sand relative to how much there is out there in all of God's marvelous creations. When once asking the Master, *"Of all the knowledge that exists, how much of it do we have on the Earth Plane?"* The answer: One-millionth to the millionth power.

The last ET communication in this chapter comes from one of the great leaders in the extraterrestrial realm. His message conveys the connection they have had with humankind and how they are assisting us as we enter into the time known as the New Earth.

Earth has always had its connection with extraterrestrial beings. We have come to Earth many times at different points in your evolutionary process and assisted you in advancing your technology, your knowledge, your wisdom, and your life itself. Sometimes we have come in physical forms; other times we entered Earth by being born with Earth bodies, and other times we have implanted ourselves among you.

We have starbases in systems that for us are very near to Earth, such as in the Pleiades and Orion systems. This makes it easy to observe what is unfolding on your planet. Humans have observed some of our starships while others are vibrationally above your ability to see them. They are all over your known outer space.

We are connected to higher beings on your planet. Usually it is a mental connection because this is the best connection. So many of your entities wish that they could see an ET, yet many do not realize they have already done so but we will not walk among you in our own forms.

We come there to help you bring in the New Age or Golden Age of Earth as some of you have termed it. We wish for you to have a more evolved planet so you may experience times of peace, joy, and brotherhood as we do upon our advanced planets. But know that you will never experience space travel beyond your own solar system until you evolve to these qualities and move beyond the tendencies of aggression and non-love throughout the Earth. All advanced beings who observe planet Earth can see the potential of their star brothers and are waiting for you to reach the point where your natures become such that you can join your space brothers in cosmic travel.

Those of you we consider starseed will, during your sleep state, be traveling with us, working with us, and are being trained by us. When the time is right, what you have learned will come into your consciousness so you may do the work you have been trained for, work that will assist in the unfolding of a more evolved planet Earth. Those who have been chosen are of the awareness level that they really care about your planet, have no fear of their star brothers, and continue to show they have open minds.

We see you as our brothers and sisters and want the very best for all who reside on the Earth plane. The problem we currently see with Earth beings is similar to what your Master, the Christ had when he walked upon your planet. Because we are advanced many of you have the awareness that we are better than you. However, we do not see this from our level but see you the same as ourselves but at different levels of technology. The truth is, we are connected in oneness with you. We see you as evolving just as we are, only at different rates and speeds.

Though you are our brothers and sisters, if some of us would approach you in our basic energy forms with consciousness, you would be very awed and that is not what we desire, nor do we wish to be worshipped. We desire you to see us only as your brothers connected in a great cosmic oneness. Until you reach the point where you see all life in equality, though unique, you will not be able to be comfortable seeing us in our true-life expressions.

It is truly a wondrous journey that we all travel in our lives. Your star brothers have worked very hard to assist in helping you create a New Earth with a raised consciousness, but without the lifting of your collective consciousness there will be no change. We are trying through many of your human expressions, to get you to understand that there is so much more to you and to your planet than you are currently able to see. If you can ever comprehend the wonder of your own being, of your planet, the wonder of all that is around you; and if you can ever overcome that which is termed fear; and if you can learn to utilize the greatest power within you which is love, then you are indeed going to have a Golden Age beyond your imagination. This will be a period of great enlightenment and I think all of you are of the awareness that something truly wondrous is going on around you in terms of enlightenment, regardless of the chaos being cleansed in your physical world. Vibrations really are getting higher.

In this chapter, we have explored a variety of other worlds. In the next and last chapter of Part One, we'll look at how our own world is changing.

True Reality Is Often Beyond Our Comprehension.

CHAPTER 12

Our Changing World

I have said elsewhere, "Change is constant while everything else in the physical is temporary." This must be if any individual, any corporation, any country, or any planet will evolve to greater levels of beingness and expression. Why then is it that so many humans resist change? Most humans are creatures of habit and therefore find it uncomfortable to change. The Internet has created a major change in the way we communicate and obtain information. The youth of today easily learn the ins and outs of computers while many of our seniors have difficulty mastering the technology. When my grandson works on a computer, his fingers fly. When I have a problem figuring out something on my computer, I call him and he usually knows right away what to do to solve the problem. We must continue to learn more all the time to keep up with our fast changing world. If we do not, we quickly find ourselves feeling lost and falling behind.

Computers are a good example of change. When I worked in the aerospace field, our first computer in the mid-1960s nearly took up an entire wall, yet it only had 128MB of memory. The advancements in memory chips have been one of the major elements that have allowed computers to be more powerful, much faster, and much smaller. However, I still remember one of my star brothers saying, "I know you think your computers have come a long way, but they are still far too complicated." Someone once wrote, "If automobiles had the same reliability as computers, the streets would be filled with stalled vehicles." Before long, I expect we will have computers that we will verbally ask to research something, solve a problem, or ask for certain information, and in a few moments we will hear, "I now have the information you requested." Voice recognition is already quickly moving forward.

The area that seems to be the slowest to change is religion. It took millennia to evolve from multiple gods to one God. It took centuries to move from a vengeful and angry God, as depicted in the Old Testament, to a loving and forgiving God. In every religion from the past to the present, the believers are sure they have the ultimate truth. Therefore, they are very slow to change their beliefs. Martin Luther broke out of the Catholic Church to enhance change. Today, within Protestant churches, there is a more progressive group developing called the "Center for Progressive Christianity." It was created because many have become disillusioned with the traditional beliefs. In the past few decades, many "New Thought" churches are growing in leaps and bounds. Why? Because they take a more open and positive approach to religion and spirituality, yet they do use Jesus' more positive teachings as examples. Moreover, they honor and accept all religions and do not condemn other religions' beliefs as wrong. They also do not get caught up in the fear aspects within their teachings or beliefs.

Now let's go a little deeper. The Earth is now going through a great evolutionary change and the culminations of three grand cycles are the catalysts for many of the changes in process. We are all very familiar with cycles, i.e., 60 seconds per minute; 60 minutes per hour; 24 hours per day; 7 days in a week; and on to cycles of months, years, decades, centuries, and beyond. There are, however, much greater cycles than these. Approximately every 2167 years we move into a new age. We have just completed the Piscean Age and entered into the Age of Aquarius. But there are even greater cycles.

Every 26,000 years we complete a much larger cycle. This is a cycle where evolution is assured and it is based on the Universal Law of Evolution. Because our Creator knows how physical beings can be distracted from the evolutionary path, this law will ultimately bring us back by the way of passing through a filter, so to speak, that only allows light or positive energy through. Some have called it the Photon Belt and it is a light energy whose essence is love. Universal truth tells us that the **Light** *(Divine energy)* always bears the truth while the ***dark*** energies will try to distort or hide the truth. We have just begun to enter into the peripheral area of that field of *Divine Light energy*.

We are beginning to see the effects of this already. Large corporations and CEOs who have been dishonest in their corporate dealings are being exposed. Politicians who have become corrupt and make dishonest deals are being exposed. Priests who have sexually abused young children in their parish are being exposed, as are parents who have done the same. Home videos are exposing inhumane acts such as police brutality. The dark secrets of many are coming to the surface. Whistle-blowers are exposing unethical operations within corporations and the government. It is becoming more difficult to cover up dark acts and operations. It is all part of a cleansing of the negative and the darkness on the planet. I'm sure you can think of even more things that relate to these cleansing changes, and they will continue to escalate. IT IS TIME that the planet is cleansed of its negativity, greed, corruption, and its darkness.

It is no coincidence that we are experiencing more violent weather and seismic activities. Humanity has, for too long, abused the planet's environment in the name of profit. Pollution and negative vibrations have made Gaia (planet's spirit) sick. She asked for healing help and our loving starbrothers began sending her healing energy. This is one of the causes of the planet warming up but is also exacerbated by the pollution in the air. Pollution of our waters is causing an unbalanced ecosystem. The governments of nations have exploded nuclear bombs within the Earth and this has been the basis for many devastating earthquakes.

Mother Nature is reacting to these abuses in many ways as anomalies of hurricanes, tornados, tsunamis, earthquakes, volcanoes, etc., ravage the planet. Yes, we have always had these disastrous events, but they are increasing in power and frequency. These are all examples of how the Universal Law of Cause and Effect comes into play. Nothing escapes this great balancing law that our Creator created for us to live by.

Our planet, often called Gaia, is a living physical entity with a spiritual essence as are we; however, the spirits of planets, stars, and all other heavenly bodies are of a more evolved nature than humanity. Earth is also going through an evolutionary process and needs to purge the planet of all the extreme negativities created by wars, pollution, and sucking her lifeblood (oil) dry. You may recall what a horse does while it is being bitten by a horsefly. It whips its tail around or shakes its skin vigorously to remove the source of the irritating bites. Our planet is doing a similar thing to rid her self of the irritations that her temporary residents (us) have been creating through many abuses.

Let's take a look at what spirit has to say about 'The Law of Cycles.'

> *The Law of Cycles states that cycles keep life in motion and lead to evolution. The motion of evolution is always in progress and so it is on the Earth today. Your planet is now in the process of culminating multiple cycles, thus there will be more noticeable changes than normal. You can see what has been happening in recent years; the significant changes occurring in world situations brought on by its inhabitants such as moral decadence, increased crime (your prisons are overflowing), increased mental and physical ill-health, plus alcohol and drug abuse to name a few. Some of this is a result of mankind's increased negative vibrations. These will create direct manifestations through the Law of Cause and Effect. Other changes will be created by divine action as necessary to ensure the evolutionary process continues to move forward. If*

the state of affairs were left to continue on its own accord, the planet could move swiftly to a mode of self-destruct. This has happened to other planets in the Universes. Such a planet was Maldek. Many of its former inhabitants are on Earth today. Because there are enough good people on the Earth worthy of saving and who will ultimately preserve the planet and bring about a new world of goodness and purity, the Creator will not allow complete destruction as has happened elsewhere. Those of you who do care about your planet and all life thereon will be given an opportunity to work on behalf of your Creator to bring about a new world filled with love and peace.

Know that good ultimately overpowers the negative, love is stronger than hate, and peace will overcome chaos and strife. It is all part of the evolutionary process but it must come from its planet's inhabitants. When it does not, other forces will come into play to ensure that it does.

Although, from a physical perspective, it will appear to be a very chaotic time as the cycles of this period on your planet conclude before entering into yet another level of cycles. Remember, the physical realm is actually an illusion. You will realize this when you return to your spirit home. During the final stages of the chaos, there will be tremendous opportunities to grow and serve. For those who have risen above the temptations of the physical, their progress will be great.

Because the Law of Cycles and the Law of Evolution go hand in hand, the Law of Evolution follows.

The Law of Evolution states that evolution is eternal. It never stops and continues throughout the life expressions of all entities. If you limit your definition of evolution to change, then it will not work. So, in this respect, think of evolution as the growing and expanding of the changeless qualities of the Lord Most High.

Spiritual evolution means expansion, growth, and unity with God. Physical evolution is not necessarily eternal. Physical species do evolve as their brains evolve and they will continue to do so as various factors within their environment necessitate. However, some species evolve to a point and then become extinct.

Evolution of the consciousness can progress or regress. It is the consciousness that determines how many times you must experience physical life. Increased consciousness parallels spiritual progress. How you think (which is consciousness) greatly determines what you do. What you do determines how the Law of Cause and Effect affects your life, plus it has an impact on your spiritual evolution. Think of how evolution of your consciousness, and thus your spirit, means learning to think and live high thoughts. Thus it means transcending to higher planes of thought. It cycles between the physical and spirit and can play a great part in physical evolution. So, raising your consciousness is important to physical evolution as well as conscious and spiritual evolution. If all humans were to raise their consciousness, physical evolution would create a physical paradise. Man's physical evolution or devolution will be parallel to his own race mind or collective consciousness as it is called. Spirit cannot move until consciousness is raised at some level.

On both the physical plane and within the spiritual realm there is a direct correlation between spiritual evolution and vibrations. As we spiritually evolve on Earth, the frequency of vibrations within our bodies increases. As this occurs, we will find we become more incompatible with many things of a lower vibration such as harsh, loud sounds including certain kinds of music; we seek to consume healthier foods; and we drift away from rude and crude friends. As the beautiful prose *Desiderata* states, "*Avoid loud and aggressive persons, they are vexations to the spirit.*"

In the spirit world, as one evolves to higher dimensions, not only does the spirit body increase in vibrations but the dimension as a whole vibrates at a higher frequency. Everything is more refined, more brilliant, and more vivid. This will be explained in greater detail in Chapter 17.

We cannot change anyone else's negative choices or over-ride their free will. All we can do is keep working at raising our own vibrations, live in the Light, and send Light to others. It is the power of the Light that can transform situations or others for the highest good without trying to force our will on anyone.

The following communication from spirit discusses how the increasing planetary vibrations are creating changes in the human body/brain and how to best handle these changes.

Why So Many Are Mentally Spacing Out

> So many on the planet have been experiencing periods of what you have termed mentally spacing out. What follows are situations that many have been experiencing.

> You may be working on a project and have a need to get something from another room or the basement or garage. When you get there, you forget what it was you came to get but you see something else that needs your attention. As you begin to take care of this new thing, it leads to another room and you notice something else that needs taking care of. Finally, you find yourself in the room where you started your original project and you realize how you have been moving from one thing to another never fully completing your tasks.

Some of you experience another mental fragmentation when you are reading. After a time, you find your eyes have been moving across the words but your mind has drifted off to another thought. Other times, you try to think of something you know that you know but it simply will not enter into your consciousness. Later, when you have given up trying to remember it, there it is, as clear as your own name. These anomalies commonly occur when people get up in age; however, this is now being experienced by people of all ages.

Some of you, while driving, have become lost in areas you are very familiar with but now you are not sure which way to turn to find your way. When these mental confusions occur, many of you become angry or fearful that you are 'losing it' so to speak. Many of you have wondered if you are sliding into dementia or Alzheimer's and many have felt the need to have it checked out.

Oh dear ones of the Earth plane, fear not for I have good news for you. Certainly you must have noticed that the Earth is changing rapidly and so it is with all of humanity as mankind moves at ever-faster paces upon this marvelous spaceship Earth as it hurtles at great speeds through universal space. Nearly everyone seems to feel that time is going faster, and so it is as the planetary vibrations increase.

For many years, messages have been sent from higher planes to many on Earth warning of the impending Earth changes often known as the period of great transformation. It is not only occurring on the Earth but so also is it occurring throughout the entire universe. It is but a completion of a movement through a grand cycle as Earth is now moving into a new phase of life. Some have called it the New Age or the Golden Age. It will be as winter's darker dreary days move into the freshness of spring and new life.

This transition is in process, and many of you are feeling these changes deep within your being. The time of transcending will not be without pain or confusion but everyone will not experience the same physical discomforts. Some will experience short periods of illness as the propensities for certain illness and disease that lie in the double helix DNA are being cleared out of the body. Meanwhile, some of the new children being born upon the Earth are coming in with a more expanded DNA, and that is good.

What I wish you to know and understand regarding the mental confusion occurring in so many is this. The body and brain are slowly being molecularly restructured to be compatible with the higher vibrations. The brain is beginning to be rewired, so to speak, and new areas of the brain that have been dormant for a very long time are now in the process of being activated. This will not happen overnight and must occur slowly or one would cease to mentally and physically function for a time. However, there will be periods of confusion and discomfort for a while. Not all disease and mental or physical illness will end. Therefore, if you strongly feel there is a real mental or physical problem that needs medical attention, by all means you should have it checked out by medical professionals, if for no other reason than to give you peace of mind.

Those who become upset or fear what is occurring will have increasingly difficult times. Those whose gods are materiality, money, power, and control over others will not be compatible with the new vibrations. I will not speak an untruth by saying that all humans will survive this transformation.

The nature kingdom is actually changing more easily because of the absence of an ego. Because creatures of nature do not have the human type of ego, they are more in the flow with the increasing vibrations and it will lessen the discomfort and confusion as they experience the changes. However, animals have more recently come down out of the wilds and into the areas of human habitat.

It is especially important to love others, love yourself, and all life expressing on the planet during these times. Mother Earth is also reacting to these changes by purging and cleansing herself. You, as entities who reside upon your Mother Earth, can assist her by expressing your love to her and give thanks to this marvelous being who sustains your life. Therefore love the wind, no matter how hard it blows for you cannot survive without air. Love the water, no matter how much of it falls from the sky for you cannot live without water. Love the trees for they give you the oxygen you need to live. Breathe it freely and deeply and it will help with the transformational changes that are in process.

Know that if this process were to happen too rapidly, you could not handle or deal with it and truly you would 'lose it' as some say. How long the transformation will take depends on how well humanity reacts to its passage. If you read what your media prints, you must surely think the world is going crazy. And yes, the ones filled with darkness are becoming darker. But know ye this also; those of the light are becoming a brighter light. So also are many in the world awakening to the greater truths and realities. Light will always overcome the darkness but darkness cannot do so with the light and the light shall indeed prevail. It is for this reason that many light beings have volunteered to enter the physical realm and be on the planet during these times to assist with the transformation.

I know it is difficult for many who view the current state of affairs upon the planet to be able to envision a time of unity upon the Earth and a time of peace; a time of oneness with all of life; a time when you will create goodness to a level never seen upon the planet; and a time when fear will no longer be a controlling aspect of the minds of mankind. When these times of great change pass, there will no longer be anything to fear. In the Golden Age to come, you will come to know who you really are and life will be more beauteous than you can now imagine. Change will always be with you as you live out your life in the physical and thereafter on to the higher realms of eternal life.

I will leave you with the words that my dear friend and brother John the Divine wrote from the island of Patmos.

"And God shall wipe away all tears from their eyes; and there shall be no more death, neither sorrow nor crying, neither shall there be any more pain, for the former things are passed away."

Know ye that I am your friend and I will be with you, even unto the end of the age.

It is through cycles and change that we progress and evolve. These times are at hand. How we deal with the changes will determine how well or difficult it will be for us to finally emerge into a beauteous time beyond our imagination.

Norie Huddle wrote an analysis of what occurs when a caterpillar is transformed into a butterfly.

The caterpillar's new cells are called 'imaginal cells.' They resonate at a different frequency. They are so totally different from the caterpillar cells that his immune system thinks they are enemies ... and gobbles them up .... But these new imaginal cells continue to appear. More and more of them! Pretty soon, the caterpillar's immune system cannot destroy them fast enough. More and more of the imaginal cells survive. And then an amazing thing happens! The little tiny lonely imaginal cells start to clump together, into friendly little groups. They all resonate together at the same frequency, passing information from one to another. Then, after awhile, another amazing thing happens! The clumps of imaginal cells start to cluster together!...a long string of clumping and clustering imaginal cells, all resonating at the same frequency, all passing information from one to another there inside the chrysalis...

Then at some point, the entire long string of imaginal cells suddenly realizes all together that it is Something Different from the caterpillar. Something New! Something Wonderful! In that realization is the shout of the birth of the butterfly!

Maybe the Universe is telling us IT IS TIME for the humans to be like a caterpillar and begin transformation into a beautiful new human like the butterfly and rise up above and beyond the heaviness and negativity of the old and into the wonders of a New World.

I end this chapter with an account taken from the writings of a diary written by Admiral Byrd. His diary was found after his death by his son. He described his experience when flying on a mission over the North Pole and accidentally flying into the 'inner earth.' While this fantastic story is not directly connected to Earth changes, it gives us a greater vision of the greater reality of the planet.

Admiral Richard B. Byrd's Diary (February - March 1947)
The exploration flight over the North Pole

The Inner Earth - My Secret Diary

I must write this diary in secrecy and obscurity. It concerns my Arctic flight of the nineteenth day of February in the year of Nineteen and Forty-Seven.

There comes a time when the rationality of men must fade into insignificance and one must accept the inevitability of the Truth! I am not at liberty to disclose the following documentation at this writing ...perhaps it shall never see the light of public scrutiny, but I must do my duty and record here for all to read one day. In a world of greed and exploitation of certain of mankind can no longer suppress that which is truth.

Flight Log: Base Camp Arctic, 2/19/1947

06.00 Hours - All preparations are complete for our flight northward and we are airborne with full fuel tanks at 0610 Hours.

06.20 Hours - fuel mixture on starboard engine seems too rich, adjustment made and Pratt Whittneys are running smoothly.

07.30 Hours - Radio Check with base camp. All is well and radio reception is normal.

07.40 Hours - Note slight oil leak in starboard engine, oil pressure indicator seems normal, however.

08.00 Hours - Slight turbulence noted from easterly direction at altitude of 2321 feet, correction to 1700 feet, no further turbulence, but tail wind increases, slight adjustment in throttle controls, aircraft performing very well now.

08.15 Hours- Radio Check with base camp, situation normal.

08.30 Hours - Turbulence encountered again, increase altitude to 2900 feet, smooth flight conditions again.

09.10 Hours - Vast Ice and snow below, note coloration of yellowish nature, and disperse in a linear pattern. Altering course for a better examination of this color pattern below, note reddish or purple color also. Circle this area two full turns and return to assigned compass heading. Position check made again to Base Camp, and relay information concerning colorations in the Ice and snow below.

09.10 Hours - Both Magnetic and Gyro compasses beginning to gyrate and wobble, we are unable to hold our heading by instrumentation. Take bearing with Sun compass, yet all seems well. The controls are seemingly slow to respond and have sluggish quality, but there is no indication of Icing!

09.15 Hours - In the distance is what appears to be mountains.

0949 Hours - 29 minutes elapsed flight time from the first sighting of the mountains, it is no illusion. They are mountains and consisting of a small range that I have never seen before!

09.55 Hours - Altitude change to 2950 feet, encountering strong turbulence again.

10.00 Hours - We are crossing over the small mountain range and still proceeding northward as best as can be ascertained. Beyond the mountain range is what appears to be a valley with a small river or stream running through the center portion. There should be no green valley below! Something is definitely wrong and abnormal here! We should be over Ice and Snow! To the portside are great forests growing on the mountain slopes. Our navigation Instruments are still spinning, the gyroscope is oscillating back and forth!

10.05 Hours - I alter altitude to 1400 feet and execute a sharp left turn to better examine the valley below. It is green with either moss or a type of tight-knit grass. The Light here seems different. I cannot see the Sun anymore. We make another left turn and we spot what seems to be a large animal of some kind below us. It appears to be an elephant! NO!!! It looks more like a mammoth! This is incredible! Yet, there it is! Decrease altitude to 1000 feet and take binoculars to better examine the animal. It is confirmed - it is definitely a mammoth-like animal! Report this to Base Camp.

10.30 Hours - Encountering more rolling green hills now. The external temperature indicator reads 74 degrees Fahrenheit! Continuing on our heading now. Navigation instruments seem normal now. I am puzzled over their actions. Attempt to contact Base Camp. Radio is not functioning!

11.30 Hours - Countryside below is more level and normal (if I may use that word). Ahead we spot what seems to be a city!!!! This is impossible! Aircraft seems light and oddly buoyant. The controls refuse to respond!! My GOD!!! Off our port and starboard wings are a strange type of aircraft. They are closing rapidly alongside! They are disc-shaped and have a radiant quality to them.

They are close enough now to see the markings on them. It is a type of Swastika!!! This is fantastic. Where are we! What has happened. I tug at the controls again. They will not respond!!!! We are caught in an invisible vice grip of some type!

11.35 Hours - Our radio crackles and a voice comes through in English with what perhaps is a slight Nordic or Germanic accent! The message is: 'Welcome, Admiral, to our Domain. We shall land you in exactly seven minutes! Relax, Admiral, you are in good hands.' I note the engines of our plane have stopped running! The aircraft is under some strange control and is now turning itself. The controls are useless.

11.40 Hours - Another radio message received. We begin the landing process now, and in moments the plane shudders slightly, and begins a descent as though caught in some great unseen elevator! The downward motion is negligible, and we touch down with only a slight jolt!

11.45 Hours - I am making a hasty last entry in the Flight Log. Several men are approaching on foot toward our aircraft. They are tall with blond hair. In the distance is a large shimmering city pulsating with rainbow hues of color. I do not know what is going to happen now, but I see no signs of weapons on those approaching. I hear now a voice ordering me by name to open the cargo door. I comply.

End Log

From this point I write all the following events here from memory. It defies the imagination and would seem all but madness if it had not happened. The radioman and I are taken from the aircraft and we are received in a most cordial manner. We were then boarded on a small platform-like conveyance with no wheels! It moves us toward the glowing city with great swiftness. As we approach, the city seems to be made of a crystal material. Soon we arrive at a large building that is a type I have never seen before. It appears to be right out of the design board of Frank Lloyd Wright, or perhaps more correctly, out of a Buck Rogers setting!! We are given some type of warm beverage which tasted like nothing I have ever savored before. It is delicious.

After about ten minutes, two of our wondrous appearing Hosts come to our quarters and announce that I am to accompany them. I have no choice but to comply. I leave my Radioman behind and we walk a short distance and enter into what seems to be an elevator. We descend downward for some moments, the machine stops, and the door lifts silently upward! We then proceed down a long hallway that is lit by a rose-colored light that seems to be emanating from the very walls themselves!

One of the beings motions for us to stop before a great door. Over the door is an inscription that I cannot read. The great door slides noiselessly open and I am beckoned to enter. One of my Hosts speaks. "Have no fear, Admiral, you are to have an audience with the Master..."

I step inside and my eyes adjust to the beautiful coloration that seems to be filling the room completely. Then I begin to see my surroundings. What greeted my eyes is the most beautiful sight of my entire existence. It is in fact too beautiful and wondrous to describe. It is exquisite and delicate. I do not think there exists a Human term that can describe it in any detail with justice! My thoughts are interrupted in a cordial manner by a warm rich voice of melodious quality, 'I bid you welcome to our Domain, Admiral.' I see a man with delicate features and with the etching of years upon his face. He is seated at a long table. He motions me to sit down in one of the chairs. After I am seated, he places his fingertips together and smiles. He speaks softly again, and conveys the following.

"We have let you enter here because you are of noble character and well-known on the Surface World, Admiral."

"Surface World?", I half-gasp under my breath!

"Yes," the Master replies with a smile, "you are in the domain of the Arianni, the Inner World of the Earth. We shall not long delay your mission, and you will be safely escorted back to the surface and for a distance beyond. But now, Admiral, I shall tell you why you have been summoned here. Our interest rightly begins just after your race exploded the first atomic bombs over Hiroshima and Nagasaki, Japan. It was at that alarming time we sent our flying machines, the "Flugelrads", to your surface world to investigate what your race had done. That is, of course, past history now, my dear Admiral, but I must continue on. You see, we have never interfered before in your race's wars, and barbarity, but now we must, for you have learned to tamper with a certain power that is not for Man, namely, that of atomic energy. Our emissaries have already delivered messages to the powers of your world, and yet they do not heed. Now you have been chosen to be witness here that our world does exist. You see, our Culture and Science is many thousands of years beyond your race, Admiral."

I interrupted, "But what does this have to do with me, Sir?"

The Master's eyes seemed to penetrate deeply into my mind, and after studying me for a few moments he replied, "Your race has now reached the point of no return, for there are those among you who would destroy your very World rather than relinquish their power as they know it..."

I nodded, and the Master continued, "In 1945 and afterward, we tried to contact your race, but our efforts were met with hostility, our Flugelrads were fired upon. Yes, even pursued with malice and animosity by your fighter planes. So, now, I say to you, my son, there is a great storm gathering in your World, a black fury that will not spend itself for many years. There will be no answer in your Arms, there will be no safety in your Science. It may rage on until every flower of your culture is trampled, and all Human things are leveled in vast chaos. Your recent War was only a prelude of what is yet to come for your race. We here see it more clearly with each hour..do you say I am mistaken?"

"No," I answer, "it happened once before, the Dark Ages came and they lasted for more than five hundred years."

"Yes, my son," replied the Master, "the Dark Ages that will come now for your race will cover the Earth like a pall, but I believe that some of your race will live through the storm, beyond that, I cannot say. We see at a great distance a new world stirring from the ruins of your race, seeking its lost and legendary treasures, and they will be here, my son, safe in our keeping. When that time arrives, we shall come forward again to help revive your culture and your race. Perhaps, by then, you will have learned the futility of war and its strife...and after that time, certain of your culture and science will be returned for your race to begin anew.

You, my son, are to return to the Surface World with this message....."

With these closing words, our meeting seemed at an end. I stood for a moment as in a deam....but, yet, I knew this was reality, and for some strange reason I bowed slightly, either out of respect or humility, I do not know which.

Suddenly, I was again aware that the two beautiful Hosts who had brought me here were again at my side. "This way, Admiral," motioned one. I turned once more before leaving and looked back toward the Master. A gentle smile was etched on his delicate and ancient face. 'Farewell, my son,' he spoke, then he gestured with a lovely, slender hand a motion of peace and our meeting was truly ended.

Quickly, we walked back through the great door of the Master's chamber and once again entered into the elevator. The door slid silently downward and we were at once going upward. One of my hosts spoke again, "We must now make haste, Admiral, as the Master desires to delay you no longer on your scheduled timetable and you must return with his message to your race."

I said nothing. All of this was almost beyond belief, and once again my thoughts were interrupted as we stopped. I entered the room and was again with my Radioman. He had an anxious expression on his face. As I approached, I said, "It is all right, Howie, it is all right."

The two beings motioned us toward the awaiting conveyance, we boarded, and soon arrived back at the aircraft. The engines were idling and we boarded immediately. The whole atmosphere seemed charged now with a certain air of urgency. After the cargo door was closed the aircraft was immediately lifted by that unseen force until we reached an altitude of 2700 feet. Two of the aircraft were alongside for some distance guiding us on our return way. I must state here, the airspeed indicator registered no reading, yet we were moving along at a very rapid rate.

2.15 Hours - A radio message comes through. "We are leaving you now, Admiral, your controls are free. Auf Wiedersehen!!!!"

We watched for a moment as the flugelrads disappeared into the pale blue sky. The aircraft suddenly felt as though caught in a sharp downdraft for a moment. We quickly recovered her control. We do not speak for some time, each man has his thoughts....

Entry in Flight Log continues:
2.20 Hours - We are again over vast areas of ice and snow, and approximately 27 minutes from Base Camp. We radio them, they respond. We report all conditions normal.... normal. Base Camp expresses relief at our re-established contact.

3.00 Hours - We land smoothly at Base Camp. I have a mission.....

End Log Entries:

March 11, 1947. I have just attended a Staff Meeting at the Pentagon. I have stated fully my discovery and the message from the Master. All is duly recorded. The President has been advised. I am now detained for several hours (six hours, thirty-nine minutes, to be exact.) I am interviewed intently by

Top Security Forces and a medical team. It was an ordeal!!!!
I am placed under strict control via the National Security
provisions of this United States of America. I am ORDERED
TO REMAIN SILENT IN REGARD TO ALL THAT I
HAVE LEARNED, ON THE BEHALF OF HUMANITY!!!
Incredible! I am reminded that I am a Military Man and I
must obey orders.

30/12/56: Final Entry:
These last few years elapsed since 1947 have not been kind...I
now make my final entry in this singular diary. In closing,
I must state that I have faithfully kept this matter secret as
directed all these years. It has been completely against my
values of moral right. Now, I seem to sense the long night
coming on and this secret will not die with me, but as all
truth shall, it will triumph and so it shall.

This can be the only hope for Mankind. I have seen the truth
and it has quickened my spirit and has set me free! I have
done my duty toward the monstrous military industrial
complex. Now, the long night begins to approach, but there
shall be no end. Just as the long night of the Arctic ends, the
brilliant sunshine of Truth shall come again....and those who
are of darkness shall fall in it's Light. FOR I HAVE SEEN
THAT LAND BEYOND THE POLE, THAT CENTER OF
THE GREAT UNKNOWN.

Admiral Richard E. Byrd
United States Navy
24 December 1956

On the Physical Plane, change is constant.
Everything else is temporary.

PART TWO

The Transition Process

Introduction

In this part I have shared some of my experiences as a hospice volunteer for over 13 years. You will also learn the importance of moving beyond fear when our lives come to an end on the physical plane and move on gracefully to the next life in the realm of spirit, which by the way, is much better than the one we will leave behind. Those who have had the near death experiences of dying and coming back to tell about it have substantiated how absolutely wonderful it is on the other side.

Also in this section, you will read about the experiences of a few who have passed on and have not come back but are now in their true home on the spirit side of life. Although physical death is something most people do not like to think about, in these pages, detailed accounts of what some have experienced in the process of crossing over are presented so you, the reader, will see why there is nothing to fear about leaving this temporary journey on the Earth plane, something we will all eventually experience. It is the last experience that we, as physical humans, will have in an inevitable forthcoming time. IT IS TIME to better understand what a marvelous trip it is.

CHAPTER 13

The Hospice Experience

Dannion Brinkley wrote a series of books about his near death experiences and how they completely changed his life. A summary of his experiences is covered in the next chapter. As a result of his spiritual experiences while being on the other side, he began to serve others by volunteering at a hospice. Though he experienced the pain he had caused to others, he also experienced the great love and peace that exists in God's spiritual kingdom. I had a chance to meet him at one of his presentations. One of the key things he expressed was, have no fear of dying and do not take life on Earth so seriously. He had acquired a great sense of humor and had his audience frequently laughing during his presentation. In his first book, *Saved by the Light,* he expressed what a great service it was to volunteer at a hospice. After I retired from Corporate America, I remembered what he said about what a good thing it was to do hospice volunteer work. Feeling I had been blessed with a good life, I decided it was time to give back to life by spending time with those whose time was nearing the end of their physical journey.

Dannion Brinkley had the experience of dying and knew it was nothing to be feared. While I had no such experience, I did have experiences of communicating with friends and family on the other side and from them I knew there was nothing to fear about leaving the physical form to enter into a new life on spirit side. With that knowledge, I could help those close to passing know that there was absolutely nothing to fear. Therefore, I took the training and have, at this point, been a volunteer at a local hospice for over thirteen years. I have now interacted with hundreds of beings who were in their last days of physical life. Many of them really open up and share things they had kept to themselves for years on end. I think it is often a matter of getting things off their chest or clearing the air before passing on. The best thing a social volunteer can do is to be a good listener.

I have experienced quite a variety of patients passing on from their physical form. One thing that became clear to me was those who had a great fear of dying had a very difficult time releasing from the physical. Spirit explained this as a reaction of the ego resisting the passing because the ego knows that when the body dies, the ego is no more. When the ego is stronger than the spirit within, the ego wants to be in control to the very end. I have seen patients who were flailing their arms and body around and some even hollering and screaming, fighting against the ultimate release of their spirit. On the other hand, those who had a religious or spiritual faith were more likely to accept that their time had come to return home to the spirit plane of life. These patients had no fear and were peaceful, relaxed, and some were actually looking forward to "coming to be with their Lord."

As a means of negating any anxiety about passing on, I would often try to make patients understand that there is nothing to fear about physical death. It's something we are all going to do; some go sooner and some later because there are no guarantees of how long we will live in our physical journey of life. Then I add, "What I've learned about our transition to our next life adventure indicates it will be a most wonderful experience when we leave our heavy physical form and be able to move freely into the beautiful Light of God where great love and peace will be experienced beyond our imagination."

I also emphasize how important it is to release any fear about dying because it will make the actual release of the spirit much easier and more peaceful. To others who were not afraid to discuss the subject, I say things like, "Because life is eternal, yet the physical experience is comparatively very short, this life is like taking a vacation from the spirit plane and going on a physical adventure. We can experience things here that are not available on the spirit plane. Creating, having, and raising children is just one of them. Participating in competitive sports is another. Also, there are opportunities to achieve spiritual growth on the physical plane that do not exist on the spirit plane.

The criteria for being accepted into a hospice is, one must have been diagnosed as being in a terminal state of health with less than a specified time of life expectancy, for example, six months or less to live. The patients or their caretakers must agree that nothing will be done to extend life, such as no resuscitation, no feeding tubes, etc. There is, however, the greatest effort to make their time as comfortable as possible including administering pain control. While the average time one spends in the hospice is around two weeks, I have experienced some patients being there for two years.

Because the environment and care are so much more positive than a nursing home, some of the patients have become well and a few have come back as volunteers. For the most part, it is a very special type of person who becomes a hospice nurse or a hospice volunteer. They do all they can to make the time left for a patient as pleasant as possible. There is a pastoral staff available for those who wish to discuss or practice their religious beliefs, no matter what their religious affiliation. All religions are honored. Volunteers go through several hours of training and then spend some time with an experienced volunteer for floor training before they go out on their own with the patients.

Some volunteers work with patient care, assisting patients with physical help such as feeding, dressing, etc. Others are there for social interaction.

Here the volunteer interacts socially with the patients, but mainly listens to their stories about experiences they've had in their lives. Sometimes, when weather permits, we take patients out to the garden area for fresh air and conversation. This is an area I love to take them because it gets them out of their room and they can enjoy trees and beautiful flowers. Sometimes, I have spent hours with one patient when we really get into the depths of life. Some have completely opened up about very personal experiences or sensitive feelings. I sense some need to release pent up things or possibly guilt feelings as if lightening the load before departure. I have taken patients who are still mobile out fishing, to museums, and sporting events. Volunteers must always maintain a level of confidentiality, even with the patient's families.

I will now share a few meaningful experiences I've had with patients. I will not use their real names, even though they have now graduated to the spirit world.

Mary was admitted to the hospice with a serious heart problem. She was not expected to last very long but she actually hung in there for nearly a year. Every week on my volunteer day, I would spend an hour or more with Mary. She developed a trust in me and we actually became good friends. After spending time with her week after week, she began to share some very personal feelings. One day, she shared her psychological impacts of having a breast removed. I will not get into that but share a very cute story she told me about her grandson. She had just got out of the shower when her five-year-old grandson barged into the bathroom. He looked up and stared at her for a moment, pointed up at her, and then said, "OH! My mommy has two of those," and then quickly ran back out. We both really laughed at her humorous and amusing story and I know she got a kick out of telling it to me.

Here is another one. Jack was admitted to the hospice after he had surgery for throat cancer. He could no longer talk except for a very weak whisper. Jack had no family and as far as I knew, he didn't have any close friends, either. He appeared very lonely so I attempted to befriend him. Not many volunteers came to visit Jack because it was so difficult to communicate with him. He would often use a marker board when he couldn't communicate clearly. Jack didn't like or trust women so the nurses had a difficult time dealing with him.

One day, Jack asked if I would go to his apartment and pick up a few personal items for him. One of the items was a revolver he had hidden on the back of a top closet shelf. When I returned, I gave him all the items except the revolver, which I turned over to the hospice administrator.

When Jack was near the end of his days, the nurses wanted to know if he preferred a burial or cremation. Jack refused to answer their request so they asked if I would intercede and get the answer from Jack about his preferences. I explained to Jack that he would probably not last much longer and had he thought about whether he would prefer a burial or cremation. Because Jack developed a trust in me, he immediately answered the question. He preferred cremation. Jack lasted about another week before he passed and the administration then knew what to do with his remains.

A well-known performer on the stage came to the hospice with a rare form of palsy. Marie's body was almost non-functional. When I would come in on my normal Tuesday mornings, Marie would be in a wheel chair, her head slumped over to one side because she could not hold it up, and she would have a blank stare at nothing in particular. The only thing she seemed to be able to do was to scoot the wheelchair along backwards an inch or two at a time.

One morning when I came in, Marie was in the lobby just off the hallway; however, this morning was different. Though her head was slumped down and over, she lifted her eyes and made eye contact with me. At that point, something stirred within me to try and communicate with her. I knelt down on one knee right in front of her and looked directly into her eyes. They were still focused on me and I was encouraged to try to make a connection. I began by maintaining our eye contact and I said, "Marie, I know you can hear and understand me. I would like to ask you some questions to be answered with a yes or no. If you understand, answer by blinking your eyes twice for yes and once for no." There was no response, so I repeated my request. Still no response with her eyes but I caught a movement with her index finger lifting on her right hand. "Marie, if you understand, lift that finger again." She slowly lifted it twice. I then proceeded to ask her other questions that she could answer with our established response signal. She answered every question with a finger lifting response of yes or no and I was elated.

I shared what I had achieved with the nurses and they were very pleased that now they could at least get yes or no answers from her. I later shared all this with her husband when he came to visit later that morning and he was pleased, as well. I asked him if there was anything I could do to help lift her spirits during my visits. He explained that he had a box of various photos and newspaper clippings of her performances during her days of performing on the stage and he knew from earlier discussions with her before entering the hospice that she wanted to organize and put them all into an album. So he asked if I would work with her to complete this project.

In the following weeks, I worked with Marie by sorting the various photos and newspaper articles into groups with her agreeing or disagreeing on what should be together and in what order in the album. Working together through our established means of communication, we put together the album of Marie's professional stage career. I had the feeling she really loved doing this instead of just scooting up and down the halls. Moreover, I would leave the hospice with a great feeling of satisfaction knowing I helped bring joy to a dear soul in her last days upon the planet.

Oftentimes, people I meet or who know that I volunteer at a hospice will ask me if it is depressing to be around all those people who are dying. I answer by explaining it is very rewarding to spend time with someone in their final phase of life because I can bring joy to them by just listening to their life's stories. I let them know I care about them and I can give them hope by letting them know that there is nothing to fear in letting go of the physical because they will move into a new world of peace and joy and great love. A patient's frequent response will be something like, "Thanks for coming in to visit. You've made my day." When I get that kind of response, it makes my day!

There are physical signs when someone comes very close to passing, excluding sudden heart attacks or strokes. For example, the soles of the feet usually turn blue; or the breathing becomes erratic and sometimes even stops for short periods. When these signs are apparent, a patient is put on 'watch' which means they usually have anywhere between 48 and 72 hours of life left. The families are then notified so they may have their final visits.

One day, as I was walking down the hospice hall, I passed by a room where the patient was on watch. Several members of the family were in the room saying their goodbyes and the patient was very close to passing. A family member came out and asked me if I could come in and help. As I entered the room, the patient was wailing and thrashing back and forth, and I guessed that was because he had a great fear of dying. I approached this man on his bed, leaned over and put my hand on his forehead and I said to him, "You are about to experience something very wonderful. It is nothing to fear. It is a glorious experience that lies before you. So, now it is time to just let go. It is okay to let go and be at peace." He immediately calmed down and relaxed. I then left the family with their beloved and left the room. About 10 minutes later when I passed that room again, a member of the family came out, thanked me for what I had done and told me that his father just passed peacefully a few minutes ago.

It is these types of experiences that remind me of what very good work it is to be a hospice volunteer. While it is not for everyone, for those who are comfortable with doing this type of volunteer work, it is a wonderful thing to experience making a positive difference with someone who is in their final days on the Earth Plane.

Grief

There are usually stages of bereavement one will go through when losing a close friend or relative who graduates to the other side of life's ongoing journey, especially if the one passing on is a long time spouse. There are four basic stages of grief that are both normal and healthy to go through. The first stage is one of shock and numbness. Events may lose their importance after the death of a loved one. This rather numb feeling is a way of helping you to carry on the necessities of life.

The second stage is an emotional turmoil. Emotional extremes are common during the bereavement period. Some emotions that may surface are feelings of anger, bitterness, resentment, and even fear. You may also have guilt feelings that are accompanied with thoughts of, "If only I had…." Some of these feelings may arise over many months. During this time, a friend's emotional support with sympathetic ears and a few reassuring words will be most needed.

The third stage involves feelings of emptiness, loneliness, depression, and even despair may be experienced in this stage and may last for some time. This could become a dangerous time by leaning too heavily on someone or something else like alcohol. The bereavement process can take time, and patience is required to get through it.

The final stage is one of acceptance. It occurs when you have gone through all the previous stages and have come to grips with the loss of one who has been very close to you. You realize the loved one is gone from the physical world forevermore. It will help to believe you will see and be with this loved one again when your time comes to graduate into the next plane of life. However, you may continue to miss this person until that time. Meanwhile, you will know you have reached the stage of acceptance when you find you have an interest in becoming involved in life's activities again.

Finally in this chapter, let's go through what you might experience if you find yourself in the final days of your current life expression on Planet Earth. Many times, the person dying will quickly accept what lies ahead and is the most realistic and comfortable of all. But those around, the family and friends, may be having a difficult time accepting what is occurring. You may want to make clear who gets your personal or otherwise possessions, but your mate or other loved ones may not be comfortable with that. You can help make your loved ones more comfortable by telling them you are okay with your situation and you will be there to welcome them 'home' when their time comes to pass on to the other side.

If you are apprehensive of your actual departure from the physical, you may find your passing will be very difficult and thus you will fight against letting go to the very end. However, if you are at peace prior to passing on, you will most likely have an easy passing unless pain medication is not working well enough. But even then, it will be easier than also having the emotional pain. Most people associate dying with pain, but pain is only a precursor to the actual passing. Once the spirit releases from the physical, the experience is beautiful beyond words and is a great relief to the spirit, and that is part of the reality of who you really are.

Everything in the physical, including life itself,
is temporary except change ... and that is all that death is.

CHAPTER 14

Near Death Experiences

Death itself is a very pleasant experience, one that is more spiritual than physical. The actual dying part is what many people fear because it is often accompanied with illness, pain, and suffering. The actual moment of death is like turning off one light while simultaneously turning on another, but one that is brighter and filled with tremendous energy. What leads up to the actual departure of the spirit is our final physical experience.

However, from the moment the spirit takes its leave, it is wholly a spiritual experience. The greatest and most apparent thing the spirit body notices is the tremendous feeling of lightness and freedom from the heavy physical

How do we know what happens after death? There have been increasing numbers of individuals who have experienced a clinical death with no heartbeat, no breathing, no brain functions for sometimes lengthy periods, yet have come back to life and shared their experiences of crossing over to the other side. Moreover, a significant number of humans have been blessed with the ability to receive communications from those who have passed on to spirit side, have not come back, but have shared the story of their passing. In this chapter, we will deal with those who are considered to have a "near death" (ND) experience.

In earlier years, very few people who had such ND experiences were comfortable in discussing these experiences for fear of being labeled mentally disturbed or just plain off their rocker. However, in more recent decades the near death experience has become more readily accepted. A growing number of souls have slipped out of their bodies and traveled to the other side for a brief time and then come back to the physical and were willing to openly discuss their experiences without the fear of being crucified or labeled a heretic. This has given courage to others to also openly relate their own near death experience. While some have had just a glimpse of the other side, guides, angels, or even the Master has met others. Some have simply been told they must return to the physical because they had more things to accomplish before returning home. Others have been given special missions and some have also been given prophetic messages. Always there has been a purpose for those to have such an experience.

All those I have known who have had such an experience emphatically say they no longer have any fear of death, and some have said they look forward to the time they will return the other side because of the love, the peace, and the beautiful sensations they experienced while there. However, a few determined clinically dead by doctors have come back to life but have little or no recollection of any experience between their death and retuning to life.

I believe that those who have openly shared their near death experiences, and especially those who have written books of their ND experiences, are doing a great service by dispelling many of the myths of death and reasons to fear it.

Two such books in particular have been written and published in recent years that give two very different accounts of ND experiences though they both had experiences of going into 'The Light.' It is important to remember that details of what one experiences when going to the other side may vary greatly because it depends on many factors such as their spiritual or religious beliefs plus how they lived their lives. The two authors, Betty Eadie and Dannion Brinkley have led very different lives.

Betty Eadie wrote of her ND experiences in *Embraced by the Light*. At a young age, she was placed in a Catholic boarding school and taught of a vengeful God by the nuns. Later, she went to other religious schools and came to believe that, upon death, she would remain in a grave until resurrection day and she therefore dreaded death and the blackness that would follow. Her relationship with God became distant and was filled with fear. After she grew up, married young, and had seven children, her doctor recommended a hysterectomy. After the surgery, complications set in and she died. Here is a brief account of her ND experience.

As her passing began, she tried to signal a nurse but she couldn't move. Next, she felt a sinking sensation and heard a soft buzzing sound in her head, followed by becoming still and lifeless. Then she felt a surge of energy come from inside her and felt her spirit release and then being pulled upward out of her body. Next came a feeling of being free. Hovering above the bed, she noticed a body below her. Her curiosity drew her closer to see who it was. Finally, she recognized that it was her own body. She felt she had discarded a used garment but sadly felt there was still a lot of use left in it.

Her spirit body was weightless and very mobile. No longer was there any pain or discomfort. She was now perfect in every way. Next, she saw a point of light at the end of a black tunnel and was attracted to it. As she approached the light, she saw the figure of a man with radiant light all around him. The light which had been golden now burst forth and became a brilliant white. She felt that light blending into her own and then she experienced an explosion of love. Though she had always had a fear of Jesus and God, she now knew Jesus was her friend who had always loved her even though she thought He must hate her while in the physical. Then the Master told her it was not yet her time. That time would come when her purpose, her mission, and the meaning in her life was accomplished.

In the short time she was on the other side, she remembered so much about life that was forgotten after entering the physical realm. Before returning to her physical body, she asked and had answered many questions and acquired the knowledge of the many Universal Laws that govern life here in the physical. For four hours, her physical body was clinically dead, but considering all she learned, it seemed far longer. When her spirit slipped back into her body, she once again felt the heaviness and pain and in time lived on to accomplish her mission of sharing spiritual truths. Though she shared her experiences and what she learned on the other side in the book she published, she has shared much more than what she wrote about; as she continues to serve her life's purpose by giving talks to hundreds of audiences here and abroad.

Next we'll review the experiences that Dannion Brinkley wrote of in his book, *Saved by the Light.* His background was very different than Betty Eadie's. When he was a young boy, other kids often picked on him so his dad taught him to defend himself. Thereafter, he beat up the neighborhood bully and that created a taste for fighting. In the sixth grade, he beat up his teacher and continued to seek out fights. After his school years, he went into the military and channeled his anger as a soldier. The military noted his aggressive anger and he was therefore trained for the purpose of killing in Vietnam and Cambodia. His mission was to plan and execute enemy politicians and key enemy military personnel, and he killed many.

After his time in the military, he came back home to North Carolina. At the age of 25, he was hit by lightning through a telephone receiver. In spirit, he watched the paramedics carry his dead body away in an ambulance. Based on traditional religious beliefs, if anyone should have gone to a hell it was Dannion Brinkley. But did he? In his book, he described his experiences in great detail, but here I will give just a short overview.

Like many, he went through a tunnel and came into the presence of a magnificent being of light and then was given a full review of his life. He stated how painful much of it was for him because, not only did he have to review every negative and harmful thing he did to others, but he also had to actually experience the emotional pain it caused them including the emotional pain it caused family members who lost their loved one as a result of his military assassinations. One by one, he experienced what he had caused others to experience. These experiences he believed were the greatest catalyst for his change and, in the end of his life review, he learned that love is the most important thing there is. Nearly everyone who has gone through a life review and returned to the physical is never the same again. He stated that the 28 minutes of his death included all the emotions of the universe.

After his life review, he traveled with his guide and visited a crystal city where he received visions of the Earth's future from 13 different beings of light. He was also given over a hundred predictions, many of which have already come true. Dannion was also shown many changes that would occur to the planet, to governments, the economy, and good things like the positive strides in medicine. Finally, before returning to his physical body that had been badly burned from the inside out from thousands of volts of lightening, he was given the mission to create spiritual centers where people could find themselves through stress reduction. He stated that the 28 minutes of his death included all the emotions of the universe.

His physical recovery was slow and painful, but he brought back the vast knowledge gained while on the spirit plane. Considering all the emotional pain Dannion experienced on spirit side relative to what he inflicted on others in his earlier life, plus the pain he went through recovering from the damage of the lightning strike after returning to the physical, I would think Dannion now considers this a part of balancing his life's actions as it relates to the Universal Law of Cause and Effect.

After returning to the physical, Dannion began living a life of love. He works often in hospices helping the dying understand death and thus move beyond the fear of it. Due to his weakened organs from the lightning strike, he died a second time and returned once again to the spirit plane. He later told how much more positive the experience was when entering the spirit plane the second time. This was possible because he had already balanced his cruel deeds from his earlier years on the Earth Plane during his first ND experience. The wonderful truths he learned on the spirit plane at a place he calls "The Hall of Knowledge" could be another book.

Many who return from a ND experience come back with acute psychic abilities. Dannion Brinkley came back with the ability to know great truths about people just by physically touching them. I experienced him do this with a complete stranger at one of his talks in Ft. Collins, Colorado. I had the opportunity to talk with Dannion before he gave his talk and shared with him my experiences of receiving messages from my sister who related her experience of going to the other side. He was collecting information from others who had crossed over and asked if I would send him a copy of the communication with my sister, and so I did.

His presentation was wonderfully enlightening and it was obvious that dying and returning left him with a tremendous sense of humor and taught him to never again take physical life too seriously.

Many of those who have had ND experiences claim that spirit beings communicated with them without the use of audible words. It is rather a matter of a transfer of thoughts taking place. In that way, there is no problem with misinterpreting what was being communicated. Actually, that is the way I receive many of my messages. Spirit beings are able to transfer thoughts from their level directly into the consciousness or minds of others. The communications do not always come in through one's native language but even so the messages are perfectly clear. For those who return from their ND experience, or for others who receive messages in this manner, it is often difficult to put the thoughts or messages into words because there is so much that is beyond physical language. Spirit has said that there is a 'universal language' that goes beyond the use of words. Universal language includes vibrations, feelings, color, and tones. At the human level, universal language is understood on our higher levels of consciousness; levels we are not aware of in our awakening consciousness.

Some of those crossing over experience a beautiful light being and feel it may be the Christ being because Christ is quoted in the Bible as saying, "I am the light of the world." The light is very different than any earthly light. Though it is extremely bright, it never hurts one's eyes.

Those who have had a ND experience have no doubt it is very real. Everything is so vivid and clear to them. They are sure their experience was not a hallucination, though some medical professionals and religious leaders believe these experiences are just that. For the majority of those who have had ND experiences, it has impacted their lives significantly. They seem to place a greater value on life. They become more spiritual and less materialistic. They become more loving and are more willing to reach out to help others but they have no feelings of salvation or being saved or being better than others. Most no longer have any fear of death and some have said they look forward to the time of their physical death. They know first hand that, in reality, there is no death but it's merely a transition to an absolutely beautiful life on the other side.

Hundreds of thousands have had near death experiences and many of them are willing to share what they have learned about life on the other side. IT IS TIME humanity learns the truth about what to expect when our time comes to return home to the world of spirit and to the reality of our beingness. For far too long, it has been a mystery. The unknowingness and religious myths have caused much fear in many when the time comes to end our physical journey, a time we can be sure will come. Those who have experienced a ND experience, and those who have communicated back from the spirit world, have emphasized that there is nothing to fear of the final physical experience we call death. Maybe it would be good to just think of physical death as the end of our physical vacation from the eternal spiritual life we are all a part of and forever will be.

In the next chapter, we'll get into details of the cross-over experience and you will read the stories from a few who have crossed over and have communicated back to us what fantastic experiences they had. I'm sure you will find them as inspiring as they were to me.

Thanks to all those who have ventured for a while into that eternal paradise and have come back to inform us of just how wonderful it really is.

CHAPTER 15

Crossing Over

What occurs when the spirit leaves the human body is varied and depends on many things. How did the death occur? Was it sudden as in an accident? Was it caused by an illness gradually leading to the expiration of the physical? The passing may have been self-created as in a suicide, but that also varies depending on the motive of taking one's own life. We will get into that a little later. Some, but not many, die of what we call 'old age' where the heart or other organs just wear out and quit functioning.

Not all beings have the same experience, but a typical one that occurs after the spirit leaves the body is that one passes through a tunnel and observes a light at its end. Most of those who have had near death experiences also pass through the tunnel. It is but an entranceway into the next dimension of light on the other side. Even the details of passing through the tunnel vary from one spirit to the next. Their experiences may vary regarding the sounds and colors, whether they go through alone or with others, and what they experience when coming into the light.

Many factors determine what a spirit will experience after reaching the other side. Those who have had a long illness and have suffered physically may go into a period of a spiritual sleep state. This may occur before they are welcomed home by their friends and relatives who passed before them, but some will enter into this state after they are greeted. The spirit is often exhausted and weakened after a long suffering illness and a sleep or rest period is necessary for the spirit to recover.

Various ascended masters such as Jesus, Buddha, Mohammed, or light beings and angels often initially greet those who have a deep faith. Following that greeting, they may be introduced to those who have passed on earlier and have come to greet them. They are loved ones, family, friends, and even those known in past lives who have come to welcome them home. A person who has died suddenly and instantly, such as in a car crash, a plane crash, or in an explosion, are often confused and may not be aware that they are physically dead. Some of these beings do not initially go to the other side but stay for a while in the astral plane between the physical and spiritual planes. Following is a story of such an individual with whom I had a personal experience.

I will use only his first name here. In June 1978, I was hired by the Solar Energy Research Institute to develop and manage a newly formed Publications Branch with the objective of producing technical reports, educational material, and audio/visual presentations. A wonderful man named Van hired me to serve in this position. As time passed and the Institute evolved and changed, Van was moved into a position that required a lot of travel.

I had a private enclosed office and during my hour-long lunch period, I would often close the door, quiet myself, relax, slip into the alpha state and tune in to the spirit realm. In those times, I received many messages on various subjects from various spirits and always documented what came through. It was also a good way to deal with the stresses of the corporate world. One day as I quieted my mind, I heard a mental voice I recognized as Van, who had recently been killed in a head-on collision while on a trip to the DC area. Though his voice was in my mind I recognized his so called voiceprint. *"Ron, Ron,"* he spoke in an anxious tone, *"Why won't anyone talk to me?"*

Having heard of his fatal accident, I knew what he, in spirit, was experiencing. His spirit had not yet gone into the light and he was not aware of his physical death. So, he came back to his work place as he always did, but he could not get a response from anyone because they obviously could not see him in his spirit form.

I mentally spoke out to Van and told him, "Van, while on your trip to DC you had a head-on collision and you did not physically survive it. You died instantly and you are now in your spirit body. No one will talk to you because they cannot see or hear you. However, I can hear you because I have been blessed with the ability to communicate with the spirit dimension. Van, listen carefully -- Look up and you will see a bright white light. When you see it, will yourself to go towards and into that light."

Two weeks later, as I was meditating and tuning into spirit I heard Van's voice again. This time he was much calmer.

"Ron, I came back to you just to say thank you so much for helping me realize my situation and directing me to enter into the light. I am fine now with my life here on this side. As you have helped me, so will I help you one day."

With that he was gone and I never heard from him again knowing he was happy and where he belonged.

It has been said many times that the only thing we take to the other side is our love. This is not entirely true. For those who are carrying guilt from their misdeeds or mistakes, it is often because they have been in a religion that teaches and emphasizes sin, Satan, and evil. So they take the fear of all that with them when they enter the other side because they expect retribution. As on Earth, fear continues to be a barrier to fully receive the light.

Many scenes or dramas are created for those who have deep rigid religious beliefs, but beliefs that do not align to the truths and realities of life on the other side. Considering the great number of different religions on this planet, obviously their doctrines and beliefs cannot all be valid as they relate to *The Truth*. So scenarios are sometimes created that give newly arrived souls the opportunity to gradually open up to the greater truths of spirit life. It is all done gently and with great love. The following is a situation as told by a spirit guide of how that might apply.

In some of the Christian faiths, being saved is essential to getting into Heaven. For those who have been saved, regardless of one's earthly deeds, the traditional belief is that he will pass through the pearly gates into heaven and be with Jesus who has saved him. Each individual's beliefs become a part of what one will experience when arriving on the other side. If a person is very sure he will pass through pearly gates, when he arrives on the other side, he may join a group with the same beliefs. Here they gather in front of pearly gates, that their beliefs have created for them. There they wait for St. Peter to come and admit them into heaven. Always, when we cross over, there will be guides to assist newly arrived spirits to understand the realities of the dimension they have entered into on the other side. Spiritual guides lovingly and patiently approach the group waiting by the gates to help them understand their new life, but most of the group simply will not listen to them out of fear that these guides are from Satan's realm and are trying to tempt them away from entering Heaven. After a time of lingering near the gates and wondering why St. Peter has not come to open them, some begin to wonder if what the guides have been saying has validity and so they begin to open up and listen. At that point, their lives on the other side begin to flourish.

The guides have also shared how a newly arrived preacher will get the remaining souls all fired up again by emphatically telling them not to listen to the guides trying to lure them away from their chances of getting into Heaven. This is because they deeply believe Satan is always nearby waiting to lead them astray.

There have been many stories reported about people being killed instantly in car or plane crashes where their spirit form rises out and up from their mangled bodies and they become observers of the crash site. Looking at those mangled bodies, they would suddenly become aware that one of the motionless bodies laying there was their own physical form. With that recognition they would come to realize what had happened to them. Oftentimes, a spiritual guide will come to them and guide their soul into the light and on to the other side.

The following is a story about a friend of mine who died suddenly in a plane crash and shared his experiences on the other side. He was a member of the Army's Golden Knights Parachute Team. He was also a pilot so we had much in common. We saw each other from time to time while judging sport parachute competitions. During weather delays, we often had lengthy conversations and got to know one another very well. Upon returning to his Army base after one of his trips with the Golden Knights' demonstration parachute team, their plane ran into a severe storm and crashed. There were several team members and crew on board and all were killed instantly.

He came through to me a short time after the crash and he seemed disturbed about dying so young. He really wanted to come back because he felt his life here had been cut so short. I connected with him a couple more times after that and then I quit hearing from him for a while. Finally, he came through again and explained what he experienced subsequent to entering the spirit plane. Here is his story.

*"The first time I saw the Master was upon awakening. I shall
try to describe in physical terms so you may understand.
We see here but it is not the same and I'm sure that's hard*

to understand. When I awoke from a spiritual sleep after first crossing over He was sitting beside me. He was the most beautiful person or entity I had ever seen and I knew Him for I had seen him before. I wondered how I could have forgotten Him so much on the Earth plane. He was no stranger to me. Then He called to one named Daron who came and also sat beside me. All I wanted to do was go back. I had been called so quickly that I just was not ready and you know what happened."

Shortly after crossing over, he entered a human fetus soon after a woman's conception. The next thing he knew, he was back in the spirit plane because his potential mother had an abortion. That made him realize he had been given a great lesson. He was loved while in the physical and dearly loved when he entered the spirit plane, but now he was rejected and sent back to the spirit plane because he was not loved. This experience brought him to the realization that he must study and prepare himself if he still wanted to return later. Now I'll continue with his communication.

The Master teaches in the temple. He is so wonderful. He shines brighter than any light known to man. "When I awoke again, there He (the Master) was once more with a gentle smile upon his lips; not an 'I told you so' smile, but one filled with warmth, compassion, and understanding. He was my friend and He always had been. Oh, when I think of all the times I betrayed Him and hurt Him. Well, He called to Daron again and Daron became my first tutor. He taught me all the things I needed to know; you know, the basic things. Then I started going to hear the Master teach. He wears a white robe, but not the same white you have. It is so pure that you can see all colors in it and it's so very beautiful. His hair is shorter than most pictures of Him. He looks much the way you have presented Him in your painting Ron. He is not flesh, as you know it. He is spirit and here you can see spirit form if you wish and when you do, you see the reality of things. When He speaks, it sounds like the most beautiful music your world has and more. And when he laughs it rings all over. Yes, he has a wonderful sense of humor. You really feel the power of his love. I know it is hard for humans to really understand all this. He is worth every sacrifice you make for Him.

My friend, don't let the world get a hold on you. Seek to help others whenever you can. All believers have work to do on the Earth plane. He is warm and kind and all know him and love Him here. Please don't ever fear coming here. Listen always to Him. He will help make your life happier and smoother. Hold tight to His hand and He will guide you and protect you. Thank you dear friend for listening to me."

Most of the material in this chapter deals with what happens when we cross over, but what about the survivors? The following communication from the Master should help the survivors of those whose loved ones have transitioned to the other side.

When a loved one passes on from the physical, the first thoughts are usually regrets. You may think that perhaps you should have been more loving, more understanding, and less judgmental. Regrets burden the living with guilt. As you are well aware by now, when one dies or lets go of his physical shell he is much happier. He comes to a place of warmth and joy and after sleeping for a while, he awakens and sees many who love him. The one who crosses over suffers no more. But what about those who are left behind? How should they react? I am so saddened at funerals when I see so much sadness. If people really had faith there would be no tears. Most of the time, tears are not shed for the dead but for the living. Now why do people feel such loss? Most often it is a lot of regret. They find themselves wishing they had been perhaps kinder,

Now let us be realistic. In the first place, because they are human, people will sometimes utter an unkind word; they will feel dislike, and they will not always do their best with regard for another person. So when the person dies, there you sit in guilt, wishing you could undo things. If all could, or were willing to communicate with this plane, all the misunderstandings could be cleared. Those of the Earth plane could tell those here how they really felt. Also they could become aware of how those who have come here have developed so much love and understanding for you there, especially when becoming free of the ego.

Let's use an example. A loved one crosses over. You, of course, will miss their physical presence. If that loved one left you right now, you would feel that you still had much to say to him or her. Well, you could still tell your loved one and they will receive your thoughts. Then know that your loved one who passed would know all the things you wanted to say or do but didn't and would therefore understand and would not want you guilt ridden.

Sometimes, the living really suffers when a loved one crosses over. You may be surprised but I do not agree with that. It takes courage to live on the Earth plane and it takes faith. This is what I want you to learn from this. Seek joy in living. You never know when I shall call you home. Live your life with each other so that you have few regrets. Place value on each other. Get the most from each other's presence. Be assured that, no matter which of you is called first, there will be an understanding. If you weep, weep not just in your sorrow. Weep tears of joy that will mingle with your tears of sorrow. So also feel joy because that person has gone to a greater place where he no longer suffers. Feel happy and secure in the knowledge that you will see him or her again. Never dwell on how the death occurred. Don't discuss the horrors of a car or plane crash or years of cancer. In reality it is all irrelevant and only makes the living more fearful. The point is that no matter what happens to the physical shell, at that point it is but a vehicle that has freed the spirit.

I do not even like the word 'death' because it has a negative connotation and people fear it. Wouldn't it be wonderful if you could just say, "John's spirit has been set free" instead of saying, "Isn't it sad that John died in that car crash." or," Isn't it sad that Mary had to suffer so much before she died of cancer." Life does and should go on for the survivors.

Have faith in me and I shall not let you spend your days in loneliness. Keep on living until I call and then you will be united with those who have come here before you. The whole concept on your plane is wrong. What is so sad is, those people who do not believe in anything beyond the physical.

What regulates how long a person may spiritually sleep when they cross over are their actions, their beliefs, and their attitudes while on the Earth plane. Sometimes, if one had a great amount of physical suffering, he will sleep longer. But if he has become very spiritually evolved, he may not sleep at all. This period is like being in a void but it is very happy from my point of view. In Earth time, the maximum period of sleep would be 500 years but the average is between one to five weeks unless long suffering had occurred.

What About Those Who Commit Suicide?

What occurs to those who have taken their own life when they cross over varies considerably and it depends on what their motives were in choosing to take their life. Therefore, there is no black and white situation that a suicide will experience. Let's look at a few motives.

A person is having a difficult time continuing to live with a certain life situation. This could be for a variety of reasons. Here are just a few of many:

1. A very close loved one just died and they do not feel they can continue without them.
2. They just lost their fortune and are addicted to wealth and power.
3. They lost a job they loved of many years and feel they will never find another.
4. They were addicted to alcohol or drugs and lost their family and job and feel life is closing in on them.
5. They are deeply depressed and feel they are trapped and can no longer continue with life.
6. Great guilt can be yet another reason one takes their life.

I'm sure there are many more reasons but basically the suicide opts to end physical life thinking it will end their misery. The thing is, it doesn't because it is a selfish act and did not consider the great sadness they will cause to those who love them, regardless of how low they fell in life.

After they arrive on the other side, they invariably regret what they have done, primarily because they now realize how much pain they have caused to the many family and friends who have loved them. Some who have communicated back have said they regretted it the moment they jumped or otherwise initiated their demise. Though the suicide act is selfish, the higher wisdom of our Creator understands the deeper reasons behind this action of self-destruct. Those souls who have done so have repeatedly communicated back that they were in such a state of mind they did not fully comprehend the seriousness of their act but just needed a relief from their mental torture. It is as if it were a depressed state of mental illness and will not be punished per se, but must enter into a period of learning the true value of the gift of physical life. The suicide also realizes that if they had not been so quick to escape from their self created perils and asked for help, they most likely would not have come to the point of destroying their life. Once on the spirit plane, they go to an area of self-reflection and are able to see their problem with greater insight and realize how it could have been avoided. This is the beginning of their mental healing.

Survivors of suicides are usually as distressed as parents who lose a child. After the suicide arrives on the other side he or she may be met by a few close relatives who have passed on before and they show the suicide person and let them feel the anguish they have caused and possibly the guilt he or she has created by close family or friends who wonder what they could or should have done to prevent the suicide. They are not cast into an eternal Hell, as some religions believe. In reality, there will be no judgment except a self-judgment of how they have caused pain in others and see the lost opportunities the self-destructive act caused them to miss out on in a completed life. However, with the help of guides they usually go through a long period of learning how to value life and how to better deal with their self-created negativities. Eventually, the suicides want to return to the physical where they ultimately are confronted with similar situations they could not handle in their previous life. This they must do in order to continue their spiritual growth. Hopefully, they will be stronger in their next lifetime and apply what they have learned while on the spirit plane so they will not make the same mistakes.

As I was writing this, I recalled what Archangel Michael told me not long ago. "What is the difference between someone who puts a bullet in his head and one who smokes two packs of cigarettes a day knowing the statistics that indicate it will cut his life short?"

I said, "Tell me." He answered, "It's just a matter of time."

I wasn't sure if it was some of his humor or whether he was serious. The more I thought about it, the more I concluded that probably both were true. Since then, I think of smoking as 'subconscious suicide.' I started smoking after I graduated from high school. It was one of the worst choices I've made in my life. Then I quit for four years when I started sport parachute activities. I thought I could handle one cigarette at a party. One week later, I was buying cigarettes again. After I began communicating with spirit, in December of that year, I promised myself, on the first day of January of the next year, I was going to become a non-smoker for the rest of my life, rather than just thinking I would try to quit. In the interim, I meditated on that promise and mentally programmed into my consciousness a positive outcome. It worked surprisingly well and I've kept that promise knowing it was one of the best things I ever did.

Next let's consider the individual who has become mentally ill and takes his life not fully comprehending the impact it has. He or she may have suffered from a chemical imbalance, a bipolar condition, or another mental disease. But they, too, will experience and realize the sadness of the family and friends left behind. Always there will be help there from the guides.

Finally, we will look at those who have a serious illness and are terminal with no clear hope of surviving. Here, the motive to end their life is not selfish. They simply do not wish their loved ones to go through a period of dealing with their slow and often painful death. Also, the medical expenses may be depleting the family's estate. This is sometimes called a mercy suicide. In this case, they have merely shortened their inevitable departure and also the strain and hardships on loved ones. Their entry into the spirit world will have few if any negative results. Once again, it is the motive behind the suicide that determines at what level they will enter in the next world and what they will experience.

These have been just a few examples of different motives when someone chooses to take his own life. There are obviously many more situations that will determine the action of ones choosing suicide. Now we'll return to normal situations of crossing over.

Mediums Who Connect with the Departed

George Anderson is a medium of national fame. In his book *Lessons from the Light*, he shares many stories about connecting with loved ones on the other side. Many on the other side say to those who are the loving survivors who have grieved for a considerable time that they should get on with their lives and let those on the spirit plane get on with their lives there. Some from the other side have even said to their surviving spouse, "It's okay to find yourself another mate and when you cross over we can all be friends."

Another very interesting thing Anderson learned in his other side connections, the souls on the other side who have been murdered have the ability to forgive and understand their attacker and they encourage their family and friends to do the same. However, those still in the physical, in all likelihood, will have difficulty doing so because of the human ego and the need to know justice has been done.

Anderson also relates that those who have lost a loved one to a violent death are heartsick with the thought that their loved one experienced great pain or torture before passing. However, the souls in the hereafter state they "never felt a thing." My wife had a friend who was beaten to death by an attacker and he stated from beyond that after the first blow, he did not feel a thing before he passed. I talked to a fellow pilot who crashed his plane. He said his spirit left the body just prior to the crash. He actually survived the crash but felt no pain from the injuries he sustained at the moment of the crash.

From these stories, it becomes clear that the understandings, attitudes, and the ability to forgive are much different when one sheds the physical and ego after transitioning into the spirit plane.

The Effect One's Belief System Has After Crossing Over

One's belief system can play a significant role relative to what one might experience immediately after reaching the other side. This might become clearer by sharing the communication I had with my sister who passed on at age 37 as a result of a brain tumor.

My oldest sister Marilouise was an LPN (nurse) and had two young children from a bad marriage to an alcoholic who she met as a patient under her care in the hospital. One day her husband left and no one ever saw him again. She lived close to my parents in south Florida. Marilouise called me one day and said she would like to spend a week's vacation with me in Huntsville. She had been having dizzy spells and felt getting away might help. So she left her children with our parents and flew to Huntsville. She had many things she wanted to discuss with me, being aware of my connections with spirit. She opened up about the difficulties of being married to an alcoholic, and how hard it was on all of them, even after he left. But she also shared some of the wonderful experiences of being a nurse and how she enjoyed helping people with physical problems. She was a very spiritually focused and giving person, and would often stay past her normal hours to continue administering to patients.

During her stay, I invited her to go on a short canoe trip down a lovely stream with beautiful scenery and a few mild rapids. She liked the idea so off we went with the canoe on top of my van. It was a lovely day and she dearly loved the time we spent lazily cruising down this beautiful stream plus the excitement of going through a few rapids. When we arrived back at the house, I pulled up into the driveway that was on a slight incline. My sister got out of the passenger side but immediately lost her balance. She fell backwards and split her scalp open when her head impacted on the driveway. The impact left her dazed and bleeding so I decided it would be best if she went to the emergency room. Before leaving, I trimmed some of the hair off either side of the split on her scalp and taped it together as best I could. There the medical personnel cleaned and stitched up her scalp.

After returning home, her dizzy spells continued and even became worse, so I changed her return flight reservation by a couple days so she could return the next day. I called my parents and asked them to pick her up and take her to the hospital for further examination. After being admitted for tests, they discovered a tumor located at the base of her skull. It was the tumor that was causing her dizzy spells.

Her condition declined rapidly and soon the tumor became so enlarged it paralyzed her lower body. Four weeks after entering the hospital, her spirit left her nearly paralyzed form and she transitioned into the world of spirit. My parents had been keeping her six year-old son and four year-old daughter, so they continued to stay with my parents for a time. Some time later, my next youngest sister, Jan, who was married but had no children of her own, took the two young children and raised them.

Six days short of three months after Marilouise passed on, I connected with her on the spirit plane. After she initially greeted me, I told her I was sorry I missed her funeral because it was the first day I started a new job in Colorado. She humorously said, "Don't feel bad, I missed it too." Then she shared her experience of crossing over. What follows is exactly as she described it.

When crossing over, I could feel myself lifting and speeding headlong in a soft pink tunnel. Ahead I could see a blue and shining light. I could hear rain gently falling. I touched the blue light and it felt cool and refreshing. The pink in the tunnel had been warm. The blue light was, in reality, a mirror. I looked at myself and saw that I was healthy, strong, and perfect. Oh I felt so light and so free. I ran and ran through a green meadow with millions of flowers. You couldn't believe the sweet smell.

There was a rainbow, all shimmering there and in the distance at the end of the rainbow I could see a figure. Then I again ran freely. Oh, it felt so good to run after being confined to a bed for so long. Then I became tired and sat down by a beautiful silver stream. Butterflies danced near me. Birds sang their sweetest songs and soon I drifted off into a gentle sleep. Then I really slept.

When I awoke, I was near the figure I had seen at the end of the rainbow. Guess who it was. Yes, it was the Master Jesus. He is too beautiful to describe in human terms. He was total love and it radiated from him and encompassed everything near him and oh how I could feel it.

The reason it is hard to describe in human terms is because much of what I experienced was totally sensed as opposed to just physical sight. So you sense and see so much more here rather than just seeing. Colors here are symbols. To sense pink is to sense warmth, gentleness, softness, and birth. The color pink itself was not the actuality but what it represented is its reality.

The Master was total compassion and forgiveness. I guess the thing I noticed most were his eyes. They contained all the wisdom of the Universe as well as all the pain for nothing that man or other entities had suffered was unknown to Him. He smiled and the world here became brighter. Then he laughed and bells sounded throughout. I sensed Him touching my hand and I heard Him say, "Welcome home child."

*I felt so happy -- not lonely or sad. I was **not** dead. Then the Master beckoned and so many familiar entities came to welcome me. Uncle George, Simon, and many of those you knew but are now here came to welcome me, plus so many more you did not know. You would not believe how many there were.*

After being welcomed back home, I slept off and on for a while but now I am permanently awake. My teacher, who is also my guide here, is called Laganda and I have so much to learn. Even though I was only 37 Earth years of age, I did not, what you might consider, return early. In reality, there is no such thing as a normal life span. For me, this was the normal or right time for I had accomplished what I came there to do. Remember, no one is called until the Father's will is fulfilled. However, most people do not complete or accomplish their own set of goals or missions. Even though I would like to have stayed there until my children were raised, I know I am here because of the Father's will and I know my children will be well cared for.

Tell the family not to grieve for me, for I am very happy here and I will continue my life here, which is much better than the one I left behind. I will continue to learn more here and I will live in the love of the Master. We will speak again.

I am your sister, who loves you,
Marilouise.

There were more communications that followed and I have learned much about the death experience and of life on the other side, not only from the communications that have come from my sister, but also from both my parents, other relatives, and a few friends. I will share some of their experiences later.

One of the things I really took notice of was that colors are experienced to a much greater degree on the other side. The essence of colors is experienced which is far beyond the mere perception of the colors and shapes alone. Next, I noticed that the name of Jesus was almost never used except for new arrivals. Most often He is referred to as "The Master." I was not really surprised at this because others on the spirit plane and even those on very evolved planets have always referred to Jesus as, the Master. Yes, they know of him too. In my early stages of connecting with the Master, He told me He would prefer to be called Sananda because it is a spiritual name that better aligns with His spiritual vibrations. I have read other publications where He was also referred to as Sananda or Lord Sananda. While Sananda is one of His spiritual names, the name of Jesus, suggested by spirit before becoming physical, was vibrationally compatible with his physical being.

I certainly do not have all the answers about what our spirit experiences after leaving the body because there are considerable aspects unique to every human on the planet that determines what they will experience after crossing over. Following, are some of the key aspects that make a difference, relative to what our spirit might experience when it reaches the other side.

In the New Testament, Jesus was quoted as saying, "In my father's house there are many mansions." What spirit has explained about this quote is, the 'many mansions' Jesus referred to are actually many dimensions, also known as planes. The dimensions primarily equate to vibrations and a level of spiritual evolvement. The more spiritually evolved we are, the higher our vibrations. Pure or unconditional love is the highest of vibrations while hate and fear are the lower vibrations. Therefore, what dimension we will enter when crossing over depends on many things.

How much love did we give and receive? Were we hateful and spiteful or kind and giving? Did we do hurtful (emotional) or harmful (physical) things to others, or did we extend love to others; were we giving, caring, and helpful? Did we criticize, condemn, and complain frequently, or did we see the good in others and look for the good in all situations? How did we react to perceived negative situations or events? Did we get angry and try to blame others or even God, or did we try to understand why things happen as they do and did we take responsibility for our own actions and attitudes?

All these and many more factors determine what dimension we might enter and thus what we will experience in the process of transitioning to the other side. I use the term 'we' here because we all will experience departing our physical form one day and have a personal experience when crossing over into the spiritual realm. The guides and teachers can readily identify the spiritual level one has attained during one's physical sojourn by the color and magnitude of one's aura.

If the thought of dying is a fearful one, please take notice. What kind of quality of life can we experience when we spend our time here fearing or worrying about death? How many things have we not experienced or how often were we overcautious and circumvented our children from experiencing something joyful because there was a slight element of potential risk or danger involved with probably less danger than driving them to school? How often have we experienced fear just thinking about the possibility of something happening that could potentially cause the destruction of our physical being? Based on passenger miles, the statistical chances of dying in an automobile crash are 7 times greater than dying in an airline crash. Yet how often has it crossed your mind, "The airplane might crash," or, "I could drown if I go out too deep in the pool or lake," or, "I might fall off the cliff if I get too close to the edge"? 99. 9 percent of all our 'what if' fears never materialize unless the emotion of the fear is so powerful that it brings into being what we fear so strongly.

Remember the saying, "What you fear most will come upon you," for it is very true.

In February 1996, while I was caring for an elderly friend who was recovering from pneumonia, I received a call from my younger sister telling me my father had passed away a little earlier that evening. At that time, it was past midnight in Florida so I told my sister I'd wait until morning to call mother and let her know we would fly down and arrange for his funeral service.

Early the next morning, I called my mother and received the details of his passing. She told me dad had been watching television and after a while, she could not get a response from him. He was not slouched over and his eyes were open but they looked glazed so she called 9-1-1. When the paramedics arrived they determined he was gone and took him away. He had quietly and simply left his physical body with no signs of a problem. My parents had bought two grave sites some years earlier; however, my mother said she did not want to see him laid out so, she decided to have him cremated.

Immediately after she told me that, I clearly heard my father's voice in my head say,

> *"Cremation, eh? I'll tell you what. I could care less what you do with that old bag of bones, I don't need it anymore."*
> Yes, my father had a great sense of humor.

My flight down to Florida from Denver was at night. I looked out the window of the plane into a very clear and starry night but I was thinking about my dad. Once again I heard his voice in my head. *"Hey, sonny boy!"* He always called me that. *"I just want you to know we don't need to make airline reservations here. All we need to do is think of where we want to be and we are there."* I chuckled, again experiencing his humor.

We used to talk on the telephone almost every Sunday morning. After he crossed over, we connected mentally for some time but gradually that faded as he got on with his life on the other side. Now it's just occasionally.

Although I had connected with dad quite often after he passed on, he never discussed his experience of crossing over. It was almost six months after he departed when my friend Jean, who is an excellent channel, was visiting one day so I asked her if she would connect with my father. Jean had met dad several times. She tuned in to him and there he was ready to communicate. I asked my dad if he would share his experiences when crossing over. He agreed and I began by asking him a question: ***"Did you have a sense that you were going to leave the Earth plane before you departed to the spirit plane?"***

> *"Yes, I had known for about a year. I had been communicating during my sleep state on other levels of myself with, not only my higher self, but also with my guides and teachers. The human personality had, for so many years to the best of its understanding, taken responsibility and care for your mother. I wished for her to have the experience she requested of me several times, that being she would pass on first so she would not have to deal with the every day details of life that I always handled. However, I did not fully understand about letting her blossom into her own awareness. So I resisted that for a year and I did suffer some because of it. Some I shared with you and some I did not. Through my will I kept my personality and soul awareness within the physical body beyond the time allotted to me. Thus I suffered physically where I did not need to do so. That was a choice and it is water under the bridge and it's OK now. So I knew for about a year that it was my time but I kept resisting because of your mother's desire to go first, but she was not yet ready to go.*

Through that time and through the awareness that finally came to my consciousness of what I was learning in my sleep state and the reveries of old age, I decided that it was all right for me to let go of the responsibility of her life and in the greater understanding that it would be beneficial for her. She had chosen to live beyond my allotted and choice of time on Earth from the higher levels of herself. I finally came to understand that in my last days and was then able to release from my physical body and begin the ascension into the light and into the dimension that I exist in now.

Music and beautiful angels and people I had known gathered about me as I rose up out of my physical body into the higher consciousness with my soul body. The process of leaving the physical plane, as has been explained by many, is pretty universal and so I experienced the tunnel and into the great light and the angelic hosts as it is called, plus seeing the relatives and friends whom I knew. Immediately I felt released and free and I experienced the beautiful music of the spheres that cannot be heard on Earth that is so soothing and peaceful. The transition for me was very family oriented and very familiar in the sense that there was immediate recognition that I was now in spirit.

As I was escorted, so to speak, into the tunnel and into the light, the experience of this, as has been reported in many near death experiences, was very familiar to my own. I also experienced a review of my life as has also been reported by others. Also, I immediately lost any sense of time. So, through that experience, it seemed as normal as getting up in the morning and going to bed at night while in the body. There was no anxiety or questioning it, it was just occurring. But please realize, when crossing over, everyone's experience is unique to them, based on their life experiences, how they passed, their belief system, and especially, if they have fears of dying.

I was escorted through seven levels of, what you might term, rainbow energy. Through each level there was a corresponding color and a releasing of earthly bonds, so to speak. It was not that my awareness was erased, but the bondage disappeared. I passed through seven levels of consciousness and each one corresponded to a different color. Also, each of the seven levels had a corresponding music with a peaceful transition through each. Some people have described this experience as "crossing the river of eternity." For me it occurred through color and sound as seven levels of bondage disappeared, but not the awareness. Then, as you would term it, I rested for a while. It was as if I was in a void, like there is nothing, -- no fear but just a peaceful rest.

There was no sense of time when I came through that and then there was a celebration into my new birth and new life. Friends, relatives, and others I had known during and before my recent lifetime joined me in this celebration. Since that time, I have been experiencing, as you do on Earth, the many opportunities to learn that are available from birth of the young child, to the teenager, and to the adult. So it is that all these learning experiences are available to me here as well, and there are many. Then I can make choices about what learning experiences I will pursue. Part of it is that I have chosen to understand, to the best of my ability, my recent lifetime and how that correlated to the other lifetimes I had on the planet. I am now working at learning about love to the extent that any other experience in the 'New Earth' would be oriented toward love rather than some of the issues I dealt with as my recent being as well as in other lifetimes. I am dealing with the issues I had, such as control issues, power issues, and not listening and allowing others to have their own experiences. I used whatever leverage I needed with people close to me to choose their experiences for them. I even did that a lot with your mother, with you, and your two sisters. So, I missed some experiences with people because I drew people around me that I could have leverage with.

I am now learning, through the direction and experiences I have chosen, what you would call a spiritual education, of how unconditional love allows all consciousness within the oneness of the all, to be expressed through individual choice. I have had many willing teachers here and my personality as me is now dealing with a lot because of my last life expression on Earth and how it correlates to other lifetimes elsewhere. It is oriented towards what we think of as the Christian religion. So, I am going through an educational process about that and it is relative to how I expressed myself on Earth as I lived that understanding about love. Many of my teachers are those whom we knew on Earth who had been teachers of Christianity. They are those you, Ron, termed the Ascended Masters such as Jesus and also some of whom you know as the highly evolved extraterrestrial beings you told me about.

Here there are, what you term, the higher ascended beings who teach or experience with us and share their wisdom and knowledge in the same way that parents share their life's wisdom with their children. So, there is constant, but with no time involved, the continuation and evolving of choosing and experiences with teachers. Many of those teachers whom I have come in contact with you know of through the Christian religion because that is what I have dealt with while on Earth. Those from other religions, such as Buddhism, have teachers from that line of religious teaching, but always love is the center of all major religions. Later I will share with you more about life in the realm beyond the Earth plane."

Next I asked him another question: "Did the discussions we had about the things received from spirit that related to a greater understanding of spiritual truths have any impact on what you experienced when you crossed over to the spiritual plane?"

"The talks we had, the books we read, as well as all the communications from spirit side were all useful and helpful, not only when coming here but they were also particularly helpful to my human self as a preparation for coming here. Yes, all these things were contributing factors to what I experienced when coming here, but it was not the total picture because all that I had experienced was a contributing factor.

Like life on Earth, the transition process is like a chess game. How it's going to turn out depends on each move you make and each move can affect the next. No one, no consciousness ever plays a chess game in exactly the same way. Though there are common elements, there are many differences and so it is in the transition process. There are many things about it that have common elements, but there are also many aspects of it that are very related to the individual. And so it will be for you and all others. It is all in the Divine Plan in an evolving way.

It is like sediment in water placed in a container. The sediment sinks to the bottom because it is heavier and leaves the clear water on top. So I rose through the sediment and rose through the seven levels of different colors to where my soul has evolved into the purer form that I have attained through my soul evolution. The container represents my soul and it holds the water that allows the sediment to sink to the bottom. All the water is representative of all the experiences I have had yet there is always the sediment. Those things I am dealing with from my human personality are the sediment, so to speak, and it is just that. So where I am now, I am more of the light than the pure water. I am grateful for that and do not regret the sediment because it has allowed me to recognize the light that I am.

So, my son, as you have helped me by sharing the knowledge you acquired from the spiritual plane about spiritual truths, so shall I help you by sharing what I have learned from my current level of greater understanding on this plane of life. Always keep in mind what you told me while I was on the physical plane, for it is a great truth -- Love is the Key.

Know that my love is always with you,
Your father on high (ha ha)"

I learned some very interesting things from my father's communication. First he seemed to negate the thinking that when one's time is up, we die. His discussion about waiting to go past his allotted time so that my mother could go first indicated we have the option to change that to a certain point. However, he indicated that he paid the price by going beyond that. He never had any major physical problems or periods in a hospital, but during the year past his time he suffered from fluid on the lungs and cataracts on his eyes. He was almost 91 when he finally made his transition to spirit side. I found it interesting how he passed through several dimensions until he reached the level he was spiritually and vibrationally compatible with. My mother also indicated her experience of passing through various dimensions. Her transition experience follows. I liked dad's spiritual perception of experiencing his entire lifetime to a day of physical life, i.e., waking up in the morning (birth) and going to sleep at night (physical death).

Why do so many have a preoccupation with death? It is one of the greatest fears the human body will ever experience. As far as the spirit is concerned, it does not fear death because it knows there is no death and realizes that our spirit is our true reality. It bears repeating, the existence of everything on the physical plane, including us, is temporary. In reality, all of our fears come from the physical ego self. As my mother said after her passing – well, I'll just go ahead and share her entire experience after she crossed over as best as she could describe it in words. The point I want to make about fear in her message will be in bold but it also offers to the imagination of how beautiful an experience it is to enter into the love and peace of the spirit plane. My mother made her transition to the other side three years and three months after my father. The following is what she shared about her experience when crossing over to the spirit plane.

"The walls disappeared from my room and it was as if a band of angels with snow white wings and a heavenly chorus took me up to the horizon where I could really see. All earthly material and Earth people disappeared with all things physical. Those who had promised to be with me at the end of my physical life came en masse as had been given to me during my meditation and prayer states, those times when you visited me and thought I was out of it, All around me were angels and singing and Henry (husband) and other people I knew. Mother Mary and Jesus, who had promised to be with me, were there to greet me also. They were too beautiful to describe in words and emanated a very powerful love. I was reminded of the saints who were born on angel's wings. So indeed my journey into spirit was on angel's wings and it was accompanied with beautiful music that filled every cell and awareness. It was beautiful beyond words and it filled all that I could perceive with such great beauty. And there was golden light all around as far as I could see. Even sunlight could not compare with the beauty and brightness of this golden light and then it turned into the whiteness of angel's

wings and I was born, so to speak, upon the wings of these beautiful beings of light.

Very slowly I moved through various levels of sound and what appeared liquid, at times, of color. Light became tangible in a sense because I could experience it through sound. In a sense, I felt one with everything I perceived. I felt a part of it all as I was born up on all this. I had never felt really special in any way on Earth so I thought of what a glorious way that God would create this beautiful pathway into His home as I was taken into these beings of light and angel's wings and those that were with me, into what would be called a heavenly place that I had traveled to many times while my spirit went out of body during my sleep state, and so it was very familiar.

In this place, or dimension as I have learned here, there was a beautiful reception and what I perceived as a party, like a birthday party celebrating my birth back to spirit. I was overwhelmed at the people there who had remembered me and had come to welcome me back home again. I am home now and I feel so very happy and peaceful here. Henry was looking so young, like when we first met. He said that I could look any way I wanted to look relative to my past life. So, I made myself look refined somewhat. I am still Helen but I prettied myself by regressing my spiritual form to appear beautiful, like when I was in my twenties. We can all do this here on this dimension.

Yes, I am so happy now. After we arrive here we come into the fullness of our being. We are, in reality, so much more than we know ourselves to be in our physical life. I am going to school here and I am going to make myself useful in some way, probably working with newly arrived children for a while. Your sister Marilouise is also working with children at times. I will be here with all of you in the family at the end of your physical Earth life when you come here and you will have a reception also with many people you've known, and I'll be one of them.

(Bold for emphasis)
Know that there is no need to fear death for it is like closing one door and opening another. Because I knew that from you, it helped me to cross over more easily because I was not afraid and therefore I could more easily close my eyes to the physical and open my eyes to this life here through that understanding – and so, if you choose, will all of you who are not afraid. I have become aware of what a great barrier fear can be, not only in crossing over but also in all aspects of physical life.

In this dimension where I am now, it is very much like Earth. There are magnificent buildings, etc., but everything is of a higher vibration. My mother and daughter Marilouise are in a higher place or dimension. They can visit Henry and I here but we cannot go to a higher dimension because it is too intense until we spiritually evolve to a higher dimension. We can go to lower dimensions but we would have no desire to do so unless we wanted to visit someone we loved or knew. We will continue to learn and grow into higher dimensions. As the Master said, "In my Father's house, there are many mansions." Whenever you think of me, I will be with you.

Auf wiedersehen and God be with you.
I am your mother who loves you."

The above communication from my mother was received two months after she transitioned to the spirit plane. While there is no actual sense of time on the spirit plane, she was there long enough to become adjusted to her new spirit life before sharing her experience of crossing over. She was therefore better able to share some of her insights of life on that side of the veil. Immediately following my mother's communication, my father greeted me and shared his thoughts as follows.

> *Greetings, sonny boy. Thanks for taking care of your mother, and also to you Jan for the time you both spent with her, loving her, meeting her needs and supporting her. That support and that love were more important than you can begin to perceive. How many times have you said, 'Love is the Key?' In reality, love is all there is.*
>
> *You and I, Ron, have talked many times since I have been here, for as I have said, I am only a thought away. Think of your mother or me and we will be there for you as you were for us while in the physical. Listen deep within your mind and open your heart and we will be there to help you with your journey.*
>
> *You see, regarding guardian angels, it is not only as you perceive from your theology. We too can act as guardian angels for both of you -- all of you present. We all work together in love of the Father to become more than we ever think we are. In that love we all grow and become even more of who we were. Once again, thank you both. Be at peace, love yourself, and love all others. I am, as you knew me on Earth, your father. We will speak again.*
>
> *Auf wiedersehen*

Both of the above messages came through when my sister Jan and the rest of our immediate family gathered for a memorial service for my mother. It was rather ironic that she ended up being the key speaker at her own memorial service. In Part Three of the following pages we'll get into much greater detail about what exists in our "Life Beyond."

We'll close this chapter by imagining you have died and will now experience crossing over to the other side. If you've had any fear about dying, going through it mentally might help you release any fears you may have about it. Most people I've talked to about dying wish they could just die in their sleep. So let's assume that is how your passing will occur. Okay, here we go.

"Begin now by imagining you are in a deep sleep. Gradually your heart slows down and finally stops completely. Now your spirit slowly rises out of your physical body and you look down on it and see it laying there still below you. You are aware of how easily your spirit slipped out of your body. For a moment, you think about how that body carried you through your journey on the Earth Plane with all the many experiences it went through. Even so, now it seems like you entered the physical just a short time ago. Being released from your physical form, it becomes clear how so many negative feelings related to the human ego, the aspect of you that had fears, apprehension, guilt, self doubts, and feelings of insecurities. Even so, you thank your body with its ego for the journey it allowed you to experience on the Earth. You know now it will no longer be needed any more than you will need an aircraft after you complete a flight. All of these thoughts are but a quick flash through your mind.

Oh, you feel so light and free of the heaviness you had in that now empty physical shell beneath you. There is no more pain, no more illness. Then, all the physical surroundings of this place where your physical form lies begins to dissolve and for a moment you feel you are in a void. Then you feel movement as you enter into a somewhat dark tunnel. You

*feel tremendous speed now without any feeling of wind. As
you move toward a dim light ahead it becomes larger and
brighter as you pass through a beautiful array of soft blue,
pink, and violet colors that make you feel warm and safe. In
another moment you emerge out of the tunnel and into an
indescribable brilliance of light, brighter than anything on
Earth, but it does not hurt your eyes because you are no longer
seeing with physical eyes and you can easily and clearly see
everything around you. Oh, what a wonderful feeling of
great love and peace and it overwhelms you. Now you see a
beautiful being that also glows with a brilliant light. You
experience a powerful feeling of love coming from this being
and somehow you know He is of a divine essence. This place
feels very comfortable and, yes, it feels like home to you for in
reality it is your true home.*

*The being welcomes you and then waves his arm. Immediately,
you begin to see your entire earthly life unfold before you from
its very beginning. You see all your times of ups and downs;
your good deeds and the ones not so good; your times of giving
of yourself and the times of your selfishness; every significant
thing you experienced during your time on Earth. Yet it all
occurs in a brief moment of time. You remember Judgment
Day and you ask the being if this is what you are going to be
judged on. The being gently replies that it is you who will
now judge yourself and what kind of life you have lived on
Earth. He also tells you that there is no one here who will
judge you, condemn you, or find fault with you. What you
may have perceived as sin on Earth are only human mistakes
and missing the mark because of an absence of love.*

*Now the beautiful being asks you to follow him. As you do,
you are aware that, if there is a temperature here, it is
perfect – no heat or cold, just perfect. You notice there is*

light everywhere; no shadows, only beautiful golden light. Everything is pure. Beautiful music fills the air. Beautiful flowers are everywhere with brilliant colors never seen on Earth. You are walking on marvelous grass whose softness is like walking on air. Ahead is a beautiful setting near a small lake. Trees surround the lake that seem alive and sparkle with vibrating energy. There is a clearing next to the lake where people are gathered. As you approach the gathering you begin to recognize relatives and friends who have passed on before you. They seem so glad to see you. As they hug you one by one, you feel their love, their energy, and their beauty. They are all here to welcome you home. Then the being of light introduces you to one he says will be your teacher and your guide to help you adjust to your new life here. He also tells you that the learning and growing here will never end and when you are ready, you will evolve to an even more beautiful place in a higher dimension. You now look forward to all that you will experience in this most wonderful place that many refer to as Heaven."

Though the above journey to the other side is only typical of many who have crossed over, your own experience will be unique to you but know it is nothing to be feared. In Part Three, we will go into much greater detail about life beyond, that life which is on the endless, ageless, and timeless part of our forever life expression.

Life in the physical can be a grand journey, but when it is over, the journey home will be overwhelmingly beautiful.

PART THREE

The World Beyond

Introduction

Nearly everyone who believes in an afterlife has wondered at times what the next life will be like. Traditional religions believe in a literal Heaven and Hell. But the veil between the physical plane and the spirit plane is becoming thinner. Many now have crossed over and have communicated back to us and shared their impressions of life on the other side. While there are many dimensions, no one on the other side has made mention of a literal hell. Many on this side have communicated with spirit masters and guides. They have given us an idea of what realities are there for us when we eventually transition to the world of spirit.

IT IS TIME that humanity comes to a greater understanding of what God has forever created as the place for all life in the eternal realm of spirit. The accounts in Chapter 16 are from those who have already transitioned to the other side. They transform many religious myths into the greater truths of the spirit realm as they have experienced and perceived life in the world beyond. Because of the beauties they describe, these accounts will actually give us something to look forward to when our time comes to join them. In reality, the beauty and wonder of it is actually beyond the comprehension of our finite minds. Moreover, there are no words to adequately describe the wonders of the afterlife. With this understanding, I have made an attempt to at least touch on the realization of its magnificence. Chapter 17 explores the many levels or dimensions that exist in the spirit world and include detailed descriptions of the various levels from the very low dimensions to the marvelous world where the ascended Masters reside.

CHAPTER 16

Beyond the Myths of the Spirit World

Most myths are created from remembrances of fact. As myths are passed down from generation to generation, from century to century, and from millennium to millennium, the distortions continue to become farther and farther from the real truth.

The place many call Heaven has many other names. Some psychics and mystics call it the "Summerland." Indian mystics know it as "Devachan." Some entities on the other side refer to it as "Nirvana."

While many look to the Bible to learn more of what Heaven is like, within its pages there is very little information about the afterlife. Many preachers give more details of the horrors of a hell with fire and brimstone than they give about the specific glories of Heaven. They do not describe much more about Heaven than it having Pearly Gates one passes through if a good life was experienced on Earth and that its streets are of gold, and God sits on a throne with Jesus at His right side. They see it as a place somewhere up in the sky. This must be symbolic because the people on the other side of the Earth would have it in the opposite direction.

In the good, book Jesus said, "In my Father's house there are many mansions." When I queried the Master on this quoted statement, He explained that the many mansions are actually many dimensions. When referring to the 'spirit plane' it encompasses all the dimensions. There are an infinite number of dimensions and what determines the differences between them is their vibrational frequencies. The more spiritually evolved one is, the higher a dimension one will enter upon crossing over from the Earth Plane. Most of the descriptions of the other side in this chapter will deal with the dimensions that the average person who lived a basically good life might enter and experience. However, some details are covered about the lower dimensions and of a very high one.

While communications with spirit beings on the other side have been going on for many centuries, not many have shared or written about their communications because of the fear of being considered off their rocker or being possessed by the devil. Some of this thinking may have come from the few deranged persons who said God told them to kill various persons or led them to do horrific deeds. But humans who have connected and communicated with the higher spiritual dimensions are much more accepted in current times as minds become more open and the veil between the physical and spiritual continues to get thinner through the increasing vibrations of the Earth and her residents. Whenever we raise our vibrations, we become closer aligned to the world of spirit. As previously stated, Love is the Key to raising our vibrations.

Many on the other side have been trying to connect and communicate with the physical plane for a considerable time. Actually, John the Divine telepathically received the entire *Book of Revelation* in the Bible. Within the chapters, Jesus said to John several times, "He that hath an ear, let him hear what the Spirit saith unto the churches." The 'churches' were known then as the body of believers.

Now many thousands of humans are communicating with spirit beings. Many are being open about it while others are still afraid of possible ridicule. The *Course in Miracles* was all telepathically received by a Jewish woman and communicated to her from the Master Jesus. He also channeled the material in the book, *Jonathan Livingston Seagull* to Richard Bach. The story in that book is actually a symbolic parallel to our lives on Earth. Years ago Time Magazine published Richard Bach's story about how he actually received the material for the book. The first two parts came and then the communications stopped. Bach did not know how to finish the story until much later when finally part three came through to him.

The process of channeling information from discarnate spirits, spirit guides, angels, ascended masters, and from our Creator God has now become commonplace. Why? Because, IT IS TIME for humans to become more enlightened to the truths beyond the myths. New thought churches are springing up all over. In Neile Donald Walsch's *Conversations with God* books, God stated that the Religious Science religion is closer to the truth than most. Most of the New Thought Churches acknowledge and accept all other faiths. Even the more traditional religions are opening to more progressive thinking. In a recent newspaper article, a story was written about a minister who has joined a number of pastors disillusioned with traditional Christianity and ready to try the Center for Progressive Christianity, one that breaks away from the belief that traditional or fundamental Christianity is the only way. Their approach is to create more ways for people to enter the church and provide more options for them, especially those who have been hurt by the church.

Spiritualist Churches have mediums who, during their services, connect with their members' loved ones on the other side. They receive loving messages from family and friends who assure them they are doing wonderfully well on the other side. The medium John Edward, in his popular TV program, connected with beings on the other side who were the loved ones of those in his live audience. John passed on messages from the deceased with information that only the recipients of the message had any knowledge.

IT IS TIME for the planet and all her residents to spiritually evolve to a higher level of life expression. A man who had been a clergyman in the Church of England and then converted to Catholicism, became a priest, and eventually became a Monsignor, crossed over and later communicated back to a medium on Earth. He related a great deal of what he experienced after arriving on the other side. An overview of his experiences is given a few pages later. First, let's look at a different type of communication that exists from the spirit plane to our physical world.

A group of spirit beings on the other side have created a project called Timestream. Within that group are some of the great minds of beings who had lived on Earth including Edison, Madame Curie, Einstein, and Nicola Tesla, plus numerous scientists and physicians. Though they often work by transferring thoughts to human minds in a positive way to help achieve technological and medical advances, now they are also communicating to us through technical devices. The goal in Timestream is to establish a solid link of communication between spirit side and the Earth plane. The process is known as Instrumental Trans-Communication (ITC).

Actually, experiments in instrumental communication have been going on since the early 1900s. The process works like this. Those from the Timestream group on spirit side send voices and images from their side that are then received and recorded here on a variety of electronic equipment such as audiotape, TV screens, and even computers. Voices have also been received live on telephones from spirit side. Creating audible voices from the spirit plane is rather complicated and involves the creation and use of ectoplasm. Though this may seem far-fetched to the average person, there is considerable documentation of these communications, including photos of the images received on computers. There is an extensive amount of information about ITC on the website, www.worlditc.org. Dr. Pat Kubis and my friend Mark Macy have published a book titled, 'Conversations Beyond the Light that extensively covers all aspects of ITC, including conversations and photos received through instrumental communication.

Before leaving this subject, I'd like to share an actual telephone conversation between the spirit world and a woman here on Earth. The entity speaking from spirit was Konstantin Raudiva. He had been a psychologist professor in Sweden before he died in 1974. He had also been a pioneer in Electronic Voice Phenomenon (EVP). Since his death, he has been helping his colleges and friends on Earth to make better contact. This was the second of three such telephone contacts. The woman was Sarah Estep. Sarah had been working for some time to help make instrumental contact with the spirit plane. One day, she was sitting next to her phone when it rang. When she picked up the phone, she heard a very different voice. When she heard, *"Good morning Sarah, this is Konstantin Raudiva"*, she turned on the tape recorder she kept near the phone. Her first words were, *"Oh! How are you Dr. Raudiva?"* He replied, *"I'm as fine as a dead one can be, dear Sarah. Thank you very much for the propagation of the voices. We have been trying and have now succeeded in building this bridge to the states. You are one of the first to be contacted by this means. Thank you for all the work you did. We are very proud and honored that we could contact you. I must interrupt now. This is Konstantin Raudiva speaking."*

She replied, *"Thank you so much."*

His voice sounded like someone who has lost his vocal cords and holds a voice vibrator against the throat to talk. There was also a lot of electronic background noise but the words were distinctly clear. Apparently, they cannot keep the energy required to hold the call very long. All the contacts do not last very long and end with *I must interrupt now.* I will repeat what I said earlier. The veil between spirit and the physical is getting increasingly thinner.

The more information I received about life on the other side, the more fascinated I became and the more I tried to learn about it. It must have been the Universal Law of Attraction working when I began experiencing books coming into my possession that were communicated from the spirit plane and dealt with the life beyond. I became friends with a wonderful lady who had been pursuing spiritual truths the greater part of her life. My dear lady friend was a wonderful source of spiritual knowledge. We had been close friends and discussed spirituality for over 23 years before she recently passed on one month before her 105th birthday. When she sensed her physical adventure was coming to an end, she gave me a book titled, *Life in the World Unseen.*

The book was channeled from the other side to a medium in Great Britain and published in 1954. The individual who shared his afterlife story from the other side was in his physical life a Monsignor, a priest in the Catholic Church. He had been heavily involved in the writings and teachings of the church while still in the physical. During a brief illness, he became aware that his time on Earth was coming to an end. I'll cover a few of the highlights of his journey into the world of spirit and integrate them with what I have learned from my spirit communications in the following pages.

When finally the Monsignor's Earth life ended, he became aware of lifting out of his body and then sensed a great feeling of freedom after releasing his heavy physical body. He was also now free from his illness. Below him, he saw his lifeless body in hospital clothing. When he wondered what clothing he now had on in spirit, he saw that he was in the clothing he had normally worn while he was well. Next, the frightful idea that orthodox religion teaches of 'Judgment Day' was completely swept from his mind. He began to realize that the conception of a literal heaven, hell, and Judgment Day now seemed completely un-natural. While still at the death scene, he was greeted and welcomed by a former priest friend he had known but who had passed on several years before him. His priest friend told him to close his eyes and prepare himself for a great number of pleasant surprises that were beyond the myths of traditional religious beliefs. The Monsignor felt himself guided from the place of his passing to a wondrous location and dwelling already prepared for him in this new world.

When they arrived, he opened his eyes and saw before him what looked like the old house he had lived in while on Earth, but it displayed great improvements and was surrounded by beautiful flower gardens that quickly caught his attention. The house he had known on Earth had been recreated for him to help make his entrance into spirit more comfortable. The flowers were like nothing on Earth. When they approached any group of flowers, there poured out great streams of energy that spiritually uplifted them and gave them strength. At the same time, heavenly scents were present like no human had ever experienced. They also became aware of beautiful music that seemed to correspond to the marvelous colors of the flowers, but it was music unlike any on Earth.

I remember what my father said about experiencing flowers on the other side. "As you see only the physical aspects of flowers, we experience the true essence, the life force of the flowers here," he told me. And regarding the music, my father termed it "the music of the spheres."

The priest was about to experience a new world of life, one so vast, so beautiful, and one far beyond anything he imagined during his time on Earth. He quickly noticed things that were very different from Earth. There were no signs, no walls, no fences, nothing to mark individual properties. There was no sense of ownership, yet he was aware of his domain. He saw that everything was pure, pristine, and so alive. He became aware that volumes of his orthodox teachings, creeds, and doctrines were melting away. They were of no consequence there because they were not accurate and had no application in the eternal world of spirit. He began to see how all of that orthodoxy was man created and that the world of spirit was God created. He realized that so much of the fear on Earth was created because of the theological created belief in a literal hell and how it created more emotional suffering than any of the other erroneous doctrines.

I, too, have been enlightened about a literal hell. Spirit explained that the Old Testament writers in the Bible passages talked of and created images of hell as a means of creating fear in those who would disobey God's laws. I'll describe some of the lower dimensions where souls end up who have committed gross acts against humanity in the next chapter, but it is not a literal hell of fire and brimstone.

Many who were so engrained in their religions on Earth attempt to continue practicing their religion in the world of spirit until they finally become spiritually enlightened. When this happens, they experience the real meaning of freedom for the first time. All this new knowledge was especially enlightening to the Monsignor because he was so entrenched in the traditional writings and teachings of his church on Earth. When he became educated on greater realities and truths of the world of spirit, he felt a great concern over how he had spent so much of his life teaching the old traditional beliefs with their ceremonies and rituals, those that were actually misaligned with the greater truths of the spirit world.

Once people become adjusted to this life, they will want to begin giving of their beingness by performing deeds of kindness and service for others, and it is a real pleasure to do so. While on Earth, if people were involved in hobbies they loved to do, they can also perform the same kind of functions in the spirit world but at a much higher level of perfection. They can also learn something new, maybe something they always wanted to do but never had the chance or the financial resources to do so. But in the spirit world, anything they choose to do will never be a great effort or burden because all efforts are performed out of the power of the mind. If one had been a gardener, landscaper, architect, or a clothes designer – all these efforts can now be accomplished through the power of the mind. A musician can now create wonderful music for the pleasure of others. A minister, after being spiritually enlightened, can help teach spiritual truths to new arrivals. Always there will be available a purpose and a service for one to serve others. I might add that doing this on Earth would certainly lift one's spiritually.

After the Monsignor had experienced more of the realities in the spirit world, one particular religious book he had written on Earth began to plague his mind and he wished he had never written it because he realized the facts were distorted and the truth was suppressed. For the first time since coming to spirit, he had a regret about an earthly effort. As this book continued to be distributed and read, he knew it would be regarded as absolute truth and there was nothing he could do from the spirit plane to stop its distribution. So, he asked his friend if there could be a way to make it right on Earth. Was there a way he could connect back to the Earth plane and communicate the truths he had learned on the spirit plane? At first, his friend told him that many had tried to do this but few were believed, so why did he think he would have any better success. Moreover, if he were to connect to a medium back from where he came, would they call him a 'devil' or even the Prince of Darkness!

His friend asked him to think carefully about the consequences of what he wished to do.

Because, if he identified himself as the Monsignor, the readers of his previous works, being aware of the material he had written and what he was now trying to communicate, surely they would think he is an imposter and maybe even the devil. After his friend made him aware of the extreme difficulties of completing his desired task to communicate his newfound truth back to Earth, the Monsignor was persuaded to let it go for a time and later consult wiser beings to explore the possibilities of carrying out his intensions. Meanwhile, he would continue to learn as much as he could about all aspects of life in the spirit world.

One can travel in the spirit world by thinking himself where he desires to be. Nothing can possibly create any unhappiness, unpleasantness, or discomfort while on this level of the spirit plane. Most people on Earth have no conception of the magnificent realities that exist in the world of spirit because of limited thinking and a lack of knowledge about the spiritual life.

At the most common dimension are beautiful streams, lakes, and waterfalls. When water flows it gives off beautiful melodious sounds. When the light hits it, it glitters with all the colors of the rainbow. If you walk into the water or bathe in it, you will experience being stimulated and charged by its energy. When you come out of the water, it will flow off with sparkling drops and leave you completely dry.

As one advances in knowledge, wisdom, and spirituality, the appearance of the spirit body becomes younger, more like the appearance of the physical form at its earthly prime of life. My father made me aware of this from spirit side. Spirit has also said, when a baby or child comes to spirit, as it advances in spiritual knowledge he or she will gradually mature in appearance, close to what it would have looked like in one's physical prime around the mid to late 20s.

I think it's important to note here that what the Monsignor experienced and expressed was based on the spiritual dimension into which he entered. As I stated earlier, there are an infinite number of dimensions and the one a newly departed spirit enters is always aligned to their spiritual evolution and related vibrations. What determines their vibrations depends on many things, e.g., their spiritual faith, how they lived their life according to Universal Laws, and the key as always – how much love did they give and receive and how much good did they do for others. The basic thing that will determine if one will enter into one of the lower dimension is, were they selfish and uncaring of others; did they misuse a position of power and climb in status at the cost of others; did he or she inflict any harm or abuse others, either physically or mentally?

The higher one's vibrations, the higher dimension one will enter into. It is Universal Law and can be no other way. One cannot enter into a higher dimension than one is vibrationally compatible with because it would just be too intense to endure. An example would be that while in a physical body, we could not look directly into the sun on a clear day. Our eyes are not compatible with experiencing and taking in that much light, yet our eyes can see just fine in less intense light levels short of total darkness. So it is the same in the spirit world; we cannot enter into a higher dimension than we are compatible with but we can visit lower dimensions. However, at this level, if we were to go into very low dimensions it would be both unpleasant and can even be dangerous for our well-being.

It is as my mother indicated after she and my father first transitioned to the other side. Her mother and daughter (my sister) can visit them by coming down from their higher dimension, but they cannot travel up to visit them on their higher dimension until they spiritually evolve to the next higher level.

After the Monsignor became more in-tune to the world he entered on spirit side, he became friends with a lady who was also a newcomer. Together with his old Earth friend acting as their guide, they continued exploring their new world. They delighted in every new thing they learned. Their movements were always in direct response to their minds. It was not necessary to walk to get from point A to point B. If they wished, they could glide quickly over the surface as well as rise up vertically or even fly. This is easily done merely by the power of one's thoughts.

Some of you may have had dreams of flying with your physical form and you could do so by willing yourself to lift off the ground and just hover, or soar, or even glide. And so it is in the spirit world and it is not possible to harm one's self or ever have an accident. You can enter water while clothed, be energized by it, and never sink unless you choose to, and then exit the water perfectly dry. There is no night or darkness, only a golden light everywhere from a great celestial sun that emits its light everywhere forever. There is never any hunger or fatigue nor is there an apparent sense of time or urgency as is often experienced on Earth.

Without the sense of time you may wonder how anyone would know when a gathering or event was to begin. If one intended to attend a gathering such as talks given by the Masters from the higher realms or a musical concert, you would just know at what moment it would start and then will yourself to the gathering place.

I found the following very interesting. The lady who had joined the Monsignor had never been an active churchgoer on Earth, but she was a very lovely and kind being. It became clear to the others that her lack of church attendance made no difference as to what level or dimension she arrived in the spirit plane. By giving service to others, she had done more good for her spiritual welfare than being a committed attendee to a religious church. This is not to say that a deep spiritual faith and church attendance is of no value, for truly it is. However, church attendance is not a prerequisite to being a good loving person with a sincere faith and ultimately achieving a high level of spiritual growth.

The newcomers were reminded that religious contentions and controversies are the basis of a lack of knowledge of real spiritual truths, yet people bring their religious contentions and controversies with them to the spiritual world. Moreover, religious intolerance is the basis for most wars on the planet. I came to believe during my search for the truth that it is better to be spiritually focused than to be religious. Why? Because when we are spiritually focused, we will usually seek the greater depth of spiritual teachings and live by them. However, if one is just a religious churchgoer, he may adhere to the teachings of a particular religion based on its doctrines and dogma and never think for himself or attune to his higher self. I have heard it referred to as a mindless fundamentalism.

As these newcomers learned, there is a greater difficulty adjusting to the spirit world if one is a diehard religious fanatic and truly believes one has the absolute truth. In this situation, the individual resists opening up to the possibility of greater truths. Remember, if one truly wishes to evolve spiritually, one must be willing to let go of any aspect of one's current beliefs, for there will always be higher truths to accept on one's path to spiritual growth. Now, let's get back to life in the spiritual realm.

After newcomers arrive from Earth, their normal attire is of their earthly type of clothing. However, after being in spirit for a while, they shift to more spiritual attire such as robes that are of a flowing form and of full length with varying colors and degrees of density. The type and degree of the light that composes a spiritual robe determines the texture of the material. For those who have evolved to the level where they desire to transform their attire to a spiritual type of clothing, they just express the wish and their old clothes immediately transform into a spiritual robe, one that is best suited for them. The more spiritually evolved one is, the more vivid the color and radiance the robe appears.

For those who need to heal their spirit from physical distresses from Earth, such as pain and suffering, there exists what is called a Hall of Rest. It is not necessarily an enclosed building. Here, patients who have gone through a long illness before passing over enter into a restful sleep state for recovery. Such long physical illnesses have a debilitating effect on the mind and that also has an effect on the spirit body. In order to recover, the new spirit will need a great rest of varying durations depending on the severity and length of the illness or injury. The rest is very complete and is like being in a void. The Master recently told me the void is very pleasant and soothing.

A friend who had a very long illness before crossing over recently told me his recovery was like a very pleasant dream. His recovery lasted about 17 months, but he had no awareness of the Earth time it took, but he did say that he was somewhat aware of being administered to and it was all like a pleasant dream. After his complete recovery, he said something that really caught my attention: "We here are in a constant state of joy and happiness, but what is so sad is that there is so much sadness on the Earth Plane."

My sister had such a rest and recovery period after passing on from a brain tumor. Her recovery lasted about three months Earth time. She awoke long enough to be welcomed home by the Master and other friends and family then drifted into another slumber for a while longer before full awakening.

There is a different Hall of Rest for those whose passing is from a sudden and violent nature. Here the suddenness of the death creates a great confusion of the mind, especially if the spirit had been suddenly forced out of the physical body as in an explosion or a car or plane crash. Often, the spirits do not know they have passed and are very confused. Always there are souls who are there to help with their recovery and stay with them as long as is necessary. If souls have just a basic awareness about the spirit plane, their recovery is so much easier, faster, and joyous.

When one there focuses on or thinks about another spirit there, whether the thoughts are a definite message or merely of an affectionate nature, the recipient will receive the thoughts and associated feelings instantly. Moreover, when we here think of those on the spirit plane, they become aware of our thoughts. People often wish they had said certain things to loved ones who have departed the physical, such as, "I really loved you" or, "I have truly forgiven you," or any other personal message they wished they had said before the loved one or friend passed over. You can be sure that if you think of an individual over there and speak to them as if they were still here in your presence, they will be aware of your mental thoughts, your expressions, and your feelings. Therefore, it is never too late to say good-bye, "I love you," or whatever else you wish to express to a departed one. You may wonder if they really heard you because you received no feedback, but know that they have.

In the next world, there is no pollution, crowded streets, rush hour traffic, decay, and never any darkness. Everything is pure and pristine. Everything we can think of as beautiful here is much more so there. My friend I recently connected with said, "Regarding the statement we've heard so often from spirit regarding life on the Earth is but an illusion, now I know what that really means since I now really know reality. Everything here is so real and so pure."

In reality, there is no sense of time or space. It is all in the here and now. Therefore, there is never a feeling of being rushed or crowded because of unlimited space. Never will you feel hurried or pressured by time constraints. If there is a gathering, there are never lines to get in or space limitations, no matter how many attend any gathering, be it a symphony or the presentation of a master teacher.

There are types of cities, but they are always centered on higher spiritual learning. I might add that the learning never ends as we evolve to higher levels of spiritual beingness and expression. Always there will be higher levels to achieve and higher dimensions to transition into. Moreover, we can be sure there will always be guides and teachers more than willing to help any entity evolve. Long ago, I learned that one of our primary purposes of life is to evolve to a higher level and expression of life. A great way to spiritually evolve here is to reach out and help others. Giving of one's self will always be rewarded in some way. Remember, what goes around comes around.

Colors are more brilliant and sound is more pure in the spirit realm. Learning is fast and easy because there are no memory limitations when one functions with a pure mind without being restricted by a limited physical brain. You will also find the powers of mental perception are no longer impeded.

If you had a love for any of the arts, there are many opportunities to experience and even participate in them there. If you had a talent in music, art, voice, or acting here, you can also develop these abilities to a much greater degree there. You will never be bored or lonely in the world of spirit because there are unlimited things to involve yourself in without any financial concern, as is so often a problem in the physical realm. Money or any other medium of exchange does not exist in the spirit realm. I might add, it is the same on most of the more evolved planets.

Because we here always think in terms of time and space, it can be difficult to imagine the true way of life in the spirit world. They have no such restrictions as we do in the physical world. You may wonder how they can involve themselves in many things there and yet accomplish them all without any problems. This may help you understand. The more spiritually evolved a being is, the more places they can be at any moment. I'm sure it is obvious that Christ can be everywhere at once -- healing, nurturing, and blessing those who need Him. I was communicating with Archangel Michael not long ago and he suddenly said, "I must take leave now, duty calls" and he was gone. Knowing the angels are not limited to be in one place at a time, I later asked Archangel Gabriel why he had to leave when not being so limited. The answer surprised me. When a major Universal crisis occurs, Michael needs his total energy to deal with the crisis. Gabriel also said that Michael has responsibility for the entire universe whereas Gabriel's responsibilities are only to the Earth plane.

In one of the Halls of Art is a large gallery where hangs every great masterpiece of art created by man. My guide told me that every painting I created exists on the spirit plane, not that my paintings are masterpieces, but I found that interesting. Actually what exists on the spirit plane are the originals created by the artist's thoughts and what exists on Earth is but an earthly counterpart. Because of any limitations of the artist, the earthly version may not be as perfect as the version created by the artist's thoughts which are much more multi-dimensional, and they are actually alive, i.e., they vibrate a radiance. In other areas of the Halls of Art are students being taught in every artistic aspect without the many limitations that exist here. While they call the many places of learning Halls in the spirit realm, they are nothing close and so much more than what we know as a hall.

The spirit world also has a Hall of Literature. I found it interesting that, in areas of this hall, there exists the true history of all countries of Earth. I say the **true** history because the victors of the many wars that were fought in most countries, created most of the published histories that exist on Earth. Those who believe the Bible is very literal and accurate may be disturbed at hearing this. The Monsignor learned that the truths of all the treachery, torturing, inhumane acts, distortions, and exaggerations have been made clear. The historical literature there is as it really happened. The literature also includes all church history and that discloses the diabolical deeds that were committed by those who professed to be of and serve God. However, the writings also give truth to the many deeds that were both great and noble. These historical writings that are bound in beautiful books are as alive as the paintings are in the Halls of Art.

There are also other halls such as the Hall of Fabrics. Here there are beautiful materials and cloths that are not to be found on Earth. There are many other halls but there is not room here to cover them all.

It's important to realize that all tasks, all efforts, all involvements in this and higher spiritual dimensions are performed very willingly by all the beings. Never is any being commanded to do anything in these realms. Guides may make suggestions for one's greater growth but they never dictate or command. Actually, I experience the same gentle suggestions when I communicate with my guides, angels, and masters.

The boundaries of a dimension are not limited by size or distance but rather as it relates to the range of vibrations within each dimension. One can visit a higher dimension if there is a specific purpose, but a guide would have to put you in a protective shield, so to speak, to protect you from the greater intensities in the higher realms just as we on Earth would need to protect our eyes with very dark glasses to be able to look directly into the sun.

Another book just appeared one day and I have no idea where it came from. One day I noticed it on my desk and I never did figure out how it got there. It is very old and was originally written and printed in Germany in 1836. The fourth edition was printed in 1900. The copy I have was published in Boston in 1912. The title is *The Little Book of Life After Death*. This book was translated from its original German language. The style of English around the turn of the century appears very different.

It was not a big surprise that the book makes many of the same points and indicates various truths that align with those herein, but they were written in a somewhat different style of language.

Evolving spiritually on the other side is not as easy as when embodied on the Earth plane. When my wife first read this, she thought I had it backwards. To explain it best, the difficulty factors on the spirit plane are not as great to overcome as they are on our plane. We have greater negative influences and distractions to overcome, such as materiality, social influences, greed, power and control, addictions, and sometimes we get so caught up in our careers we abandon any thoughts of spirituality. Not only can these things retard our spiritual growth but also there are traps that many fall into that actually reverse spiritual growth. Whenever we get so focused on self and have no concern for the good of others, we lower the dimension we will enter when our time comes to cross over to the world of spirit. Fear can be a great barrier to our growth and it is very difficult to conquer deep ingrained fears. But fear is something that does not exist in the world beyond because there is nothing to fear in that realm of life.

Many of the things we fear on this planet are threats to life itself. Governments of power continue to develop bigger and more effective weapons. Terrorists with distorted beliefs and agendas, usually motivated by religious convictions, continue to use bombs, rockets, and other weapons to kill innocent beings in the process of achieving their intensions. People are starving by the hundreds of thousands because of greed and self-interests. All acts of aggression and destruction are holding back the progress of beneficial advancements. Let me explain why.

On spirit side is a Hall of Science where there are those who had been scientists and engineers on the Earth plane. They do not need things like improved methods of travel because they travel at the speed of thought. They do not need better means of communication because they communicate through thought. They do not need life enhancing drugs or better surgical procedures because they never become ill, never injured, and never die. However, when we on Earth evolve spiritually and move beyond warring, murder, acts of aggression, controlling one another, greed, lusting for power, and all other negative deeds; and when we become peaceful beings who always work for the good of the whole, it is then that we can expect many marvelous material and medical advancements which will ultimately come from spirit or the extraterrestrial realm and dramatically improve our lives. And why will this be so?

There are those who are part of the group within the Hall of Science on spirit side that have devoted themselves to serve us on Earth through the use of their evolved scientific and engineering abilities. Their beneficial developments are years ahead of those on Earth. This is also true of the highly evolved beings on other planetary systems. They cannot share their knowledge until a planet's beings will use the technology responsibly. When humankind grows beyond our primitive ways and spiritually evolves beyond our destructive ways and the need to control other nations, an endless amount of help is waiting for humanity from these devoted scientists and engineers on the other side, as well as from other more evolved planetary beings who will help us create beneficial advancements not yet dreamed of. We may have seen a glimpse of some in futuristic films such as advanced robotics to do grunt work, anti gravity vehicles, quiet and nonpolluting. Other possibilities include completely automated agricultural systems producing healthy wholesome organic foods. More natural health products will replace prescription drugs with their many side effects. Medical advancements will make surgery obsolete. The development of solar energy will evolve far beyond the present. It has not advanced to such a level now because it would be made into another weapon. The list of technical and medical advancements is endless.

Let's look at some things that provide continued growth after we graduate to our new life on the spirit plane. As an example, both my sister and mother, now on the other side, have nurtured and worked with the souls of newly arrived children, those who have died of hunger, diseases, disasters, or accidents. They take them under their wing, give them lots of love, and help them understand and adjust to their new life. They also guide them to opportunities for continued growth. There are also beings who basically do the same for adults who have recently crossed over. Sometimes it is more difficult to work with adults because of their rigid belief systems.

If you have achieved a high level of a talent here, you can serve as a teacher and help others develop these talents there, but you can also help those back on the Earth plane develop talents, just as Van Gogh helps me with my skills in art here. There are endless opportunities there to serve and grow. It is always about getting out of self and doing good things and helping others, be it on a one-to-one basis or offering to help many. This is easily accomplished there in a volunteer capacity. There is a noteworthy quote that alludes to this line of thought. The Master Buddha gave it many years ago:

> *When a person long absent from home returns safely from afar, relatives, friends, and well-wishers rejoice at his return.*
>
> *In the same way, when one who has done good and then is gone from this world to the beyond, his good deeds receive him, like relatives receiving a returning loved one.*

In summary of this chapter, my intention is to help you get beyond the many myths of the limited traditional religious beliefs of the afterlife, especially the horrific images created of a literal hell. Moreover, I am hopeful the material in this and earlier chapters have helped you to move beyond any fears you may have had about this thing we call 'death.'

I have come to think of our physical passing on as 'Graduation Day.' I really believe it is actually something to look forward to when our time comes to leave Planet Earth because of the extraordinary experiences that await us. As my mother told me shortly after she passed on, "My dear son, you cannot begin to comprehend how absolutely beautiful it was moving into this plane of life."

No matter how many stories and images I or others have presented about the other side, I'm sure they all fall well short of the true beauties and wonders are present in the life beyond.

After we release from the physical and enter into the world of spirit, loved ones and magnificent beings of light will greet us. Guides will help us adjust and become oriented in this most wonderful world. Thereafter, in all probability, we will choose a means to serve life, either within the spirit realm or by helping others here. We will find great joy by helping others in ways best suited to our greatest abilities. We might even want to develop a special knowledge in an area such as science or medicine that would be helpful if or when we return for another visit to the physical plane.

There are so many ways to serve life while on the spirit plane. Many are beyond our imagination and it is in these services to life that we will continue to evolve spiritually. Remember, it is always about giving, never getting; however, it is in giving that we will receive.

There are even higher dimensions that await our evolved beingness; dimensions that are beyond our physical comprehension and the words to adequately describe them. I hope you now have some idea of what you might experience when your inevitable day of transition arrives and you ascend into the magnificence of the world of spirit.

In the next chapter, we'll explore both the lower and higher dimensions beyond the one most humans initially enter when crossing over.

There are more things in Heaven and Earth
than are dreamt of in your philosophy.
---Shakespeare

CHAPTER 17

Exploring Other Dimensions

I had previously understood there were a total of 12 dimensions in the spirit realm of life. In various books and articles I've read, I noticed some writers referred to certain numbers when referring to the levels of various dimensions. Some have referred to them as planes. I recently asked spirit source how many there were. My answer was, "There are infinite numbers of dimensions in the spirit world."

With that answer, I quit trying to identify numbers to dimensions, except as it relates to the physical realm. As I pondered on that, I found my mind begin to open up to other probabilities. Then it came to me. Of course, stars and planets are living entities. When a star dies, as they do, where does the spiritual essence of a star go? When we see photos taken by the Hubble telescope, we can see myriad celestial formations. All that is physical in all universes has a spiritual essence. Then there must be spiritual dimensions for all of celestial life and I'm sure there are other realms of life we are not even aware of. The cosmos is vast beyond our wildest imagination. Being human, we fall short in our ability to understand infinite reality so we'll stay with that which we humans are directly concerned with.

In the range of spiritual dimensions that humans enter after leaving the Earth plane, they vary from very dark and bleak to ultimate light and beauty beyond our human comprehension. The dimension that most of us will enter when we pass on is very much like Earth but everything is more refined, more pure, very pristine, and absolutely amazing. The inhabitants and all else appear more vivid and alive, and nothing ever dies. The water is pure and filled with energy, the grass is very green, soft, and lush. Flowers are abundant and emanate wonderful scents and energy, many we've never seen on Earth. If flowers are picked for decoration, they never die. If you no longer desire them, they simply dissolve into the energy of flowerness.

There are sounds and tones of music not heard on Earth that are soothing and uplifting. Harsh sounds such as hard rock and heavy metal are non-existent. Music is an important part of life in the spirit world, though it is quite different than earthly music. Concert performances with musicians playing instruments similar to those here are held in very large amphitheater settings that may be surrounded by groves of tall and graceful trees. If you wished to attend a performance, you would receive a thought from the producers that the concert was about to begin and, in a few moments, you and other interested souls would fill the amphitheater, and never would there be a shortage of space to accommodate the attendees.

When the performers begin playing, the energy of the music may create a beautiful bright light that will rise up as an iridescent cover to the whole area and will change in intensity and color with the vibrations and movement of the music. The shapes, size, and colors of the light change with the type of music being produced. In the world of spirit, all music emits color and all color emits music. That is why colorful flowers emit pleasant tones when you come close to them and it is always in perfect harmony. It is all very natural.

Everything has a certain frequency of vibration, both on Earth and in the spirit world. However, the vibrations of spirit are much finer and of a higher frequency. Most of us in the physical, with some rare exceptions, cannot see spirit matter because it vibrates out of the range of our physical vision. As an example, we all see water clearly. If it is heated to a certain level it is less visible as steam. When the steam evaporates into the air, it is still there as water vapor but we can no longer see it except as a haze across a far distance. When a spirit leaves the physical body at death, the spirit form is of a much higher vibration and is not visible to human eyes, yet it still exists and is more real than the physical with its many limitations. In the case of those beings who are in spirit, but have not gone on to the other side, they may be considered "haunting" spirits, because their vibrations are at the lower end of the spirit scale. Therefore, they can sometimes be seen by human eyes and are usually called 'ghosts.'

Some humans have been gifted to be able to see spirit forms. Their mission, if they accept it, is to help those who have passed on but have not yet actually crossed over into the light. They become trapped in between the physical and the spirit worlds. Usually this is because of their beliefs, or the lack thereof of a spirit life beyond the physical. This follows their belief of a non-existent spirit plane. Spirit guides cannot help them because the disbeliever will not see them. They become 'lost' so to speak, and wander aimlessly. Because they are out of the time dimension, they can roam between the two worlds for years or even centuries and not realize time has passed. Some become attracted to the vibrations of familiarity, such as places they have experienced or homes they have lived in. Also, they may have some unfinished business they strongly feel they need to settle. Their vibrations are low enough to effect noises, such as footsteps in the quiet of night, or move physical objects.

The gifted ones who can see them try to help them become aware of their plight by making them aware of a spiritual world they need to enter. They tell them to look for a light and go towards it. They also may be the emissaries who help resolve a past issue, thus allowing the spirit to move on into the light of the next world. There are many other situations that apply to this in-between world situation but there is enough here to understand why there are so-called hauntings by ghosts.

Each dimension on the spirit plane contains a range of vibrations within that dimension. At the highest end of the dimension, everything is at its brightest and most vivid, yet not as much so as the lowest of the next dimension above it. At the lowest end of a dimension, there is less light, the colors are more muted and everything is less vibrant, but still brighter than the dimension below it.

During the process of writing this book, spirit guides promised that I would receive some of the material for the book during my sleep state. One night I had a dream, or at least I thought it was a dream when I awoke at a very early hour. I was in a very dull looking place. It seemed I was to start a new job and was shown a drawing board where I was to work. It was similar to the one I had when I did test stand design drawing for a large company many years ago. I thought it strange that I was just left there, with no one telling me what I was supposed to do. So I went around looking for someone whom I could ask questions. I tried to stop a few people but they just passed me off. I walked up to two men who were having a conversation and waited for a break. They totally ignored me. Then it seemed to be time to quit. I asked for directions to the parking lot. No one seemed to know where it was. Others totally ignored my questions. When I went outside the building, there was no parking lot in sight and I had no idea where home might be. Feeling desperately lost, I walked into an area that appeared very old and worn. The streets were composed of very worn cobblestones. Nothing appeared to have any colors of significance. No one or no vehicles were in sight. I entered a building through a large open entrance. A very plain looking woman was sitting on the floor in front of a small group of children in a large open area. It appeared she was trying to teach them something. When I awoke, I felt as if I had really been in that place, so later I asked my guide about it. I was told I had visited one of the lower dimensions on the other side so that I might see first hand how beings existed in a dimension consisting of beings who had been all into themselves while on the Earth plane and were rather materialistic, and didn't care much about helping others. Moreover, they didn't have any kind of spiritual faith.

Seeking more information on lower dimensions, I learned that, as we explore lower dimensions, the beings become less joyous, less vibrant, and rather lonely. This is because they had never cared about others, and now no one cared about them. Their dwellings are rather unappealing. The flowers and trees are less vibrant, and at even lower levels, they are no longer present. The sky is dull and the landscape is rather barren. At this level are those who, while on Earth, used and abused others to get ahead. Their god was money and they did whatever it took to get more of it. While money is not the root of all evil, the love of it is.

Here you would find the Ebenezer Scrooge type of individual. He may have been a very successful businessman but was unscrupulous in his dealings with others. He was probably so immersed in his successful business ventures that he had no time for anything or anyone else, including God. He may have given to charity but only if he received recognition for it or a tax write-off. He most likely would have felt above everyone else and demanded respect. He would need to always be in control of everything and everyone. He may have attended church regularly to look good in his community. Maybe he gave money to his church because he thought it would buy him a high place in the next life whether he even believed in such a place. Everything he would do had a selfish motive for the ultimate purpose of gain and self-aggrandizement. A genuine love for others was never given or received.

In these lower dimensions, everything reverses itself. When the time on Earth ends for the individual who used or abused others, was greedy, loved little, and lived with the attitude of getting but giving little, he enters the spirit world in amazement of the life he created for himself, one that is bleak and lonely. His dwelling is incomprehensible and uncomfortable compared with what his selfish riches provided for him. He is bitter

EXPLORING OTHER DIMENSIONS

and feels he has been judged unfairly, not realizing he created all of this himself.

All his selfishness and unconcern about the welfare or happiness of others had been at a great expense. His spiritual vibrations will not allow him to enter the spirit world into a great and wonderful life at a higher level where he may have found joy and love had he expressed more love and been giving of himself while on Earth. He may spend considerable time in this meager existence until he changes his attitude, quits trying to blame someone for his perceived misfortune, and begins listening to guides who are available to help him understand his plight and begin to move onward and upward to the higher levels. As Ebenezer Scrooge in the Christmas Story entirely changed his attitude toward life and others after the ghosts of his past showed him the error of his ways and how it negatively affected others, so can those who enter into these levels rise out of their plight when they seek the light.

If one on a higher level was curious and strong enough, and desired to visit the lower dimensions, as he or she descended, it would become colder, drearier, darker, and even slimy.

At the lowest levels are those who have committed horrific acts against humanity. Also, there you would find the Satan worshippers. Their appearance would be hideous, even demon-looking. Those who enjoyed killing humans are down at these levels, still trying to do each other in, even though no one in spirit can die. They are still filled with hate and aggression. Also there are those who tortured others and found joy in doing so, but at this level, there is no joy. Those who have willingly been involved in genocide, raping, torturing and killing men, women, and children also enter at these levels. As for those who instigated the extermination of the Jews in WWII, spirit has said they are continually haunted by the piercing screams of those they killed as well as the terrible smell of burning flesh. The spiritless bodies they have murdered lie all around them. This is their mental torture for the horrors they have committed on Earth and they scream for relief of it.

If you were in spirit and wanted to visit these lowest dimensions -- not that you would ever want to -- you would first need protection from a high and powerful being. You would find it extremely uncomfortable; however, those there would not see you because of the great difference in your vibrations. It is rather the opposite of a literal hell. It is very dark, dreary, and cold. According to the Master, there are thousands of thousands in even the very deepest levels. They do not even know they are evil. They exist even below the lowest of dimensions. However, unlike the fundamental beliefs of an eternal damnation, if they choose, all have the opportunity to be redeemed by going through a long and very slow progression to eventually reach higher levels. This may take hundreds or even thousands of years, and higher beings are always available to help them.

Remember, all aspects of life on all levels are one with God and He would not eternally damn an aspect of Himself. It is humans who believe in a duality of life and believe that the dark side is separate from God. Though some may find it difficult to believe, all life in all realms and in all levels of spirit are one with our Creator God. In reality, God is all there is.

So much for the lower dimensions. Next let's get some idea what the higher dimensions in God's Kingdom are like. I say some idea because so much of it is beyond our comprehension and words fall short of being able to adequately describe it. From several sources, including sources of my own, I've been told that the higher the dimension, the more difficult it is to adequately describe it in earthly terms.

My sister Marilouise first crossed over in 1978. She contacted me recently and shared, as best she could, her latest experience of evolving to a higher dimension. This is as she described it.

Evolving into the next dimension was beautiful, wondrous, and even unimaginable. The colors and music were as soft as angel's wings. Did you ever look at a peacock's tail spread out like angel's wings? Now put a neon light behind them with a continuous light giving it shaded colors like Joseph's coat. It is like the softness of a gentle breeze off gentle waters.

Imagine yourself as the only person around. Bring your mind into focus and gently breathe. Then bring your mind to focus on the stillness and you will feel the gentle breeze, the breath of God washing over your entire being. Do not stop the breath until you feel God's breath. Only then will you begin to see the colors in your naked state of awakening to your true self. You will feel feather light and a floating sensation. You will hear the whisper of angel's wings and feel their gentle brush as they come close to your body. Sounds are sweet and soothing as the angels sing in harmony and hum in unison. Even in this state, you can only get a glimpse, a fraction of what is in store for you.

You can only cross over into this level from the Earth plane if your life was lived in a very spiritual manner. You must live as a thoughtful person to yourself as well as to all of mankind. Relatively speaking, life on the Earth is so short lived. In a flash, it is ended, but you will not realize that until you have crossed over, whether you are 20 or 90. However, when you do, you will review your life, whether you were good, bad, or evil. In the blink of your eye or the nod of your head it will seem as if it was not your life but an illusion of another being. You will only see this once. Then you put it behind you, for it will not serve you to go back to the past. Now you will only move forward.

She indicated she is very busy now working with and nurturing the children who came to spirit from the recent hurricanes and tsunamis.

There are only two ways one can enter into the higher dimensions after crossing over. One must spiritually evolve to higher vibrations and thus be compatible to move up into a higher dimension. I'm not aware if there is a special celebration when such a spirit entity evolves into a higher dimension. My sister did not say, but she did tell me at an earlier time that she would soon be moving into the next dimension.

The second way is to be invited by some higher being to visit in the higher realms and only if there is a very specific reason. However, if not spiritually ready, you must be protected or shielded from the higher intensity. When you encounter beings in these higher dimensions, they are even more loving, radiate an even brighter light, are very light-hearted, and have a wonderful sense of humor, but always in a positive manner.

Unlike some religious leaders on Earth who have attained a high status and then become more serious and pious, those on the higher dimensions are very pleasant and even humble because of their greater service to all in all realms. I have personally experienced this while communicating with the Master and those in the angelic realms. They often greet me as a dear friend with warmth and love. They enjoy laughter and a cheerful attitude in us, and will even laugh with us. I recall what my sister said when crossing over and meeting the Master, "…when He laughed, bells sounded throughout."

In the book, *Life in the World Unseen,* the Monsignor and his woman friend received an invitation to visit the higher realms. Since he had received permission to communicate the greater truths and realities he had experienced on the other side, he was given the opportunity to visit the higher realms so he could give some description of these higher vibratory levels where the spiritual teachers and even avatars reside. Though they reside on the higher planes, they continue to teach in the lower planes as well as the Earth plane. I can certainly attest to how loving and patient they are when dealing with us humans and our very limited capacity to comprehend spiritual truth.

At times, I have had to ask for further clarification so my finite mind could make clear their message. When the Creator comes through, I feel a wonderful energy sweep over me, one that gives me goose bumps. When I later transpose the tape to document the message, that feeling comes over me once again. I always try to let them know how grateful I am. In fact, when I awaken each morning, I give thanks for my many blessings including the many messages I've been given. Then I have a short dialog with my Creator to start off the day.

The Monsignor described how they were shielded and given special films over their eyes to protect them from the greater intensities of light. They were escorted by the two higher beings who extended the invitation to them. When the higher realm opened to them, they were amazed at the unparalleled beauty of it that was beyond the imagination of any earthly mind. He quickly realized he could give at best an inadequate description of what they experienced using the limitation of language. He explained how the structures were composed of the celestial equivalent of diamonds, sapphires, and topaz that embodied the crystalline colors of white, blue and gold, the same colors of the robe of the celestial teacher who they had seen in one of the temples in their own plane. The crystalline colors of the jeweled palace-like structure were touched by pure rays of the great central sun and were magnified a thousand-fold as they sprayed outward in every direction with beams of the purest light. Enchanting gardens surrounded the magnificent palace structure, displaying a huge intricate pattern. Others buildings they saw were of other precious stones. Magnificent flowers were displaying myriads of colors, while the stream wandered gracefully below, glistening in the light. They were told this was very normal for this dimension of beingness.

A flash of light came from the palace and to their guide. That was the signal they were now expecting within the palace. They were amazed at the beauty of the interior with its jeweled floors, plus beautiful art that was alive with what appeared to be liquid light. They were greeted by very warm and gracious beings along the way to see their host. They were told there were no rules of etiquette, just use good taste.

When finally they arrived at the room of their host, they immediately knew they were in the presence of a supreme being. Their host came forth and bid them a warm welcome. They recognized him as one who spoke in one of the temples where they came from. His hair appeared as a bright golden light. His voice was like pure music and he had a rippling laugh. His presence breathed forth affection, kindness, thoughtfulness, and consideration. There was a feeling that their host held the key to all knowledge and wisdom. He laughed and joked with them and they felt very much at ease and at home with this magnificent being.

Finally he explained why he had invited them to this domain. Since they had already visited the darker realms, it was only right they should visit the higher realms and experience firsthand its great beauties, yet also realizing the inhabitants of these realms were not above the understandings of all others in all realms and could express cheerfulness, joyfulness, and laughter.

There was yet another thing he wanted them to know. The realms they were now visiting were within the reach of every human who had ever been born upon the Earth and, though it might take eons to spiritually evolve to these realms, they had eternity to do so. He also made it clear that it did not require adherence to any orthodox religion, for none had the power to secure a soul's salvation.

At this point, the guide who brought them to this high dimension advised them that, though they were shielded from the intense vibrations, there was a limit to how long they could comfortably handle it and it was now time to depart. I will end here the highlights of the Monsignor's experiences and some of the knowledge he gained when returning to their true home beyond the Earth plane.

The Monsignor ultimately connected with a medium on Earth and communicated the many great truths back to Earth dispelling many of the religious myths of what happens to those who complete their physical journeys and reenter into the magnificent world of spirit. Before I completed this chapter and described some of the key points of the Monsignor's life in the spirit world, I asked spirit if all that was portrayed in the Monsignor's testimony of his life beyond was basically accurate. I received confirmation that it was indeed accurate, considering the limitations of language.

I'm sure we all get so involved, busy, and occupied in the affairs of our physical lives, that we seldom seriously think about just what occurs to us and what we will experience when our time comes to depart and close down the physical part of our lives, and enter into the next life in the realm of spirit. I am aware, though, that the older we get, the more aware we become of our mortality. As was given earlier, the more we understand what the realities are beyond religious beliefs and teaching, the easier and faster we will adjust to our renewed life on the other side.

It is my wish that the material and evidence in the last two chapters, as reported by those who have gone on before us, will not only better prepare us, but will also dissolve any apprehension about making the transition from our physical life to the magnificent life our spirit will enter into when passing on to the world of spirit beyond.

It's important not to forget that our spirit being is the reality of who we really are and, in that beingness, free of the physical, we are so much more than we ever knew ourselves to be while in the physical. May Love and Peace be with you the rest of your days.

Amen and amen.

God is the 'isness' that is in all that is.

EPILOGUE

Throughout our life in the physical realm, it is often difficult to understand why things happen as they do. For some, it is good and for others it is not, but we are co-creators with the Infinite. We create the life we are experiencing this moment, and we do so by our choices and our actions. Remember, there is a reason for everything and there are, in reality, no victims. If our health is bad, what have we taken into our bodies throughout our life that was counter to good health? If we have incurred injuries in our life, have we done harm to others in some way? If not in this life, then most likely in a past one. If we have ongoing health or injury problems, it is usually a balancing in process through the Law of Cause and Effect.

As a knight in England, I killed and maimed many. The Universal Law of Cause and Effect is unfailing and determines so much of what we experience in life, be it good or difficult. I've had many injuries from parachuting and a couple while skiing. The ongoing structure problems that have resulted from those injuries are but a means of balancing my destructive deeds during knighthood in a past life. By understanding that, I can accept why without thinking, why me?

Often, we incur what we think are negative experiences but they may be for our ultimate growth. They may also be learning experiences to prevent greater negative problems. If we truly understand there is a reason for everything, we can often see the good that comes from something we initially perceived as negative. If we take our life too seriously, it will in all probability be filled with stress and difficulty, but understanding that everything on the physical plane is temporary except change, it can help defuse our seriousness. We are all just passing through this life and the good we do will always be rewarded when we return home to our never-ending life in the world of the spirit realm. There is an enormous amount of good we can do when we get out of ourselves and focus more on doing what is the greater good for all of life. The most monumental task we must achieve in this life to truly evolve is, to become consciousness of 'who we really are.'

We all come into this life with goals to achieve or a mission to accomplish. Some have referred to it as 'writing a contract' for this life. Sometimes, we get sidetracked from our mission or break our contract. It has been written that Hitler was a mighty spirit and had the potential to do much good, but he became influenced by negative energies and fell into the earthly trap of developing a lust for power and control. It is a great challenge to avoid the many traps that are present in this world and often it takes great courage and a strong faith to stay free of the entrapments.

Whether we are successful or not in completing our purpose for this life, or the mission we have accepted, we will all return to our true home in the world beyond. In that realm, we will no longer experience disease or pain, stress or discomfort. And in that realm, great love, peace and beauty will overshadow anything that exists on the Earth plane. There are great opportunities available for us to continue learning there and ultimately growing to even higher levels of life, expressing in a greater understanding of the oneness of all life.

When the Creator challenged me to write this book, I thought the primary purpose was to share the messages I had received from spirit over the last 33 years of my life. Little did I know until now that another great purpose was achieved. This project was not only a great refresher course for me, but it has also led me to seek and find even greater truths, and I have gained tremendously from it. My awareness has been heightened relative to all the major aspects of life, death, and where this great journey takes us when we leave this beautiful planet we call Earth. I give thanks to the God within and all those wonderful guides, angels, family, star brothers, and friends who reside in the world of spirit for the marvelous messages of greater truth and enlightenment they have shared with me for over three decades. I feel so very privileged to share them with you the reader and hope these writings have helped you understand in some way the greater purpose for our choosing to enter the Earth plane and ways to better achieve the goals we set for ourselves in this lifetime.

I do not claim to be a medium by any means, and my Earth mission is not to be one but rather to be a teacher of higher truths. I cannot choose whom I will connect with when I quiet myself and tune in the higher realms. I never know who will come through or what realm I will connect with, be it one of the Masters, the angelic realm, loved ones on the other side, the extraterrestrial realm, or the Creator of us all. It has become clear to me that all those messages were not just for me but also for my sharing with anyone and everyone who is open and searching for the greater truth of life. My search for the greater truths discovered more than I ever imagined, and it is not yet finished. I imagine it never will be. I am thankful for the methods of communication I have been blessed with, both receiving and sharing. In the Universal Law of Descending Knowledge it is given that, as knowledge of life is given to us, so shall we pass it on so all may grow in a greater understanding.

I conclude with one primary thought. In all that we do, and in all of our thoughts, **Love is the Key,** a love without judgment, without prejudice, without guilt, and without conditions attached to it. Love is the greatest power in the universe. It is the common thread that flows through all the religious writings on the planet. It has the power to balance out any negative karma; it is the greatest catalyst for tremendous growth, and it is a power that innately lies within us all. If we master just this one thing, all else will fall into a perfect balance and it will bring us untold joy and happiness. Are you ready? IT IS TIME!

Go forth with great love and let your light shine for all to see. Do this and know you will lift the vibrations of the world. I guarantee it!

ABOUT THE AUTHOR

For over three decades Ron has been receiving communications from the higher realms including guides, archangels, ascended masters, and from the Most High. Additionally, he has communicated with highly evolved beings throughout the Extraterrestrial Realm. Several Star Beings have shared details of their world with Ron. This includes their culture, their purpose, and how they live in oneness with the Most High, or as some have referred to Him, the Supreme Commander.

In 1982, Ron founded a spiritual group called Universalia, meaning *Of the Universe.* Those within the organization explored the many facets of spirituality, Universal Laws, and extraterrestrial life, all under the guidance of the spiritual realm. Eventually, all the members learned to communicate with the higher realms. Selected communications from the members were collected into a periodic publication and sent to subscribers throughout the U.S. and several others countries. Through trusting the Universe, all production and mailing costs were covered by free will donations.

Over the past several years, Ron has given many lectures to a variety of organizations. Additionally, for several years he was part of the organizing staff, and has given lectures at symposiums of the International Association for New Science. 'New Science' is one that combines science and spirituality. A scientific researcher once told Ron, "If you do not include spirituality in your research, you are only dealing with half the formula."

Expressing his creativity, Ron has produced a variety of oil paintings, most of which have a symbolic message, such as on the cover for this book. You can visit his website at www.starlightmessages.com.

CPSIA information can be obtained at www.ICGtesting.com
263262BV00001B/17/P

9 781452 534305